"Emily Miller's reporting shows how stricter gun control laws would make it nearly impossible for law-abiding citizens to get guns—while doing nothing to stop the criminals from arming themselves. This is an eye-opening story and a great read."

—**Donald Trump**, entrepreneur, star of
The Apprentice, and author of *Trump: The Art of the Deal*

"Emily Miller is the patron saint of the Second Amendment."

—**Tom Marr**, talk show host, WCBM 680 AM Baltimore

"The fundamental right to exist pivots upon the irrefutable, God-given, U.S. Constitutionally guaranteed individual instinctual right to self-defense and the inherent right to keep and bear arms. That this is debated represents an indictment of the soullessness of the anti-gun zombies who want more gun-free slaughter zones like Chicago. Emily Miller destroys this sheeplike curse of unarmed helplessness and the monsters who attempt to force it upon us with her every written and uttered self-evident truth-driven word."

—**Ted Nugent**, rock-and-roll legend and author of *Ted, White, and Blue, Kill It & Grill It*, and *God, Guns, & Rock 'N' Roll*

EMILY GETS
HER GUN

If you only follow liberal media and listen to President Obama, it would be easy to believe that gun owners are all bitter clingers, reckless hicks, or criminals. The truth is that the 100 million gun owners in America are among the most responsible, patriotic, family-oriented citizens in our nation. To dispel this mischaracterization, I'm deeply grateful to all the law-abiding gun owners who sent in photographs of themselves that are published in this book. The photos are a beautiful demonstration of Americans—men and women, young and old—exercising their Second Amendment rights.

EMILY GETS
HER GUN

...BUT OBAMA WANTS TO TAKE YOURS

EMILY MILLER

REGNERY
Publishing, Inc.

Cataloging-in-Publication data on file with the Library of Congress

ISBN 978-1-62157-192-6

ISBN autographed edition 978-1-62157-197-1

Published in the United States by
Regnery Publishing, Inc.
One Massachusetts Avenue NW
Washington, DC 20001
www.Regnery.com

Manufactured in the United States of America
10 9 8 7 6 5 4 3 2 1
Books are available in quantity for promotional or premium use. Write to Director of Special Sales, Regnery Publishing, Inc., One Massachusetts Avenue NW, Washington, DC 20001, for information on discounts and terms, or call (202) 216-0600.

Distributed to the trade by
Perseus Distribution
250 West 57th Street
New York, NY 10107

A portion of this book was adapted from material that originally appeared in the *Washington Times* and is reprinted here with permission.

*For Dad, who taught me by word and example
to always do the right thing and tell the truth.*

CONTENTS

The Second Amendment of the U.S. Constitution

A well regulated Militia,
being necessary to the security of a free State,
the right of the people to keep and bear Arms,
shall not be infringed.

CHAPTER 1

FROM CRIME VICTIM TO GUN OWNER

"I'm here to get a gun."

I was standing in the empty Firearms Registration Section of the D.C. Metropolitan Police Department Headquarters, just a few blocks from Capitol Hill. Behind the counter—which came up to my chest, as I'm only 5 feet 2 inches tall—there was one female police officer sitting at a desk.

The uniformed officer got up and walked slowly over to the counter. I read her nametag: "D. A. Brown."

"You want to register your gun?" Officer Brown asked.

It was October 2011. I had never owned a gun, or even tried to get one. I have lived in Washington, D.C., since I started college at Georgetown University. Handguns had been banned completely in the nation's capital for thirty years, until 2008 when the Supreme Court struck down the ban as unconstitutional in the landmark *District of Columbia v. Heller* decision. It took the city until 2009 to pass a new law regulating the possession of handguns. That law included the requirement that every gun has to be registered with the police.

But I didn't know anything about the process then. I was just trying to get started.

"No, no, I don't have a gun yet," I told her. "I mean I'm here to get a gun permit."

I assumed the process was like buying a car—first you get a driver's license and then you get the car.

I didn't know that in the gun world, "registration" and "permit" are two entirely different things. A "permit" enables you to carry a gun outside your home—bear arms. Somehow that is still illegal in Washington, despite the Second Amendment of the U.S. Constitution being quite clear about our right to both "keep and bear arms."

Officer Brown quickly knocked down my naïveté. "This is D.C., you can't get a gun permit," she said. "You can't be just carrying a gun around with you. It's for home protection."

I asked her to explain. "You can't carry it around like I do," she said, pointing at the black gun in her side holster. "You can't get a license. You can buy a gun and register it."

She started putting piles of paper on the desk between us. "Here's everything you need to know," she quickly ticked through advice on each form as she handed it to me. "Fill out this form. This one has a trick question, so be careful. This one you give to Sykes." I was totally confused. Who was Sykes? How do I buy a gun first if I'm not allowed to have it in Washington without it being registered? The mound of papers just kept growing.

"So, what do I do first?" I asked, picking up the messy papers and knocking them against the counter to make a neat stack.

"You get a gun and then get it registered," she said.

"Okay, well where do I go to buy the gun?" I asked. I can see now that it was dumb to ask a Washington, D.C., police officer for advice on buying a gun, but I had never gun-shopped before, and I was thinking she might direct me to a store nearby.

Instead, she got annoyed.

"You can go to any licensed dealer in another state or on the internet," she said. I later learned that there is only one legal gun dealer in Washington—and he doesn't buy or sell guns. He only transfers them from out-of-state dealers to D.C. residents. That's the Charles Sykes that Officer Brown had mentioned earlier. There is actually no place in the city where you can legally buy a gun. It's easier for the criminals—they just buy them on the streets.

Office Brown raised yet another issue. "But you can only get a gun on the D.C.-approved list," she pointed out.

I had no clue what she was talking about at the time, but later learned that D.C. has a ban on so-called assault weapons and high-capacity magazines. The list is actually a compilation of guns that California, Massachusetts, and Maryland decided were allowed under their bans. D.C. saved time and effort by just using those states' lists.

"You can get a Glock if that's what you want," replied Office Brown. Of course I'd heard of Glocks from TV and movies. I later learned that Glock is the standard sidearm for many police. "You just buy it and then give the form to Charles Sykes downstairs, and he'll go pick it up for you and transfer it." I still didn't know where to find a seller, nor what it meant to transfer a gun.

Officer Brown was still doling out the rules. "And if you get a semi-automatic, you can only get a ten-round magazine."

"A ten what?" I asked. I'd never shot a gun. To me, "magazine" still sounded like *Us Weekly* or *Allure*.

"Magazine, magazine, where the ammunition is," she said in exasperation. "Look, it's all in the packet here. I'm only telling you these things to help you, but you need to go through the packet."

Officer Brown wanted to get rid of me, even though only one other person had come into the registration office (and already left) while I was standing there. The whole time I was in the office, the phone rang one time, and the call was resolved in a few seconds.

Over time, I learned that the office was typically empty. The registration process is so arduous that few have gone through it. The bad guys, of course, aren't going to tell the police about their weapons. The good guys may not want the government knowing about their gun, or they don't have the time, money, or patience to jump through all these hoops.

The year before the Supreme Court decision, 512 guns were registered to police and licensed security in the District.[1] Once civilians were allowed to own handguns in 2008, the number of guns registered went up to 916—these could be new or old guns.

Dick Heller told me that he took advantage of his newfound rights on August 18, 2008, and registered a gun during the initial ninety-day amnesty period. He said re-registration three years later was "no hoop, hassle, at all."[2]

However, after the complex registration laws were enacted in 2009, the number of firearms registered decreased to 864. It went down again in 2010 with only 854 guns registered. The convoluted process discouraged people from telling the police about their handguns.

Perhaps because of dramatic increases in sales throughout the country, D.C. had an increase of newly registered guns—1,215 in 2011. This was when I started exposing the onerous process in the *Washington Times*. As the series led to the city council passing a law in 2012 to make registration a little less expensive and time consuming, D.C. saw the biggest jump in registrations—to 1,701.

Still, these are bizarrely low numbers for a city of 630,000 residents. Nationwide, nearly half the population—47 percent—has a gun in the home.[3]

Anyway, I thanked Officer Brown and walked out of the glass doors to sit on a chair outside the office and try to make sense of all the documents. After a few minutes, she opened the door, holding yet more paper.

"Here, you need to take a safety class, these people teach them," she said, handing me pages with lists of names and phone numbers. "It's all in your packet, but here are some names." This was the first I'd heard of the required classes. I just added the paper to my pile and kept reading.

At 3:15 p.m., Officer Brown walked briskly out of the office carrying a large black folder. She locked the door and taped a piece of paper with a typed note: OUT OF OFFICE BE BACK SHORTLY on it. Apparently any government office, even the Firearms Registration, can arbitrarily close with no return time.

I've seen a homemade sign just like that at the post office.

——————

I decided to get a gun because I wanted a way to defend myself in a city in which violent crime continually increases, while it decreases in the rest of the country. Assaults with a gun jumped 12 percent in 2012 in D.C.[4] Robberies with a gun were up a frightening 18 percent. And sexual assaults—which include rapes—were up a staggering 49 percent. Total violent crime was up 4 percent in 2012 in D.C., according to the Metropolitan Police Department's website.

The idea to get a gun first came to me after I was the victim of a scary home invasion on New Year's Day 2010. I was dog-sitting for friends, who were on vacation, and staying in their large house, which sat prominently on a road lined with some of the most expensive and beautiful houses in the Northwest quadrant of the city.

My friends' house is one of the few in Washington on a cul-de-sac, with only about half a dozen houses on the street. It was pleasantly quiet staying on a street with no through traffic, but that was also a draw for criminals who want to do their job in daylight hours.

I was headed to a New Year's party and needed to take the old Golden Retriever for a quick walk beforehand. The street seemed so safe and quiet to me that I had not been locking the door behind me when I took out the dog. It was a stupid thing to do just to save myself a few seconds turning the key.

The slow-moving dog and I went down a private driveway along the woods, then turned around and came back to the house in about ten minutes. As I got inside the yard gate, I saw a man coming from the house. At that point I wasn't scared, just surprised and confused.

"What are you doing?" I asked him as I walked toward the front door. The old dog stood next to me on a slack leash. He wasn't putting up much of a defense of his home.

"We're here to clean the pool," the man said. He looked nervous. He was white, about six feet tall, late twenties, disheveled—and his eyes were bloodshot. I didn't know what he meant by "we."

One thing I was sure of, my friends hadn't called from vacation about a swimming pool emergency in the middle of winter. "No," I asserted. "We didn't call for you." I said "we" in an attempt to make him think I wasn't alone with the bored dog.

"Oh, then it must be the house next door," he said and quickly walked away.

I was still suspicious, so I decided to try to get a photo of the mysterious pool cleaner. (I've watched every episode of *Law & Order* repeatedly.) I put the dog in the house, grabbed my BlackBerry, and clicked on the icon for the camera. I walked down the street after the stranger, holding the BlackBerry up in front of my face.

The street curves, so the last houses can't be seen from the main road. As I turned the corner, I was shocked to see about fifteen scruffy young men standing around two pickup trucks. Behind them, all I could see were two houses without any lights on and then the woodsy dead end of the cul-de-sac.

The men all looked up at me. No one moved. I got scared. I tried to press the camera button on the BlackBerry to get a quick photo of them and the license plates of the pickups.

Suddenly, the man I had seen earlier coming from my friends' house ran up at me, blocking the shot with his body.

"What are you doing?" he asked.

I wanted to run away, but I was terrified they would attack me if they realized I knew they were up to something.

"Nothing," I said as I moved the BlackBerry down to my side. "Um, I'm, I'm just going home." I turned away and raced back to the house, never looking behind me.

When I got inside, I looked around. Nothing in the house appeared messed up or missing. My purse was where I'd left it—in the kitchen, in the back of the house. I heard the trucks drive away. I assumed that I had been overly suspicious and paranoid. I grabbed my purse and headed out to the party.

A few hours later, my phone rang. It was my credit card company asking if my card was in my possession because there were odd charges on it. I looked in my purse again and this time opened my wallet. All my cash and cards were gone. A wave of fear washed over me as I realized that the "pool guy" had been deep into the house by the time I caught him. He must have left my wallet behind so that he would be long gone by the time I realized anything was missing.

I called 911, and D.C. police met me at the house. When they heard the story, they called in a detective, who gave me a long lecture about facing down criminals myself—even armed with my BlackBerry. He was right. I should have trusted my instincts and called the cops first.

The police said that there had been a pattern of drug dealers and addicts coming from neighboring Virginia into Washington for drugs, then hitting a few houses on their way back out of town to get quick cash and credit.

Detectives dusted for fingerprints and searched carefully through the house for any windows or doors left unlocked by the bad guys. They explained to me that criminals often take something small, then leave themselves a way to reenter the house to get more stuff. That scared me more than anything because I had committed to taking care of this dog and spending two weeks in my friends' house. I already felt embarrassed and guilty for leaving their nice home vulnerable to thieves.

I was terrified to go to sleep in case the men came back. I knew the dog was useless for protection. He probably wouldn't even wake up if someone broke into the house at night.

I finally figured out how to push a dresser in the master bedroom up against the door to barricade myself inside.

Still, I didn't sleep very much. For the first time in my life I thought, if I just had a gun on the nightstand, I know I would have a chance at defending myself if those men came in and tried to rape or murder me.

The next day, I tweeted that I was thinking about getting a gun. I was inundated with replies, and all were disappointing: "No 2nd amend in D.C." "Only one guy can sell weapons in DC—good luck with that." "Call the NRA."

I knew that the Supreme Court had overturned the thirty-year gun ban, so I didn't understand why people were so pessimistic about my idea. At any rate, my friends came back from vacation, and I moved back to my humbler, dog-free home. In a different neighborhood, and somewhat discouraged by the reaction on Twitter, I gave up on the idea of getting a gun for a while.

———

The following fall, I was walking through a neighborhood fair when I saw a bunch of campaign signs and a man shaking hands in a basketball court. I recognized Vincent Gray, the chairman of the city council, who was running for mayor that fall. Then-Mayor Adrian Fenty was very unpopular in large parts of the city at that time.

As Gray circled the basketball court glad-handing potential voters, I approached and told him that I was a lifelong Republican but would consider supporting a Democrat for mayor under two conditions. He smiled broadly, held my hand, and asked about my concerns.

"First, you've got to stop them from giving out all these tickets for things that aren't illegal, just to make money." Everyone in town was complaining about how the Fenty administration had increased parking tickets as a way to essentially raise taxes. The meter maids were renowned for giving out bad tickets, such as for meters that had not expired, with the expectation that many people wouldn't go through the hassle of fighting them.

I had gotten a $50 ticket for not having passed inspection—despite the current inspection sticker prominently displayed on my windshield. It would take three years and two appeals to win that fight. I also had to go to traffic court to fight a ticket I got on my way to church to teach Sunday school. The cop actually wrote out a moving violation for "driving with coffee cup." In court, the magistrate lectured the officer that it was not against the law in D.C. to drive with coffee.

Washington residents learn the hard way that the city is a free-for-all when it comes to the rules and laws. The voters returned Mayor Marion Barry to elected office after he was arrested for smoking crack cocaine (in the infamous "the bitch set me up" incident). Barry is still on the city council—and an ardent proponent of the gun registration laws.[5]

So when I asked Vincent Gray to stop this practice of inventing parking tickets to make extra money to balance the budget, the city council chairman and mayoral candidate smiled and promised to do that.

"Now what is the second concern?" he asked me that pre-election day on the basketball court.

"I want the city to make it easier to get a gun," I told the tall man. His smile faded. "A what?" he asked, leaning down to hear me.

"A GUN. I want a gun." I said loudly, looking up at him. "I don't know what's going on in this city, but apparently no one is listening to the Supreme Court."

"Well, um, Emily is it?" he said awkwardly. "Let me introduce you to my campaign manager." The candidate steered me by the elbow toward a guy in a "GRAY" shirt holding a clipboard. This is the politician's way of getting the crazy person away from themselves. I told the aide that I would start a "Republicans for Gray" campaign if he agreed to my two demands. I never heard back from anyone on the campaign.

———

Mr. Gray was elected mayor of D.C., and I started writing for the commentary section of the *Washington Times*. The *Times* is a daily newspaper that covers both local and national politics and is known for its conservative opinion pages.

In early fall of 2011, the new city council chairman, Kwame Brown, came to our newspaper bureau in Northeast Washington for a round-table interview with reporters, opinion writers, and editors.

There had been a wave of gun crimes in Northwest D.C. at the time. Two blocks from where I live, a man was walking along a brightly lit street when a car full of thugs pulled up next to him, jumped out of the car, and held him up at gunpoint. They took his laptop, wallet, and phone. Luckily, they didn't hurt him after he handed over the goods.

The crime spree made me more scared than usual walking from my car to my home. Although only the criminals get away with having guns on the streets, I was jarred into again considering at least getting a gun to defend myself at home.

In our meeting with Mr. Brown, I raised my hand. "Can I ask you about guns in D.C.?"

"You say guns?" the chairman asked.

"Guns," I replied as I held up both of my hands in the shape of a handgun, like they did on *Charlie's Angels*.

"Oh, you used both your fingers," Mr. Brown said, laughing. "You're a shooter, you use both of them."

I didn't laugh with him.

"Well, I'm trying to get a gun," I said.

"You're trying to get a gun?" he repeated. He clearly thought I was going to ask a policy question about the increased violence in Washington.

"I'm trying to get a gun." I said again. "I'm a city resident. And it seems the city council and the mayor have made it very difficult for residents to get guns, even though the Supreme Court has overturned the gun ban. Do you think the city is in adherence to the Supreme Court's decision?"

"Some new facts have come out, so they are now. The gentleman was able to open up shop here in the District of Columbia," Mr. Brown said, referring to Charles Sykes's problems with zoning for his business, something I learned more about later.

"People want guns now. They want to protect themselves. When you see petty crime and people breaking into people's homes, they want to protect themselves. They are like, 'The burglar's got a gun, and I don't have anything.' I understand that. The question is: Should we be helping people get more guns or should we be dealing with the real problem? The real problem is reducing crime because the fear of crime is why people want guns."

Actually, the real problem is that only the bad guys have guns so there is nothing to stop them from robbery, rape, and murder.

But politicians like to blame crime on unemployment. President Obama often gives that rationale for gun violence in his hometown of Chicago, which saw 506 people murdered in 2012, a 16 percent increase in a year.[6] He seems to believe if everyone in the Windy City had jobs, crime would just stop. Obama never mentions that Chicago already has all the gun laws he wants to enact nationally.

Mr. Brown continued in his very quiet voice. We all strained to hear him.

"How do we reduce crime? How do we get people back to work? When you do that, you can reduce crime, so it reduces the fear of crime," he rambled. "I'm not saying you want to get one because of crime, but I'm pretty sure you want to protect yourself."

"Yes, I want it for self-defense," I said.

"Ninety percent or 80 percent of people want them because of crime. Some people want to get them because they just want to carry guns," said the city council chairman.

My colleagues were patient when I pushed him on that point. "Actually, crime goes down with gun ownership because the bad guys don't know who is armed and who isn't, so it would actually reduce crime if more people were armed in this city."

"I believe that the easy way isn't just to have everyone have a gun and it may possibly reduce crime," he told me. "We need to figure out the real reasons that we have crime in the District of Columbia and tackle them. When we have 45 to 50 percent unemployment in the District of Columbia, people are going to start to do things, when they don't have, they are going to start to take..."

"Mr. Chairman," I tried to interrupt but he kept talking.

"Look what's going on with these bicycles and people breaking into homes. My car has been broken into in front of my house five times. I'm like fighting for the people. It hits home too. If they break into my home, you want to protect yourself, and I understand that. I think people want to work and take care of their families. Some people don't. They want to rob you and me and want to steal. And we should do whatever we can to make sure they are punished too..."

We were all looking around the room visually nudging each other to try to get him to stop meandering and get to the point. Finally my colleague Deborah Simmons, who reported on city hall and so was sitting next to Mr. Brown, turned to him and asked, "Do you agree it's the constitutional right for law-abiding citizens to own guns? The Supreme Court overturned the ban but now only one man is allowed to sell guns..."

The chairman interrupted her to focus on the recently resolved dealer issue. "I haven't heard of other people jumping up saying they want to sell guns in the District of Columbia. If you have people who want to sell guns, let me know. But my understanding is there's not a lot of people jumping up saying that they want to sell guns." Mr. Brown was doing the standard politician's sleight of hand of answering the question to fit his own agenda.

Deborah was having none of it. She asked point blank: "Do you support the Second Amendment?" I could have hugged her.

Mr. Brown paused a long time. Then in a low voice he admitted, "I don't support having more guns in the District of Columbia. I don't think we need more guns on our streets."

The chairman of the District city council never said whether he supported the Bill of Rights in the Constitution, but his non-answer said it all about what I was facing in trying to get a legal gun in the nation's capital.

CHAPTER 2

EXPLOITING THE NEWTOWN TRAGEDY

If President Obama gets his way and Congress enacts the items on his gun control agenda, it will be just as hard to get a gun in the rest of America as it was for me in Washington, D.C.

The biggest fight in history over Americans' right to keep and bear arms is being waged today. There were attacks on the Second Amendment in the early 1990s with the passage of the Brady bill and the "assault weapons" ban. The gun control battle of 2013, however, could easily see the greatest losses of Second Amendment rights ever.

The two key factors that make this assault more serious are a billionaire mayor willing to spend anything to win and a longtime anti-gun fanatic in the White House, applying the full power of the presidential bully pulpit to the gun-grabbers' cause.

When I started writing about getting a gun for my own personal protection in October 2011, gun control was not a major national political issue. While it was still a pet issue of the far left, a majority of Congress had been pro-gun since late 1994, the year the "assault weapons" ban went into effect and Clinton lost the House.

That's not to say liberals had given up on more restrictions to Americans' Second Amendment rights. Quite the opposite. They had just learned that they couldn't win elections by calling for more gun control, so they kept their agenda quiet from the public. They were lying in wait for the right political timing—such as the second term of a far-left Democratic president and a particularly horrific mass shooting.

Obama knew that the 100 million gun owners in the United States could sink his election if they became aware of his true views on firearm ownership. So in the 2012 election he assured voters, "We're a nation that believes in the Second Amendment, and I believe in the Second Amendment."[1] Gun owners were mocked as crazy and paranoid for fearing a second-term gun grab by Obama. Political analysts suggested that pro-gun leaders were trying to stir up fear to get out the vote for Mitt Romney. But in the end, everything the pro-gun groups predicted came true.

═══════

Back when Obama ran for the Illinois state senate, he didn't try to hide his anti-gun views. When asked on a candidate questionnaire in 1996 if he supported legislation to "ban the manufacture, sale and possession of handguns," Obama simply answered, "Yes." He also responded that he wanted laws to ban assault weapons and "mandatory waiting periods, with background checks, to purchase guns."[2]

During his 2004 run for the U.S. Senate, Obama elaborated on his views. Answering the same questionnaire again, he previewed what would be his top agenda in 2013, saying he supported mandating background checks of buyers purchasing guns at gun shows, through the internet, and through print advertisements.

On the question of legislation to ban all handguns, Obama replied, "While a complete ban on handguns is not politically practicable, I believe reasonable restrictions on the sale and possession of handguns are necessary to protect the public safety. In the Illinois Senate last year, I supported a package of bills to limit individual Illinoisans to purchasing one handgun a month; require all promoters and sellers at firearms shows to carry a state license; allow civil liability for death or injuries caused by handguns; and require [Firearm Owner Identification] applicants to apply in person. I would support similar efforts at the federal level, including retaining the Brady Law."[3]

He reiterated his support for reinstating the Clinton-era assault weapons ban that Congress let expire that same year because it had not reduced crime.[4] Senate-candidate Obama also said on the questionnaire, "I would support banning the sale of ammunition for assault weapons and limiting the sale of ammunition for handguns."[5] Going after bullets is just a backdoor way to get to guns.

True to his word, once he got to Washington, Senator Obama was one of only thirty votes in favor of an amendment sponsored by Senator Edward Kennedy to expand the definition of "armor-piercing" ammunition, a deliberately vague label that could cover regular hunting ammo.[6]

While running for president in 2008, Obama never spoke aloud about his anti-gun views, except once. At a private, off-camera fundraiser in San Francisco, he said that people in small towns "get bitter, they cling to guns or religion."[7]

The infamous "bitter clinger" comment has haunted Obama ever since.

His primary opponent, Hillary Clinton, also wanted more gun control, but used the opportunity to portray Obama as too liberal for America. She said her father taught her to shoot as a young girl. "People enjoy hunting and shooting because it's an important part of who they are. Not because they are bitter," Clinton said.[8] At another campaign stop, she talked about going duck hunting.

Obama was driven crazy by his opponent's sudden respect for the Second Amendment. "She's talking like she's Annie Oakley," he said. "Hillary Clinton is out there like she's on the duck blind every Sunday. She's packing a six-shooter. Come on, she knows better. That's some politics being played by Hillary Clinton."[9]

However, once he was elected president, Obama didn't push his gun control agenda in his first term. But Wayne LaPierre, the executive vice president and CEO of the National Rifle Association (NRA), warned gun owners for years that reelecting Obama would be dangerous to their rights.

"When he got elected, they concocted a scheme to stay away from the gun issue, lull gun owners to sleep, and play us for fools in 2012. Well, gun owners are not fools, and we are not fooled," LaPierre told activists at the Conservative Political Action Conference in Florida in September 2011. "We see the president's strategy crystal clear: get reelected, and with no other reelections to worry about, get busy dismantling and destroying our firearms freedom. Erase the Second Amendment from the Bill of Rights and exorcise it from the U.S. Constitution."[10]

The liberal media jumped all over LaPierre for using scare tactics to get out the vote for Mitt Romney. Rachel Maddow of MSNBC played a clip of the speech, then said, "The NRA says the way you can tell Obama is coming for your guns, is that he's not coming for your guns. It's genius! That is the insane paranoid message from the NRA this year."[11] Jon Stewart of the *Daily Show* mocked LaPierre for saying Obama hid his true intentions for four years: "It's just so crazy, it's f---ing crazy."[12]

Chris Matthews said the remarks were "another strain of the crazy far right." The MSNBC *Hardball* host actually said he'd known LaPierre "a long time" and then called him the "head of the NPR—not National Public Radio, National Rifle Association."[13] Apparently the cocktail party class in Washington is more familiar with the liberal taxpayer-funded radio network than the gun-rights group made up of 5 million Americans.

———

Why do gun issues matter so much in American politics? Votes. Only one of four registered voters believes stricter gun control laws will reduce firearm-related violence.[14]

Nearly 1 in 3 Americans owns a gun.[15] There are also 8 million concealed-carry permit holders in the U.S., according to a Government Accountability Office study released in July 2012.[16] Nearly half of all households have a gun—and that is just the ones who would admit to a strange pollster on the phone that they have a firearm at home. The highest rate of gun ownership is in the South (38 percent) and the lowest is in the East (21 percent).[17] Note that none of the presidential swing states is in the East.

The Democrats are split over guns, but the GOP has great strength from its party positions. Reince Priebus, the Republican National Committee chairman, told me in an interview, "I am totally on board with every sentence in our platform. More government intervention in our lives with regard to the Second Amendment is unacceptable. Those are rights that are sacred, people fought and died for, and we're a party that is going to stand up for them."

Priebus, who still lives with his family in Wisconsin, has four shotguns (in 12, 16, 20, and .410 gauges), two rifles (.300 Weatherby Magnum and Savage), and a .357 Smith & Wesson revolver, along with a collection from his father. I asked how he uses his firearms. "Hunting mainly, but my shotgun in Kenosha is not far from the bed," he replied.[18]

Texas Governor Rick Perry, the strongest defender of the Second Amendment in the 2012 Republican presidential primary, also warned about the true political objectives of Barack Obama.

Perry, who famously shot dead a coyote with his .380 Ruger for threatening his dog while on a morning run in 2010, loves all kinds of guns. The fifth-generation Texan has been shooting since he was kid. "The first gun I ever had was given to me by my grandfather when I was young—a Remington single shot .22lr. I still have it," he told me. He said that some of his favorite firearms are a LaRue OBR 5.56 rifle, a Colt 1911 .45 caliber pistol, and a 12-gauge Browning Maxus shotgun.

He uses his guns for a variety of purposes, including self-defense, target shooting, and hunting. "One of my favorite hobbies is going to target shoot at LaRue Tactical just outside of Austin," Perry said. When he was running for governor in 2010, he posted a video called "What to do on a day off" which showed him shooting at the 100-meter LaRue range.[19] Referring to it as "my form of golf," the governor said, "I'm still trying to get a hole in one—five rounds in the same hole—but I haven't quite got there yet. I think a 5.56 is my best. For me, it's really relaxing."

I met Perry for the first time in February 2012, soon after he had dropped out of the Republican primary. He was leaving the media room at the Conservative Political Action Conference in Washington, and I asked his aide for a brief interview. Knowing he was pro-gun, I mentioned my travails attempting to buy a gun in D.C.

"I read your article," he said.

"You did?" I asked, surprised.

"Yes ma'am. It was really interesting," said the cowboy-boot-wearing governor.

"What do you think of the gun laws in D.C.?" I asked.

"I think they are very onerous so you won't get a gun. They've made these rules and regulations and the cost very prohibitive so that Americans cannot have a gun. And that's their point." I asked him about his political future. "I haven't left the fight. I reloaded my mag, and I'm just fighting on a different front."[20]

In May 2013, I interviewed Perry again, at the NRA's annual meeting in Houston. He walked into the room and yelled out to me, "Gun girl!" I laughed, and we compared photos on our iPhones of different kinds of guns we'd shot lately. "You ever been huntin', gun girl?" he asked.

"No, sir, but I want to."

"Well, I'll teach you. You're comin' to my ranch this fall."

"Deal," I said.

Getting down to business, I told the governor that while he was speaking to the NRA members, Obama was just south of the border, saying that infringing on Second Amendment rights would benefit Mexicans. "Most of the guns used to commit violence here in Mexico come from the United States," Obama said in Mexico City on May 3. "I will continue to do everything in my power to pass common-sense reforms that keep guns out of the hands of criminals and dangerous people. That can save lives here in Mexico and back home in the United States."[21]

Perry was so shocked that he pushed back his chair from the table and thought before answering. "The idea that a United States president would go to Mexico and make that statement is incredible," he said. "His goal—well before he became president of the United States—was to try to disarm the American public. He just disregards the Constitution."

Perry went on to say, "He believes this. I got in trouble for calling Barack Obama a socialist, but he is. Socialists believe in disarming the public. Just go look at how he's performed on economic issues, health care, gun control, and Barack Obama is a central-control socialist."[22]

While Obama stayed silent on gun control during his first term, he started to hint about his agenda and put plans in place as it became clear he would win reelection. He assured gun control activist Sarah Brady in

March 2011 that gun control was "very much on his agenda." According to the *Washington Post*, Obama told her "We have to go through a few processes, but under the radar."[23] This was a sign to his base that gun control was still at the top of his list if they voted for him.

In the second debate with Mitt Romney on October 16, Obama came out publicly for the first time as president for banning some guns, but continued to reassure the American people that he believed in the Second Amendment.[24] At the town hall-style debate at Hofstra University, a supposedly undecided voter named Nina Gonzalez asked the president what he'd done to limit the availability of "assault weapons."

Mr. Obama started to answer by saying, "I believe in the Second Amendment. We've got a long tradition of hunting and sportsmen, and people who want to make sure they can protect themselves."

It's never a good thing when a politician suggests that hunting is the reason for the right of the people to keep and bear arms.

So it was no surprise when the next word out of his mouth was "but," followed by a list of guns he wanted to ban, from handguns to rifles. "I also share your belief that weapons that were designed for soldiers in war theaters don't belong on our streets. And so what I'm trying to do is to get a broader conversation about how do we reduce the violence generally. Part of it is seeing if we can get an assault weapons ban reintroduced, but part of it is also looking at other sources of the violence, because, frankly, in my hometown of Chicago there's an awful lot of violence, and they're not using AK-47s, they're using cheap handguns."

The suggestion that handguns should be banned based on their cost betrayed the president's extremist views—as if constitutional rights come with a minimum price tag.

Obama added, "What I want is a comprehensive strategy. Part of it is seeing if we can get automatic weapons that kill folks in amazing numbers out of the hands of criminals and the mentally ill."

He was being deliberately confusing. Automatic firearms are not on the streets or in the hands of criminals. They have been heavily regulated in the civilian market since 1934, and their manufacture for civilian use has been banned since 1986.[25]

Meanwhile, the other gun-grabbers were getting their ducks in a row to push legislation through Congress fast. The Friday before the November election, Senator Dianne Feinstein requested a meeting between her legal staff and the Bureau of Alcohol, Tobacco, Firearms and Explosives (ATF) at their branch in West Virginia. The California Democrat who wrote the first "assault weapons" ban wanted to discuss ways to reinstate and expand it, closing supposed loopholes, and even confiscating some guns.[26]

When Obama was elected to a second term on November 6, 2012, the gun-grabbing legislative agenda was already in place. Now all he had to do was wait for the right opportunity.

That day tragically arrived on Friday, December 14, when Adam Lanza murdered twenty first graders and six educators at Sandy Hook Elementary School in Newtown, Connecticut.

It was one of the most awful days in our nation's history. The death of one child is hard to bear, much less twenty. Knowing they were terrified and in pain is heartbreaking. Every American mourned as they watched TV and saw kids running out of the school and parents looking for children who would never return. I taught first grade Sunday school for six years, and I can't bring myself to even imagine those babies being killed in the classroom.

It is human nature to want to look for someone or something to blame for a tragedy like this. We want to find a way to control the world so we can avoid feeling vulnerable to pain and suffering. After the horror in Newtown, we all wanted to find ways to protect our children from another Adam Lanza, to stop the next criminal hell-bent on killing. We want to stop evil.

Yet no law could have prevented what happened at that Connecticut elementary school. The world is broken, and we can't fix everything that's wrong with it. Unfortunately, that fact didn't stop politicians from preying on Americans' fears to push their long-planned agenda.

New York Mayor Mike Bloomberg didn't even wait until the children's bodies were taken out of the school before he erupted. On the day of the massacre, the mayor released a statement that the president should "send a bill to Congress to fix this problem. Calling for 'meaningful action' is not enough. We need immediate action."[27]

Representative Jerry Nadler went on MSNBC that same Friday to call on Obama to use the dead children to push for gun control. "I think we will be there if the president exploits it," the New York Democrat told Ed Schultz.[28]

White House Spokesman Jay Carney reiterated that the president wanted to bring back the so-called "assault weapons" ban.[29] Chuck Schumer of New York, number three in the Senate, said on CBS that he was confident a bill with further restrictions could now pass.[30] By Sunday, Senator Dianne Feinstein said on NBC that she would introduce her prewritten assault weapons ban when the new Senate convened in January.[31]

The anti-gun activists had changed in the twenty years since the first assault weapons ban passed. The Brady Campaign had been eclipsed by the billionaire mayor of New York. Michael Bloomberg's organization, Mayors Against Illegal Guns, is essentially part of the mayor's administration, but with political consultants and a bottomless bank account.

The opposition to Bloomberg's gun-grabbing campaign is led by the NRA, whose power is in its grassroots operation and massive membership of 5 million; the National Shooting Sports Foundation, which represents firearms and ammunition manufacturers and retailers; the Second Amendment Foundation, which fights unconstitutional laws in the courts; the associated Citizens Committee for the Right to Keep and Bear Arms, which does grassroots politics but does not endorse candidates; and the Gun Owners of America, another grassroots organization.

Obama was appropriately nonpolitical for forty-eight hours after the Sandy Hook shooting, but he started letting his plans show at the prayer vigil in Newtown on Sunday. "Are we really prepared to say that we're powerless in the face of such carnage, that the politics are too hard? Are we prepared to say that such violence visited on our children year after year after year is somehow the price of our freedom?" He announced a plan to "use whatever power this office holds to engage my fellow citizens" in an effort to prevent "tragedies like this."[32]

Every life is precious. Obama never had much to say about the thousands of people murdered last year in individual shootings. Instead, he chose to focus on the rare mass shootings in suburban areas, which are more relatable for voters, and thus politically helpful for him.

There have been seventy-eight public mass shootings in the last thirty years that claimed 547 lives, according to an April 2013 report from the nonpartisan Congressional Research Service (CRS).[33] That averages to eighteen victims a year.

To put that number in context, there were 8,583 murders by firearm in the U.S. in 2011, the most recent year for which we have figures from the FBI.[34] And there were 851 people accidentally killed by firearms in 2011 according to the Centers for Disease Control and Prevention.[35]

That's why the CRS concluded, "While tragic and shocking, public mass shootings account for few of the murders related to firearms that occur annually in the United States." As for prevention, the congressional agency reported that, because of the rarity of the events, "potential perpetrators cannot be identified accurately, and no systematic means of intervening are known to be effective."[36]

But Obama wasn't going to let the facts stand in the way of his gun-grabbing campaign. Just five days after Sandy Hook, he announced that

Vice President Joe Biden would lead a task force to come up with "con-crete proposals no later than January—proposals that I then intend to push without delay." The president made it clear that the recommenda-tions of the task force were pre-determined, saying he had picked Biden to lead the effort because "he wrote the 1994 Crime Bill," which included the "assault weapon ban."[37]

While it was developing the agenda, the Biden task force invited pro-Second Amendment groups to just one White House meeting, on January 10. The NRA sent its top lobbyist for federal affairs, James J. Baker.

The NRA was not expecting a sincere dialogue. David Keene, who was NRA president at the time, told me the day before the meeting, "It has been clear since Newtown that the anti-Second Amendment crowd sees what happened there as giving them their best shot in years of attain-ing at least some and perhaps most of their substantive goals."

Keene explained why the threat to gun rights was more serious than ever before. "They are better prepared for this effort than at any time in the past. They have the president, the media and the messaging expertise they haven't had in the past—thanks largely to Mr. Bloom-berg's willingness to spend any amount they think they will need to coordinate and advance their activities." He warned, "This is going to be a long and tough fight because if they cannot roll back Second Amendment rights this time they may not get another chance for years or even decades."[38]

Keene was right. Obama always knew that what he was pushing was unlikely to pass on the federal level, but he kept up the campaign because it provided publicity that helped push the same agenda on the state level.

The ploy was effective. By January 15, New York Governor Andrew Cuomo was able to ram radical new anti-gun laws through the state legislature. The effort was aided by Bloomberg's money, and the legisla-tion itself was reportedly written by Hizzoner's staff.

The New York law set an example for how other liberal governors could use speed and White House influence to carve exceptions out of the Second Amendment.

The next day, Obama sought new federal gun control laws. He announced that the Biden task force had concluded with the new White House agenda.[39] The president forewarned what opponents would say, "There will be pundits and politicians and special interest lobbyists publicly warning of a tyrannical, all-out assault on liberty—not because that's true, but because they want to gin up fear or higher ratings or revenue for themselves."[40]

Then Obama acted just like a tyrant by thumbing his nose at Congress and signing twenty-three executive actions for things such as once again allowing the Centers for Disease Control to spend taxpayers' money to promote gun control.[41] He couldn't do it all himself, so Obama told Americans to call their representatives on Capitol Hill and demand his highest priorities—"universal background checks" and bans on "assault weapons" and magazines over ten rounds.

Shamelessly, he said his longtime wish list should be the law of the land "for the 25 other innocent children and devoted educators who had so much left to give."[42]

CHAPTER 3

PHOTO SHOOT

I first started trying to get a gun over a year before the Newtown shooting, at a time when gun control was not in the news. I thought it would be interesting to *Washington Times* readers to learn about what it took to get a legal firearm in D.C. I figured the whole process would take me about two weeks and maybe be five stories. In the end, it took four months to get my gun, it cost $435 in fees, there were over twenty stories in the series, and it resulted in the District's firearms laws changing.

I approached my boss, Brett Decker, the editorial page editor at that time, with my pitch. Decker, originally from Michigan and a gun owner himself, thought it was a great idea. He supported me as the series expanded and lengthened. He said "no" to only one of my requests: he wouldn't let me expense the gun.

Decker and I had been friends since we had both worked for then-House Majority Whip Tom DeLay, the Texas Republican legendary for his conservative views and hard-charging style. Decker was the speech-writer, and I was the press secretary, so we sat next to each other in a tiny, windowless office in the Capitol. We are polar opposites. Decker is thoughtful and intellectual, appreciates the arts, and has a calm demeanor. I am high energy, talk fast, bounce from topic to topic, subscribe to *Us Weekly*, and religiously watch *The Bachelor*. Decker has never owned a TV.

We became friends because we shared conservative values, and our differences amused us both. I went through a rough period in my life when I got caught up in a political scandal, and Decker was one of the few from my political career who stood by me. When he offered me a job at the *Washington Times*, I was overcome with gratitude for his kindness.

While Decker gave me the go-ahead for the gun series, he did not relieve me of my regular duties, which included writing a daily editorial on political issues. My job was intense. Decker had started his career as a researcher for the influential conservative columnist Bob Novak, who believed that opinion pieces had to be heavily reported. Novak had a rule that he had to make five calls a day for every column he wrote. This method ensured he double- or triple-sourced his information and used only original reporting to develop his opinion.

Decker instilled this principle in his staff. We were not allowed to use other outlets' reporting, nor written statements. The worst offense among the editorial board at the *Times* was if Decker overheard you mention *Wikipedia*.

In this environment, my days were full. I was under pressure to report and then write an editorial every day on a totally new topic. After my daily 4:00 p.m. deadline, I would turn in my work, stretch my legs, and then start figuring out the next day's topic—and lining up sources and interviews. I mostly reported on Capitol Hill about budget and tax issues.

So Decker gave me the green light for the gun series but let me know that I had to do it in my own time—after work and on weekends. Since I didn't think it would go on for very long, and I was excited about the challenge, I agreed.

I didn't realize it at the time, but by doing it this way, I was giving readers a realistic view of what any Washington resident has to face to get a legal gun. I discovered that exercising your Second Amendment rights in the nation's capital required taking days off or long absences from work. The firearms registration office at police headquarters is only open on weekdays, from 9:00 a.m. to 5:00 p.m. Either the police want to make it hard for fully employed people to get legal guns—or they assume only the unemployed want them.

Decker put Richard Diamond in charge of editing my gun series. Diamond was also an old friend. He had worked for then-House Majority Leader Dick Armey of Texas at the same time as Decker and I worked for DeLay. Diamond edited the editorials for the *Times*, so we worked together closely already. And he is a huge gun nut. His father taught him to shoot as a kid. He has built up a collection that the liberal media would call an "arsenal." He has all kinds of firearms—handguns, rifles, and shotguns. Of course he doesn't live in D.C. He commutes from Virginia to work at the *Times*.

Diamond laid down some ground rules for me. He told me that the *Washington Post* had done a story about getting a gun in D.C. a couple years earlier, but I was not allowed to read it. The reason was to put me on par with the average person in Washington who did not know any shortcuts or have any special resources for understanding the process in advance.

(After I completed the series in 2012, Diamond reminded me that I was now allowed to read the *Post*'s story. It turned out the story was only a single article, and it omitted all the details that make the registration process so onerous. I noticed the reporter got to expense the cost of his gun. The bias of the reporter in the *Post*'s story was evident in that he returned his free, legally owned gun at the end.)

Before I started writing, we needed a series title and photos to accompany the stories. I sent Diamond a list of title ideas such as "D.C.'s Gun

Laws" or "Getting a Gun in D.C." At the end of the email, I wrote, "Emily Gets Her Gun"—a takeoff on *Annie Gets Her Gun*, the Broadway show about Annie Oakley. It wasn't a typical newspaper title, but he went for it.

Diamond offered to use his guns for the photos, but we couldn't do it at work because the newspaper is in D.C. We decided to meet at his house in Virginia for our amateur photo shoot. We used point-and-click cameras, nothing fancy, with his giant movie screen that he uses to watch TV as the backdrop. It was October but still warm, so I was wearing a pink tank top, cut off-denim shorts, and flip-flops.

When I walked into Diamond's house, I was freaked out to see so many guns lying all over his living room. I had never even held a gun before.

———

I grew up in Baltimore. When I was a little girl, I was playing around on the floor of the backseat of my father's car and saw a revolver under the driver's seat. I wasn't curious about it. I was scared of it. I didn't touch it and never told him of my discovery. My father, Harmon Miller, never mentioned having a gun to my little sister Karen and me.

The memory came back to me as an adult when I told my dad about the series I was starting. I mentioned it a few times before he realized that I wanted a gun for self-protection, not just for the story.

"You're actually going to get the gun?" he asked, shocked.

"Of course," I said. "I wanted the gun first. The story came later."

"Well, why don't you get it and then give it back?"

"Dad, that would defeat the whole purpose."

"Oh, I don't like this at all, Em. Can't you just write the story and then give the gun back?"

"No, Dad, I'm keeping the gun. But I think you of all people would understand."

"What do you mean?" he asked, clearly not yet realizing the secret discovery I'd made as a child.

"You have a gun."

"I certainly do not."

"Yes, you do. You had a gun and kept it in the car under the driver's seat. I saw it."

There was a long silence.

"I didn't know you knew that."

"Well, I do."

It turns out my dad remembered the car incident well. He slammed on the breaks and saw the gun fly out from under the seat. He corrected my memory. "Emily, you said, 'What is that doing there?' And I said, 'Oh, it's no big deal. I use it for work.' You never asked any more about it." He said the gun was holstered with a clip to keep it under the seat.

He said he got the gun because his truck business was in a high-crime part of downtown Baltimore. The company was in a fenced lot. He had a button by his desk that went directly to the police if there was an emergency. But the safety concern was when, about once a month, an exchange was in cash, which he would have to take to or from the bank.

Dad got the revolver from a cousin who he said was "obsessed with guns." This was before the 1993 Brady Act requiring all dealers to do background checks on handgun buyers through the FBI before completing a sale. And of course back then there was no gun registration process such as D.C. has now. So it was legal for my dad's cousin to buy him a gun.

He explained what it took to get a legal carry permit in those days. Maryland was—and is—a "may issue" state, meaning you have to give the police a justification for why you want to bear arms. "I wasn't law enforcement and no one was looking to kill me. I wasn't a bail bondsman," my dad explained. "So the only reason was to be vulnerable for carrying cash—and people knowing it."

My father went to the state police several times with letters vouching for him, proof he was the owner of the company, and bank deposit slips showing the cash transfers. (Now people also get fingerprints and extensive background checks.) It took my dad about six to eight weeks for the carry permit—a card with a photo—to be issued. It was valid for two years, and he renewed it once.

"Then I didn't want to bother with it anymore," he recalled. "I'd have to go through that whole routine again with the police." Dad added that the system is much the same now. "They don't want people having guns, so it's a good way for them to prevent them—just wear them down."

I wondered where the revolver was today. "I kept it for another eight or nine years at the top of a high bureau, where you kids couldn't reach it. I kept the ammo in the same drawer, but the gun wasn't loaded." He finally got rid of it by returning it to a police "buy back" for $50.

Despite this family revelation, my dad still has not come around about my owning a gun. I have tried not to be defensive but instead find out why he is opposed to it.

"It could complicate a scenario. Even though it's for defense, it could make a situation worse than it started out to be," he told me. "You could get yourself hurt."

I think Dad's position comes more from the old-fashioned perception that guns are for men, not girls, than out of any hostility to firearms. I have repeatedly told him that I train regularly and am very responsible with my firearm. "I'm not happy about it, but if you feel more secure with it, then good for you," he finally conceded.

While he still asks all the time where I keep my gun, he is amused that I've become known as an advocate for the Second Amendment. That's not the typical path for a daughter.

My biggest fan in my family is my six-year-old nephew Christopher, who can't get enough YouTube videos of Aunt Emmy shooting big guns. My sister Karen just shakes her head. Boys will be boys.

At Diamond's house, the first gun I picked up—because I thought it was so pretty—was a Sig Sauer P226 X-Five L1 with a wood grip and stainless steel slide. I asked if I could hold it. Diamond took out the magazine and cleared the slide to ensure it was unloaded, then handed it to me.

I held the gun in my hand sideways, looking at it, too nervous to hold the grip like I would shoot it. "Just pick it up and hold it like this," he said, confidently holding the gun in his large hands. He handed me the firearm. "Just point it in that direction," he said, indicating an outside wall of his house.

Diamond doesn't say much. It was common for me to ask him for a change in an editorial and get this email response: "No." It's hard to get him to talk, but with the people he knows, you quickly learn, he is incredibly smart and knowledgeable. He has admirable integrity. I trust him completely, which is rare in Washington media and political circles.

I held it and tried to put my finger on the trigger but couldn't reach it without sliding my hand well over to the right side.

"Do this," he said, grabbing my hands and pushing my left hand onto the gun. "Now don't put your finger on the trigger. Just put your finger straight on the side of the gun."

Without moving my hands from the position he had set, I walked over to the movie screen and started holding the gun out in different positions while Diamond took photos.

He wanted photos of me holding rifles and shotguns to use in future stories. He handed me a shotgun, a Remington 870 in 12-gauge. It was so heavy that I could barely hold it above my waist. "Pick it up," he insisted. I did for a few photos and then lowered it again.

"It's too heavy. I don't like it," I said. Diamond, at 6 foot 4 inches tall and 205 pounds, hadn't thought of this issue. Neither has Vice President Biden.

Next he brought out an AR rifle with a bayonet on the end. This is what President Obama and Senator Dianne Feinstein call an "assault weapon." This was the first time I'd seen an AR-style rifle in real life, and I probably would have agreed with them that it looked like it would jump up and assault someone.

"I'm not touching that thing," I said, staring at it on the carpet.

"Pick it up," said Diamond.

"No, I'm scared. I don't want to," I said, backing away from it like it would explode on its own.

"It's not loaded. Just pick it up." I did and held it straight down in front of me. "Don't put your finger on the trigger, but pick it up to look through the scope." I did as he told me. He snapped a few photos. It wasn't nearly as heavy as the shotgun.

"Let's try something else," Diamond said, taking the gun out of my hands. He put it on the floor and told me to get on the ground and hold it.

"Just put your arm around it like you are going to shoot," he said. I did as he told me, and as he snapped, I grew more comfortable with the rifle. When I looked at the photos in the camera, I thought I looked tough and cool holding it.

These pictures weren't that important for the story, since this "assault rifle" was banned in the District. It had cosmetic features that some politicians find scary: a pistol grip to hold the gun from the bottom, which makes it easier to hold up than a gun at the shoulder; a collapsing stock, which adjusts to fit people with shorter arms, like me; and a bayonet. (I have never heard of a crime in modern history in which someone was stabbed to death by a knife on the end of a rifle, have you?)

We still needed a good photo with a handgun, which was the goal of the series. I picked up a small, shiny, silver-colored gun. It was a Kahr K40 in .40 caliber.

"I love this one. It fits my hands. This is the one I want to buy," I said.

"You have to shoot a gun before you decide what you will get. And that is a carry gun. You won't need it."

I took the Kahr and started posing with it. We found it difficult to get a photo that showed my face close up enough for a newspaper photo, while I was holding a gun in a way that is natural.

"The gun people are going to hate this," Diamond finally said, "But there's no other way to get you and the gun in the photo." He told me to hold the gun up like they do in the iconic opening of the show *Charlie's Angels*.

"What's so bad about this?" I asked.

"You're shooting out my ceiling," he said.

Despite the bad form, that photo turned out to be the best one and the logo of the series. We skipped our graphics department and Diamond somehow made the online logo himself. He's not an artist, but it worked perfectly.

Now that we were ready, I set out to buy my own gun and write about doing that in D.C.—beginning with my frustrating visit to the police registration office. After seeing Officer Brown, I had a twenty-two-page stack of confusing paperwork. But I also had a name: Charles Sykes.

CHAPTER 4

LOADED LANGUAGE: DISPELLING THE MYTHS OF GUN CONTROL

The entire public discussion of gun control issues today is dominated by terms created by the people who want to chip away at Americans' Second Amendment rights.

Anti-gun activists invented these phrases: assault weapons, high-capacity magazines, cop-killer bullets, universal background checks, the gun show loophole, and high-power ammunition. Not one of these terms actually means what President Obama, Mayor Bloomberg, and their allies mean to suggest by it. Rhetorical deception is the key component in the push for more gun control laws.

Consider Obama's remarks in Denver in April 3013. "The type of assault rifle used in Aurora, for example, when paired with a high-capacity magazine, has one purpose: to pump out as many bullets as possible, as fast as possible," the president said. "It's what allowed that gunman to shoot seventy people and kill twelve in a matter of a few minutes. I don't believe that weapons designed for theaters of war have a place in movie theaters."[1]

Politicians who talk about "assault" weapons are not using the term correctly when they are referring to modern semiautomatic sporting rifles that have cosmetic features that make them look like military arms. Obama and Dianne Feinstein and the rest misuse the term deliberately to confuse the public.

A longtime anti-gun activist revealed the scheme. "The weapons' menacing looks, coupled with the public's confusion over fully automatic machine guns versus semiautomatic assault weapons—anything that looks like a machine gun is assumed to be a machine gun—can only increase the chance of public support for restrictions on these weapons," said Josh Sugarmann, the executive director of the Violence Policy Center, which is funded by the Joyce Foundation.[2]

A true assault weapon is a machine gun or automatic firearm that continues to fire as long as the trigger is pulled. They have been highly regulated for civilian ownership since the National Firearms Act of 1934. To get one legally, you have to pay a $200 tax and go through an extensive background check by the ATF.[3]

There are now a half million machine guns registered,[4] but none has been used in a crime. Furthermore, automatic weapons have been banned from manufacture and import for civilians since 1986. The limited supply has made these weapons very expensive, often costing more than $20,000.[5] The bad guys can't afford them.

The Obama family deliberately calls semiautomatic guns "automatic" to scare people. First Lady Michelle Obama was wildly off base in her description of how Chicago teenager Hadiya Pendleton was shot with a handgun allegedly by a gang member on probation for a weapons charge.

"She was standing out in a park with her friends in a neighborhood blocks away from where my kids grew up, where our house is. She had just taken a chemistry test. And she was caught in the line of fire because some kids had some automatic weapons they didn't need," Michelle Obama told ABC News's Robin Roberts. *Good Morning America* edited out the incorrect information from the show, but the unedited transcript can be found online.[6]

Her husband told supporters at a private fundraiser in San Francisco that he wants gun control so that "we don't have another twenty children in a classroom gunned down by a semiautomatic weapon—by a fully automatic weapon in that case, sadly."[7]

It defies belief that two Harvard-educated lawyers in the White House don't know that automatic weapons are not used in crime.

The military and some police agencies and civilian federal law enforcement use "selective-fire" weapons. This type can be made to fire in semiautomatic mode or automatic mode by rotating a switch on the receiver. Some of these weapons are limited to two- or three-shot bursts of automatic fire.

But law enforcement and military guns are not the ones that these politicians are going after. They want to ban standard semiautomatic firearms—those that fire one shot with each trigger pull—which simply look like military weapons.

"Assault weapons" is now a political term referring to firearms that have certain cosmetic features. "Assault weapons" shoot the same ammunition as other guns, at the same speed and power. As the media uses the term "assault rifle" to refer to almost any black rifle, the public has picked up this terminology as well. However, the firearms industry uses the term "Modern Sporting Rifles" or MSRs.

NSSF Senior Vice President Larry Keane led his organization's effort to rename the rifles right before the presidential election in 2008 in expectation of Obama trying to reinstate the "assault weapons" ban. They considered many alternatives, including "tactical" and "utility." In the end, they chose "modern" to describe the materials the rifles are commonly made from—aluminum, polymer, and such. "Sporting" was used to differentiate the semiautomatic rifle from military firearms, which are automatic.

"We had to change the nomenclature starting with gun owners and industry members if we were ever to reframe the terms of the debate,"

Keane told me. "It has taken some time but the term MSR has grown in usage."[8]

In response to this effort, the anti-gun groups have adjusted their terminology to "military style" in order to continue the push to confuse the public into thinking that, for example, a semiautomatic AR-15 is the same as a fully-automatic M-16. The mainstream media has fallen for this trick, and you'll often see reporters use the term "military-style rifle."[9]

What constitutes an "assault weapon" for legislative purposes depends on who writes the bill. The original "assault weapons" ban that was in effect from 1994 to 2004 said that a rifle with a detachable magazine was illegal if it had any two of these cosmetic features: a folding or telescoping stock, a pistol grip that protrudes conspicuously beneath the action of the weapon, a bayonet mount, a flash suppressor or threaded barrel designed to accommodate a flash suppressor, or a grenade launcher.

Not one of these features alters how the firearm actually functions.

Currently seven states plus D.C. have their own "assault weapons" bans,[10] but there is no consistency in the definition. For example, adding a pistol grip to a rifle makes it illegal in D.C., but it is still perfectly legal to possess under neighboring Maryland's new "assault weapons" ban.[11] There is no "assault weapons" ban at all in Virginia, just on the other side of the Potomac. Of the three neighboring jurisdictions, Washington has by far the strictest gun control. It is also the only one where violent crime is increasing. That is not a coincidence.

———————

A Rasmussen poll taken the week after Sandy Hook showed that 55 percent of respondents want a ban on "assault-type weapons" and only 36 percent are opposed.[12] Just one year earlier, a Gallup poll put support at only 43 percent.[13]

Whenever I write stories for the *Washington Times* and mention polls on gun issues, readers comment about how they don't know who gets called for these surveys. They all say, "They didn't call me!"

So how do you explain the discrepancy between the poll results and the views of half the country who have a gun in the home?

Much of the contradiction is due to the loaded language that mostly liberal media pollsters use in the questions. For example, a *New York Times* and CBS poll in late April 2013 asked, "Do you favor or oppose a nationwide ban on semiautomatic weapons—including some rifles, pistols, and shotguns—that have detachable magazines, allowing them to rapidly fire a high number of rounds?"[14]

However, there is no such thing as a gun in the civilian market that allows you to more "rapidly fire." The speed of shooting for semiautomatic guns is how quickly your finger can pull the trigger for one round. Anyone not familiar with firearms would wrongly assume this question was asking about fully automatic weapons.

Similarly, an ABC News/*Washington Post* poll in April asked simply: "Would you support or oppose a law requiring a nationwide ban on the sale of assault weapons?" Fifty-seven percent said that they would.[15] But how many people called in these polls know that an assault weapon defined by Obama and his allies is a semiautomatic with certain cosmetic features? An insightful follow-up question to those who want to ban them would give them four options to define "assault weapon."

Another way to dig deeper to find out public consensus would be to ask the person to estimate the number killed each year from "assault weapons." Senator Dianne Feinstein said in January that an average of thirty-five people in the United States are killed each year by rifles with these certain characteristics. The public probably would guess many thousands.

Only Fox News polled the question, "Which is more important: protecting the constitutional right of citizens to own guns or protecting citizens from gun violence?" The Constitution was chosen, 53 to 42 percent.[16]

With public consensus seemingly at his back, Obama began to quickly work with Feinstein to get a new "assault weapons" ban in place. Having already started drafting one before the election, Feinstein was able to announce her new legislation less than two weeks after Sandy Hook.

This was her old "assault weapon" ban, but on steroids. Unlike the 1994 ban, there would be no true grandfather clause because you would have to register lawfully-owned rifles with the federal government. The legislation would then create a national gun registry in which an owner would have to submit to a background check, photograph, and finger-printing; supply the type and serial number of the firearm; and get certi-fication from local law enforcement of his identity and the fact that possession would violate neither state nor local law.[17]

"What we're looking at now is placing these weapons under the federal Firearms Act, the same act that exists for automatic weapons," Feinstein said at a press conference in Washington on December 21. She added, "We are also looking at a buy-back program."[18] (An oddly named program, since the government never owned the gun in the first place.)

The recoil was swift. This version of the bill in a white paper myste-riously disappeared from Feinstein's website, but the NRA kept a copy.

By the time she staged a dramatic press conference on January 24—standing in front of a wall of black rifles that are illegal in D.C. for everyone else—Feinstein had been forced to drop the federal gun registry and allow for a true grandfather clause for existing firearms.

However, she broadened the definition to grab more guns. She changed the so-called two-characteristic test to a one-characteristic test. That means a pistol, rifle, or shotgun with just one cosmetic feature would be illegal. The scary-looking features she listed were the pistol grip, forward grip, folding or telescoping or detachable stock, grenade or rocket launcher, barrel shroud, or threaded barrel. Again, none of these accessories changes the speed of firing or power of the gun.

Feinstein also drew up a list of 157 specific models that would be banned.[19] Gun owners would have to go through a government background check to sell or transfer a grandfathered gun.

"We have done our best to craft a responsible bill to ban these 'assault weapons'—guns designed for military use, bought all over this country and often used for mass murder," Feinstein said of her ambitious proposal.[20] To press her case at the drama-filled event, she and the other anti-gun officials referred to the Newtown shooting over forty-five times.[21] They will let no tragedy go to waste.

Obama often uses law enforcement to try to sway public opinion. "Weapons of war have no place on our streets, or in our schools, or threatening our law enforcement officers. Our law enforcement officers should never be outgunned on the streets."[22]

It is patently false that law enforcement is being "outgunned" on the streets by "assault weapons." Seventy-two law enforcement officials were killed in the line of duty in 2011, according to the most recent FBI data. Of those, fifty were slain by handguns, seven by rifles (of any type), six by shotgun, six by vehicle, two by hand, and one by a knife.[23]

And anyway, law enforcement has said they don't support the ban. PoliceOne did an extensive survey of fifteen thousand active and retired law enforcement officers across the country in March 2013. Almost 96 percent said that a ban on standard-capacity magazines would not reduce violent crime. When asked what kind of effect a ban on "assault weapons" would have on crime, 71 percent said "none." Another 21 percent said such a ban on guns based on cosmetic appearance would make crime worsen.[24]

It hadn't stopped mass public shootings either. The Columbine High School shooting took place in the middle of the period when the ban was in effect.

The type of weapons used at mass shootings actually varies. In January 2011, Jared Loughner used a Glock 9mm pistol with a thirty-three-round magazine to shoot Representative Gabrielle Giffords and kill six people in Tucson, Arizona.[25] In Colorado in July 2012, James Holmes allegedly brought a 12-gauge Remington Model 870 shotgun, a Glock Model 22 .40-caliber pistol, and a Smith & Wesson M&P15 AR-15-style .223-caliber rifle to the movie theater.[26]

At the shooting at a Sikh temple in Oak Creek, Wisconsin, in August 2012, Wade Michael Page killed six people using a Springfield XD(M) 9mm handgun.[27] In September of that year, Andrew Engeldinger used a Glock semiautomatic pistol in 9mm, paired with two fifteen-round magazines and a few loose rounds, to kill six people (including himself) at the Accent Signage Systems in Minneapolis, Minnesota.[28]

In Newtown, Connecticut, Adam Lanza used a .223-caliber rifle manufactured by Bushmaster. The model was XM15-E2S, with a thirty-round magazine. The police recovered two handguns inside the school, a Glock 10mm and a Sig-Sauer P226 in 9mm. A 12-gauge shotgun, an Izhmash Canta-12, was found in his car in the parking lot.[29]

Because of persistent internet rumors that Lanza never used a rifle, the Connecticut State Police released a statement listing the weapons and the locations where they were found at the school. I get asked about this a lot by readers. I think it is disrespectful to the victims to perpetuate this gossip. Lanza definitely used the AR rifle to murder those children.

Obama's insistence that "assault weapons" are to blame for a significant amount of violence in the U.S. is absurd. Criminals don't often use rifles because they can't conceal them. Eighty-nine percent of the homicides in America in which the type of weapon is known are by handguns.[30] Even if you look at all rifles, whether or not they have the cosmetic features, they accounted for only 323 of the 12,664 homicides in the United States in 2011. More murders were committed by shotguns —353—which Vice President Biden recommends everyone buy for self-defense.

In fact, twice as many people—728—were killed by attackers using hands and feet as by all types of rifles.[31] Yet no one is calling for an assault-fist ban.

Feinstein claimed at the Senate Judiciary Committee hearing on her bill that it is an "important issue of public policy" that 350 people were killed by "assault weapons" since her last ban expired.[32] Actually, no government agency tracks the style of rifles used in murders. Feinstein's staff would not tell me how she came up with this number.[33] In any case, by her own math the reason she wants to infringe on a constitutional right is the deaths of an average of thirty-five people a year.

She doesn't take into account that the number of murders has steadily gone down since the ban was lifted. The point is that anti-gun activists and politicians know that banning so-called assault weapons is not about public safety, but about public relations. It's their way of making inroads against the Second Amendment.

There has been only one extensive government research study on firearms laws in America. The Centers for Disease Control and Prevention (CDC)—an agency with a known bias against guns—looked at the various statutes from the local to national level. The two-year investigation evaluated the following laws: bans on specified firearms or ammunition (which includes the 1994 Assault Weapons Ban), restrictions on firearm acquisition, waiting periods for firearm acquisition, firearms registration and licensing of firearm owners, "shall issue" concealed weapon carry laws, child access prevention laws, and zero tolerance laws for firearms in schools.

The final 2003 CDC report concluded, "The Task Force found insufficient evidence to determine the effectiveness of any of the firearms laws or combinations of laws reviewed on violent outcomes."[34]

Leading anti-gun activists can't even come up with a solid reason for their desired ban. Mark Glaze heads up Mayors Against Illegal Guns and is Bloomberg's top advisor on gun control. At a press conference in the U.S. Capitol on February 6, I asked Glaze why Bloomberg wanted an "assault weapons" ban if it had already proved a failure at reducing violence when it was in effect for ten years.

"We believe the assault weapons ban had some good effects," Glaze said. "Some crime was driven to other kinds of guns. And when you make particularly lethal weapons less available, you make it less easy to perpetrate mass killings."

There is no evidence that what Glaze said was factual, but it offers insight into the twisted thinking of Bloomberg and his allies. Apparently it is a net positive for the country when criminals use a type of weapon that the mayor of New York approves of, even if the same number of people are killed.

Feinstein explained her opinion of "assault weapons" at the January press conference: "Military-style 'assault weapons' have but one purpose... to hold at the hip if possible, to spray fire to be able to kill large numbers."[35]

Hardly. According to a survey conducted in 2010 for the NSSF, 90 percent of the owners of modern sporting rifles use them for target shooting, 80 percent for home defense, and 60 percent for hunting. About 44 percent of owners are former military or law enforcement. The typical owner is over thirty-five years old, married, and has some college education.[36]

The AR-15 is the target of much of the hate directed at "assault rifles." The AR, which originally stood for the manufacturer, ArmaLite Rifle, but now refers to the platform or style of the gun, is one of the most common firearms sold to civilians. The gun is black and looks like a military gun, but it does not have the lever to switch to automatic mode.

Biden was simply wrong when he said that a "shotgun will do better for you than your AR-15" and that "people can handle a shotgun a hell of a lot better than they can a semiautomatic weapon in terms of both their aim and in terms of their ability to deter people coming."[37]

I've shot several modern sporting rifles and standard shotguns, and the rifles are significantly easier for me to control. They are lighter, so I can hold them up to aim with the sights. The pistol grip on the bottom helps me to hold up the gun by using my left hand for better control. The dreaded "collapsing stock" means I can adjust the size of the gun to fit my petite frame.

Gayle Trotter of the Independent Women's Forum testified at the first Senate Judiciary Committee hearing on the post-Newtown gun control bills. She spoke about the importance of firearms for women defending themselves and their children.[38] I was seated at one of the four long press tables behind the witnesses. The hundred or so public seats in the room were filled with anti-gun activists wearing green ribbons or yellow stickers that said "Stop Gun Violence NOW."

Senator Chuck Grassley of Iowa, the ranking Republican on the committee, asked Trotter, "Can you tell us why you believe a semi-automatic rifle such as an AR-15 has value as a weapon of self-defense? And does banning guns which feature designs to improve accuracy disproportionately burden women?"

Trotter responded, "I believe it does. Young women are speaking out as to why AR-15 weapons are their weapon of choice.... They are easy for women to hold. And most importantly, their appearance. An assault weapon in the hands of a young woman defending her babies in her home becomes a defense weapon." Trotter added, "I speak on behalf of millions of American women across the country who urge you to defend our Second Amendment right to choose to defend ourselves."

Suddenly, the women activists in the audience began laughing and loudly heckling her. Several yelled out, "She doesn't speak for me."

Without thinking, I yelled out loudly, "She speaks for me!" My fellow reporters looked up in horror. The media is supposed to be impartial, and at least follow the decorum of the Senate. I squished down in my seat and went back to transcribing her testimony.

Senator Lindsey Graham—who has his own AR-15 type rifle at home—said to Trotter, "That explains the dilemma we have here.... The people who were giggling were saying to you, 'That's crazy. Nobody I know thinks that way.' Which reminds me of the Harvard professor who said, 'I can't believe the governor lost. Everybody I know voted for him.'"[39] The protesters did not burst out again.

Also at the hearing, Graham pointed to a poster of a rifle and noted that he and Senator Ted Cruz of Texas had wanted to bring in an actual rifle to demonstrate the absurdity of the gun bans posed. However, unlike Feinstein, who was aided by four local and federal law enforcement agencies in bringing rifles banned in the District to her Senate press conference, the Republicans were not able to bring in the guns. Instead, Cruz used a photo of a standard wood-stock hunting rifle and held up a plastic pistol grip to demonstrate the absurdity that simply adding this single feature would transform a legal gun into an illegal "assault weapon" under the new ban being proposed by Feinstein.

Obama barnstormed the country to push for this "assault weapon" ban until the Senate vote on it in April. But he knew it could never get through the Republican House. The real purpose of the four-month public relations push was to build support for the same ban on the state level. He has been effective in doing that. Since the beginning of 2013, New York, Connecticut, and Maryland have passed "assault weapons" bans, despite there being few or no murders by rifle in those states.[40]

Senate Majority Leader Harry Reid pretty much sunk Feinstein's bill before it even hit the floor, telling reporters, "Her amendment, using the most optimistic numbers, has less than forty votes—that's not sixty." He hit the bull's-eye on that vote count.[41]

The "assault weapons" ban is simply a means of confiscation. This is not a conspiracy theory.

The NRA's Institute for Legislative Action acquired a secret internal memo written by the Obama administration's Justice Department in January 2013 that sheds light on the real objective. The document concluded that a "complete elimination of assault weapons would not have a large impact on gun homicides."

However, the author, Deputy Director of the National Institute of Justice Greg Ridgeway, claimed, "If coupled with a gun buyback and no exemptions then it could be effective."[42]

No exemptions means existing owners are not grandfathered in, so they would have to turn their guns over to the government. In other words: confiscation.

CHAPTER 5

ONE GUN DEALER AND SEVENTEEN STEPS TO REGISTRATION

C harles Sykes is the one person holding Washington, D.C., residents' Second Amendment rights afloat. He is our single licensed gun dealer. Federal law requires that all interstate sales of handguns have to include a "transfer" through a dealer in the buyer's own state. If there was no Sykes, we would not be allowed to buy a handgun. And for a short period of time, even after the *Heller* ruling, that was the case.

Four months before I met Sykes in October 2011, he had lost the lease for his business when the building was sold. He had been a gun dealer since 1994, but since civilians were banned from owning handguns until 2009, he just did transfers for police officers and security guards licensed to carry on the job. (Dick Heller, the lead plaintiff in *District of Columbia v. Heller*, who sued the District of Columbia all the way to the Supreme Court to establish his Second Amendment rights, had a gun license for his job as a security guard. He just wanted to have the same right to have a gun in his D.C. home—and he had to sue the city to get it.)

When Sykes lost his lease, city officials made it almost impossible for him to relocate by taking advantage of a stray word in the law to classify his business as a "firearms retail sales establishment"—which it technically was not. Sykes never wanted to buy or sell guns. That was too dangerous a business to be in in D.C.

The designation meant he couldn't reopen his business within the length of a football field from a school, library, church, house, or apartment. In this tightly packed city, that pretty much meant he had to either set up shop in the Washington Monument, move his business into a multi-million-dollar stately home, or shut down. He spent weeks going around town trying to find a reasonably priced option. At one point, the city gave him a small-scale map of the places he could supposedly find leasing options—but left off all the street names.

Officials were deliberately trying to put him out of business. So from May until August 2011, D.C. residents could not buy handguns. Their Second Amendment right, recently upheld by the Supreme Court, was again being denied, this time by a backdoor scam.

Finally, public pressure built up, and city officials realized the court could rule against them again if this continued. Sykes finally proposed the wild idea of leasing government space to set up a gun dealership. The bureaucrats relented and found an open spot in a huge government building one floor down from police headquarters and next door to the Department of Motor Vehicles.

This is the problem the city council chairman, Kwame Brown, crowed about solving at our *Washington Times* roundtable. We never asked Brown about the issue, but he took full credit for solving a problem originally caused by the city government.

———

Although Charles Sykes is the key to getting a legal gun in D.C., I didn't learn about him from the firearms registration office. Officer Brown mentioned Sykes's name to me, but nothing in the twenty-two pages of paper for potential gun owners explained that he was instrumental in getting every new pistol into the city after its purchase. The only clue was a Xeroxed copy of Sykes's business card stapled to the registration form.

Using the copy of the business card, I went to find Sykes and figure out why Officer Brown told me I needed to talk to him. By then, Sykes was operating out of the space he had been given in the same hall as the DMV. This is most likely the only private business, much less gun dealer, housed in a government building in the U.S.

I found a nondescript brown door marked 1140A with a small sign on the wall that said "CS Exchange." There was a button on the door with a big sign that said "BELL." Sykes had found that so many people looking to fight dumb parking tickets accidentally rang his bell that he had posted pieces of paper on either side of the office door: "ATTEN-TION—ANYTHING TO DO WITH TICKETS AND PAYMENTS IS DONE DOWN THE HALL IN ROOM 1157."

When I got there, the door was closed and locked. I wasn't sure if I should ring the bell or not. After a few moments, a man came up to me and asked gruffly, "What are you doing?"

"I'm just waiting to talk to Mr. Sykes about getting a gun," I said. The man stared at me hard. He was African-American, middle-aged, mustached, wearing dark pants and a maroon shirt.

"Do you have an appointment?" he asked. I said that I did not, but I was just hoping to talk to Mr. Sykes briefly.

"I'm Charles Sykes. I only see people who have an appointment," he said. I waited. Finally, he relented, "But you're here, so come in for a minute."

We walked into his space, which had a former payment counter in the front. He led me through a door to his very small office. His desk and two other small chairs facing it were all that could fit in the space because of the two large safes against one wall. On the office wall were six newly framed licenses he had had to get in order to reopen inside the public building.

I didn't tell Sykes I was a reporter. I just told him that I wanted to get a gun and didn't know anything about how to do it. I kept my small tape recorder on inside my bag because I couldn't take notes and give away my secret mission, so that I would be treated like every other potential gun buyer.

Sykes is very sly and aware. We have developed a warm relationship over time.

I was in his office about six months later on another case, and he said off-handedly, "So do you have your little tape recorder on in your bag this time?" I reddened and my heart started racing. He just laughed. "You thought I never knew, huh?"

He has to be extra vigilant because the criminals know he's the man with the guns in D.C. That's why he refused to let me take his photo for the series. I took a couple of his office and have caught him in photos of other people for stories, but I always crop him out of the pictures out of respect for his safety.

Sykes charges $125 to do the transfer, which includes the FBI background check. It costs the same whether the firearm is sent in the mail or he picks it up at the relatively nearby dealers in Virginia or Maryland. The city originally charged Sykes only a token $100 a year for leasing the space, but according to him he has to spend a lot of money on expensive insurance policies in order to have guns delivered, stored, and then transferred to residents—all inside this huge government building. Aside from the other risks, one reason he doesn't actually buy or sell guns is that his insurance would be still higher.

When I first wrote about Sykes and his standard transfer rate of $125, readers around the country were shocked. They believed he was overcharging because he had a monopoly in D.C. What they were missing is that while firearm sales have skyrocketed everywhere else in the country during the Obama administration, not much has changed in Washington.

Most people with guns in the city have never registered them—and that includes both the good guys and the bad guys. Since handguns were legalized in 2009, only 4,634 guns have been registered.[1] That number includes long guns, which don't have to go through Sykes. According to Sykes, about half of the handguns are not new so they don't need to be transferred. That means he is transferring only about 250 guns a year. At his going rate, that comes to gross revenue of about $31,000 a year.

"I'm not making much," Sykes explained to me. "You don't see a big line outside that door? It's not like it's a sale on iPads or iPhones where people camp out the night for the door to open in the morning to get in here." He was laughing, but I did notice that no one else came into his office during the forty-five minutes we spoke that first day. That's why Sykes works by appointment only, generally during a four-hour midday window, then goes to his second job in the afternoon. He runs this business because he believes in the Second Amendment.

"I don't understand why they try to make it so difficult for the honest people to get a gun the right way," Sykes told me. "In all other cities, you can have guns. Why do they say, 'We don't want guns in the nation's capital?' They are here. And you can go a lot of different places and get them just like that," he said, snapping his fingers. He meant the guns that are all over the streets. The bad guys aren't making appointments with Sykes.

Since demand is so low and the government is unfriendly, no one else is trying to get in the gun business. And I doubt the city would give a dealer who actually buys and sells guns a zoned space. As Kwame Brown has said, "There's not a lot of people jumping up saying that they want to sell guns." What he meant was, there are not a lot of people jumping up and down to sell legal guns. The illegal ones are a hot commodity on the dangerous streets of Washington, D.C.

That day in October I asked Sykes for help understanding the registration process. He told me that he had worked (as a civilian) in the police department's registration office, so he knew the whole system, and he would share his inside knowledge with his clients.

"I am a notary, so I'll take care of that part," he said, though I didn't understand what he meant. "You need to go out and pick a gun and let me know where you bought it."

It is strange to have a gun dealer tell you to go buy a gun somewhere else. Sykes recommended a couple of dealers he knew in neighboring states. He asked if I knew what kind of gun I wanted. I said that I had never shot a gun. I couldn't tell from his expression if he was amused or concerned.

He handed me one of his business cards. "I take these upstairs to the registration office all the time, but they refuse to give them out," he said. "Call me if you have any questions. I know how this works A to Z."

"I'm pretty overwhelmed with all this paper. I don't know where to start," I told him.

"Take the firearms safety course. It's a requirement, and you can just get it out of the way," he said. "After you buy the gun, call me to make an appointment." He clearly didn't want any more unexpected visitors. And to be fair, if I had an office full of guns in D.C., I wouldn't have liked a stranger lurking outside my door, no matter who it was.

Sykes threw out a bunch more tips, which I wrote down quickly, but I didn't really know what any of it meant.

"Show them the bill of sale, that will cut down on the ten-day waiting period. Call the day before you want to pick it up, and I'll be here to give it to you. They'll take it back to test fire and escort you back upstairs. There are three gun lists on the website—Maryland, Massachusetts, and California—check it's the exact make and model and caliber. It has to be on the list by January 1, 2009, or it's not recognized as updated."

I was suffering from information overload. So when I got home, I decided that the only way to make sense of it all was to go through every page and write down each thing I would have to do to get a legal gun. It came to seventeen steps:

1. Fill out the "Statement of Eligibility" form;
2. Find a D.C.-certified instructor for a gun safety class;
3. Take four hours of classroom instruction and one hour of range instruction, plus get the instructor to fill out a "compliance form";
4. Provide proof that my vision is good;
5. Provide proof of residency (my driver's license would work for steps four and five—but the majority of Washingtonians who use public transportation have to get a vision test and collect documentation of residency);
6. Buy two passport photos;
7. Study D.C.'s laws and regulations for firearms;
8. Take a twenty-question multiple choice test;
9. Get fingerprinted;
10. Pay government fees;
11. Buy the gun;
12. Transfer the gun through Sykes;
13. Have Sykes fill out the section in the application for the firearms registration certificate;
14. Take all the documents to the registration office;
15. Wait five days for the application to be approved;
16. If the application is approved, wait five days for Sykes to be legally allowed to release the firearm;
17. Pick the gun up from Sykes and take it to the police department for a ballistics test.

When I had written out my list based on the police guidelines Officer Brown had given me, I felt a little more in control of the mess, but also daunted by what I had in front of me. And it wasn't until later that I learned I hadn't put these items in the most efficient order—I could have saved some time if I had been able to guess the right order. (But should citizens have to play guessing games with the police to exercise their constitutional rights?)

First, I sat down to fill out the "Statement of Eligibility" form.[2] This turned out to be the form the police use when they do the District's background check. Sykes would do the FBI background check before transferring the gun to me. Determining if I was eligible to own a firearm in D.C. was easy. I've never been indicted for a felony, for example, much less convicted.

I found out later that the questions generally overlap the information the federal government uses to determine if the buyer is in one of the categories of people who are prohibited from owning guns. However, the District's checks are broader.

For example, the feds will stop you from buying a gun if you were convicted in the last year on drug charges,[3] while D.C. stretches the time frame to five years. (So the former mayor and current council member Marion Barry, who was caught smoking crack cocaine, could still own a gun because it was a misdemeanor and happened twenty years earlier.)

D.C. also wanted to know if I "suffer from any physical defect which makes it unsafe for you to possess and use a firearm safely and responsibly?" This question is so vague, it seemed like anything from tennis elbow to having no fingers could make you ineligible. I checked "no."

Had I ever been found negligent in a firearm-related mishap causing death or injury to another human being? Apparently you could shoot yourself in the leg—but not someone else—and still be considered responsible enough to get another gun. If Plaxico Burress moved to D.C., he would benefit from this wording.

City ordinance also bans anyone who has been convicted of prostitution or operating a "bawdy house," which I learned from Google means running a brothel. You're also deemed ineligible if you've been convicted of "vagrancy." I'm not sure why hanging around the 7-Eleven parking lot too long makes you unqualified to have a gun.

For the next question, I had to go back to Google again, this time to figure out what "abrogating strikes" meant. I went through three pages of search results, and I still don't know. It sounded like something union-related, so as a political conservative, I was fairly sure I had not done it.

At this point, I had straight check marks down the "no" column on the form. I remembered, though, that when I picked up these papers, Officer Brown warned me of a "trick question" on this document. I read through each question carefully and did my research on the meaning of unfamiliar terms, but couldn't figure out the question she considered a trick. Finally, on question 9, I figured it out. "Have you provided accurate and true facts on your application for a Firearms Registration Certificate?" Bingo! The one question where a law-abiding person should check the "yes" box.

I signed my name to affirm that the information was accurate. I was about to check step one off my to-do list when I read the bottom of the form where it required the signature of a notary public. Then I remembered that Sykes had told me he was a notary, just so he could sign this form for his clients. Although I hadn't quite completed this step, I still checked it off my list.

What I didn't know was that there were even more hoops I would have to jump through to get a legal gun than the seventeen on my list. The city didn't advertise some of their requirements.

The First Amendment right to free speech has only one step: doing it. But D.C.'s politicians make you go through seventeen steps to exercise your Second Amendment rights.

The right to keep and bear arms is a basic human right. As I had told Charles Sykes in our first meeting, I just wanted a gun so I could defend myself at home.

"That's right," he told me. "It's better to have a gun and never need it, than need a gun and not have one."

CHAPTER 6

"HIGH-CAPACITY" MAGAZINES AND OTHER INVENTIONS OF ANTI-GUN RHETORIC

I
f you walked into a gun store and asked for a high-capacity magazine, you'd be met with blank stares. There is no such thing.

The magazine is the part of a gun that holds the ammunition. It
is generally detachable to make it easier to load. Every gun comes with
a standard magazine, but most can be changed out for different sizes. As
I was about to find out in my adventure in gun-buying in the nation's
capital, if I happened to decide on a gun that comes with a standard
thirteen-round magazine, I would have to replace it with one that has a
piece of metal blocking bullets one, two, and three from being loaded in
order for it to be legal.

The term "high-capacity" is secret code from anti-gun groups to refer
to any ammunition magazine bigger than they think civilians should be
allowed to own. It's terminology made up just to scare and confuse
people.

When the term has been applied under the law, it has been defined at
anywhere from seven to fifteen rounds. The federal government, D.C.,
and eight states have had their own definitions.[1]

Modern semiautomatic handguns generally can hold between 12 and 19 cartridges in the magazine, depending on caliber. Modern sporting rifles usually hold fifteen to thirty rounds. There are at least 300 million removable magazines in the U.S., and about 30 million of those have a capacity of over thirty rounds, according to the National Shooting Sports Foundation (NSSF).

That's a lot of magazines that would suddenly be illegal if President Obama gets his way. He said in January that Congress had to pass laws to restrict "magazine clips that aren't necessary for hunters and sportsmen and those responsible gun owners who are out there."[2]

For its new gun control law, New York arbitrarily chose seven rounds as the cutoff, a magazine capacity that exists only for small pistols or vintage Model 1911 pistols. Reportedly, the inexperienced Bloomberg policy staffers who wrote the New York statute didn't know enough about the firearms industry.[3] Thus, Governor Cuomo had to go back and update the law to say that magazines could be larger, but people could only load seven rounds, and to exempt the police from the ban. It's ridiculous to think criminals will carefully count out seven bullets and not fully load their magazines.

The size of the magazine is irrelevant for fighting crime for two reasons. First, criminals use way fewer than 10 rounds. A 2004 study for the Department of Justice by Christopher S. Koper, a professor of criminology at George Mason University, reported that "assailants fire less than four shots on average, a number well within the 10-round magazine limit."[4]

Second, it's very quick and easy to change a magazine. I'm an amateur, but I can't even time how quickly I reload a magazine because it's so fast. I just push the magazine release button with my right thumb, the empty magazine drops out, and I push the full magazine into the bottom of the grip frame.

Maybe it's because Biden owns 12- and 20-gauge shotguns that he doesn't know the mechanics of a handgun. He blamed the death toll in the Newtown shooting on "high-capacity" magazines. "Maybe one of their children would be alive if we didn't have a policy you could walk in and you could buy a clip—you could buy a magazine—that housed thirty rounds, or in Aurora, a hundred rounds."[5]

(AR style rifles come standard with thirty-round magazines. The Aurora shooter allegedly used an after-market extra-large magazine or drum with a hundred rounds that jammed, which happens frequently. These fifty- or hundred-round magazines are notoriously unreliable and likely to jam because of the physics of the spring under so much weight. Military personnel sometimes tape thirty-round magazines back to back to keep the reliability but have the extra rounds easily accessible.)

Government studies have said a ban on standard magazines over a certain size won't make us safer. The CDC task force concluded that "evidence was insufficient to determine the effectiveness" of the "high-capacity magazine" ban.[6] According to a Justice Department study released in May 2013, the number of criminal shootings (fatal and non-fatal) has decreased 7 percent since the decade-long federal ban on "high-capacity" ammunition devices expired in 2004.[7]

You'll often hear liberal politicians and the media incorrectly use the term "clip" when discussing ammunition magazines. Majority Leader Harry Reid, for example, argued during the Senate debate against "large clips...designed to kill humans."[8] But clips and magazines are not the same. Clips are used in older firearms with internal magazines, such as the Model 1903 bolt-action Springfield of World War I and the M1 Garand from World War II.

Modern firearms have removable magazines that are loaded externally and then inserted into the gun, so they don't require clips. We should make a deal with Obama and his allies that we will agree to ban all clips over ten rounds but leave magazines alone. They might actually fall for it.

Despite what Reid, Biden, and the president's other allies keep claiming, there are real-world reasons why law-abiding people need full magazines. Criminals are likely to carry as many magazines as they need, but individuals with their guns concealed for self-defense purposes often aren't able to bring extra magazines.

Also, the number of rounds needed to stop a dangerous criminal can be high in a stressful situation. That number goes up significantly if there is more than one assailant. At least one quarter of all violent crimes committed by strangers involved more than one offender, according to the Justice Department's most recent survey of violent crimes in the U.S. in which the number of offenders is known. The number is even higher for violent robberies—half of which are by multiple assailants who are strangers to their victims, with 15 percent involving a terrifying four or more attackers.[9]

So if a high-capacity magazine ban would not improve public safety, why are the politicians so focused on it? That internal January 2013 Justice Department memo obtained by the NRA described the Obama administration's true goal—confiscation. "In order to have an impact, large capacity magazine regulation needs to sharply curtail their availability to include restrictions on importation, manufacture, sale, and possession. An exemption for previously owned magazines would nearly eliminate any impact," wrote Greg Ridgeway.[10]

Another well-designed deceptive term in the gun-grabbers' arsenal is "cop-killer bullet." This phrase was invented to go after guns in the name of protecting the police. When the politicians can't get their hands on your firearm, the next best way to disarm you is to get rid of your ammunition. Thus Obama talks about "bullets often designed to inflict maximum damage."[11] And Biden uses the term "cop-killer bullets."[12]

Obama and his allies have effectively used this language to confuse the public. A Pew poll done the week after Newtown showed that 56 percent favor "banning bullets designed to explode or penetrate bullet-proof vests."[13] And a Gallup poll taken the week after Obama gave this presentation showed that 67 percent of voters would support a law banning possession of armor-piercing bullets by anyone other than the military and law enforcement.[14]

Here are the facts. Armor-piercing ammunition has already been banned under federal law for over twenty-five years. Neither the ATF nor the FBI could give me a single case of law enforcement killed by armor-piercing bullets.[15] It's such an irrelevant public-safety issue that the agencies don't even track it. Obama and Biden are just, once again, shamefully using the police for their political agenda.

———

I visited Winchester, the ammunition manufacturer, in August 2012 on an educational and training trip for female journalists who cover gun issues. Their engineers explained the basics of ammunition to me. There are three styles. Rimfire, the oldest style, has a one-piece casing of metal that goes around the whole shell, encasing the bullet, gunpowder, and primer. The second style is a shotgun shell—a shellcase, which is a complex mix of plastic and metal, plus either a slug or a lot of small pellets.

The third type of ammunition is the modern kind called centerfire. It is the highest-powered and most commonly used for personal defense. The brass or steel casing of the cartridge holds the gunpowder. At the base of the case is the primer that, when struck by the gun's firing pin, ignites the powder charge. The bullet, which is normally made of lead, is the projectile that leaves the gun to hit the target. It is surrounded by a jacket of copper or copper plate.

One type of centerfire ammunition is full metal jacket, which means the metal goes over the cartridge and the bullet in one piece. Full metal jackets are pointed at the top so they can't change shape. They are cheaper to make and so generally used for target practice.

Until twenty years ago this type was also used for personal defense. But the problem with it was that full metal jacket bullets would go straight through a violent felon and into an innocent bystander. That's why I was taught at Winchester never to use my target ammo at home. It could go through the bad guy, through a wall, and accidentally hit my neighbor. (It has not come out in court documents yet, but some ammunition experts surmise the Aurora, Colorado, shooter may have used full metal jacket rounds since people were hit through the walls of the neighboring theater.)

To meet the needs of law enforcement, ammunition companies developed hollow-point and soft-point bullets that could expand in tissue, reducing the chances they would over-penetrate and go completely through an attacking criminal. These bullets also make hunting safer because they will go into the game and not through it to hit a person.

It is worth noting the massive shortage of ammunition in the U.S. in 2013 because of increased civilian demand out of fears of gun control legislation and of government agencies supposedly stockpiling ammunition. Many of my readers have told me about the theory that the Obama administration is making massive purchases of ammunition in order to make citizens defenseless.

While the House of Representatives is investigating the large ammunition buys by federal agencies, such as the Department of Homeland Security, the Social Security Administration, the National Oceanic and Atmospheric Administration, and the National Weather Service, it is most likely going to turn out that this was not an effort by the federal government to seize up the supply.

Both the NRA and the NSSF have repeatedly said that the large purchases are within normal historical levels. The contracts are for multi-year purchases in order to keep the prices at current levels. Even if the federal agencies bought all the ammunition at one time, the NRA said that it would only be about 3 percent of total domestic ammunition production.[16]

So what about "armor-piercing" bullets? The military originally used the term "armor-piercing" to refer to rounds capable of penetrating armored vehicles. But the gun-grabbers have picked up on this terminology and misapplied it to describe a bullet made of hardened metals that can penetrate a soft body armor vest made of Kevlar®. Now the government also uses the term to mean these types of ammunition.

The manufacture, import, and sale of handgun bullets made of hardened brass, steel, or any other alloy has been prohibited since 1986.[17] That legislation was never intended to ban rifle ammunition. While centerfire rifle bullets can penetrate Kevlar®, rifles are too cumbersome for criminals on the street, who prefer handguns because they're less obvious.

The new scheme to ban ammunition is to replace the existing statute with a performance test to determine whether a bullet can penetrate soft body armor, which is a sneaky way to get at all rifles. Most ordinary centerfire rifle rounds can penetrate a soft body armor vest because rifles are significantly more powerful than handguns. Law enforcement and the military use hard body armor with metal or ceramic plates inserted into their vests to protect against such powerful rounds.

Mayor Bloomberg told Piers Morgan after Aurora, "The only reason to have an armor-piercing bullet is to go through a bullet-resistant vest. The only people that wear bullet-resistant vests are our police officers."[18] He flat out ignores the ATF study published eleven years after the ban on truly armor-piercing bullets concluded that there was no longer a threat to police. "Since the enactment of these laws, no law enforcement officer in the United States has died as a result of a round of armor piercing ammunition, as defined, having been fired from a handgun, subsequently penetrating an officer's protective body armor causing lethal injuries," concluded a government panel.[19]

Bloomberg also said on CNN that police officers should "go on strike" over the issue. While he may speak for the police chiefs appointed by liberal mayors like himself, he does not speak for rank-and-file cops and elected sheriffs.

That PoliceOne survey of fifteen thousand law enforcement officers asked what effect passage of the White House's proposed legislation would have on improving police officer safety. Sixty-one percent said no effect, while 25 percent said Obama's plan would actually put them in more danger.[20]

Sheriffs in Colorado are suing the state over the new gun control law. Many sheriffs in jurisdictions around the country have said they would not enforce new state laws.[21] The reason is simple: gun control laws mean wasting time going after the good guys for things such as eleven-round magazines and fewer resources to fight the criminals.

The loaded language of the gun-grabbers is effective public relations but terrible public policy. None of these proposals has been proven to reduce crime. The only effect is to make it harder for law-abiding Americans to exercise their Second Amendment rights.

CHAPTER 7

LEARNING TO SHOOT STRAIGHT

I was working my way through the seventeen steps to getting a legal handgun in D.C., but I still needed to learn how to shoot a gun.

I thought that I would learn by taking Washington's mandatory gun course, but my editor, Richard Diamond, told me that I didn't need to take a class to learn to shoot a gun. Most people learn the safety rules and fundamentals from friends and family. Diamond's father first took him to a shooting range in their hometown in southern California when he was ten years old.

It turned out to be a good thing that Diamond insisted on teaching me himself because, I found out later, the city didn't mandate teaching fundamentals or gun safety, just memorizing the law and pulling a trigger.

Diamond and I discussed where we should meet to begin my lessons before going to a range. The *Washington Times* is on the very edge of northeast D.C., but still it would be illegal for him to bring even an unloaded gun to the office to teach me there. It would also be against the law for him to bring it to my home in the District. I suggested that we could meet at a Starbucks or Panera in Virginia, but he pointed out that we might scare other customers. We decided to meet at his house in Virginia again.

When I arrived, Diamond had several handguns lying on the floor. He started by handing me the .40 caliber Kahr that I had liked at our photo shoot because it looked cool, and because I was under the impression that small guns were easier for women to shoot.

A couple days earlier, Diamond had sent me a link to the NRA safety test that you have to pass before using their range. I took the studying very seriously, but nothing made sense without having ever been in a shooting range or live fire before. I emailed Diamond. "It says to keep the gun pointed down range. Which way is that?" I asked.

Now I was going to acquire some practical knowledge. Diamond handed the gun to me by the handle and said, "Always check to see if the gun is unloaded, even if someone tells you it is." He showed me how to push a button to make the magazine pop out of the bottom of the gun. He then pushed the top—called the slide—back so I could look inside to see if there were any rounds in the chamber. Then it was my turn to do the check myself.

I pulled and pulled but couldn't get the heavy steel slide to move. "Pull harder," Diamond said. "You can't break it." I really pulled, and the top slid back so I could look inside. There were no rounds.

"Always keep the gun pointed in a safe direction. You can aim at that," he said, pointing to a pile of books on the floor with a clipboard on top.

"Why is that safe?" I asked.

He picked up the clipboard and knocked his hand against it. "Kevlar®," he said. "You also need to know what is behind where you are aiming."

"Isn't your garage under this floor?" I asked.

"I took my car out before you got here," he replied. He wasn't giving me much confidence in my ability to not accidentally shoot something in his house.

I took the gun and pointed it at the pile of books on the floor with my right hand.

"Finger off the trigger!" Diamond said sharply. "Never touch the trigger until you are ready to shoot." He had already given me this lesson when we took photos, but I didn't remember it. He was teaching me the NRA's three safety rules. Over time, these have become automatic for me, but I always appreciate when someone repeats them when I go shooting. The concept behind the rules is that even if you mess up one rule—say you have your finger on the trigger—then the other two—gun in a safe direction and unloaded—will save you from a disaster.

When we took the photos, Diamond had positioned my hands on the gun to make it appear that I knew how to hold it safely. Now I needed to learn for myself the fundamentals of handling a gun. He handed me a bunch of red bullets and explained that these "snap caps" were fakes used to practice pulling a trigger. Diamond told me to put the fake bullets into the magazine. I pushed one into the top of the column-shaped part but couldn't get it to go into the space.

"It's backwards," Diamond pointed out. I turned the snap cap around and pushed it into the magazine. Even the right way around, it did take some effort. I've learned over time that loading magazines never gets easy, and it's particularly hard for women because we don't have the hand strength to fight against the magazine springs.

Later, I learned at Winchester with the other female reporters that a magazine is easier to load if you put it on a hard surface. This lets a woman use leverage instead of upper-body strength. There are also magazine-loading tools, but I'd rather not go the girly route.

While I held the Kahr in one hand and aimed at the pile of books, Diamond held up a different gun and showed me the small ridges on top of the gun that are the front and back sights, which a shooter uses to align it to the target. He then showed me how to stand with my feet about hip distance apart. There were variations in the proper stance for shooting, he told me, but I could stick to this basic position for now.

Diamond then showed how to hold a gun with the right hand while using the left hand to steady it for more security and control. He is a foot and two inches taller than I am, so his hands fit the guns very differently from mine. I awkwardly held both my hands against the gun and kept it pointed at the pile of books.

"Now pull the trigger," he said.

"Are you sure?" I asked. Even though I knew the gun had the snap caps in it, I was nervous.

"Yes, pull it. You need to get comfortable."

I pulled.

"It's stuck," I said.

"It's fine. You're not pulling hard enough," he told me.

I pulled the trigger harder. The gun started to move away from the books. I repositioned the gun and finally pulled the trigger. Click.

"Is that it?" I asked. "Did I do it?"

"Yes, that's it," he said. I pulled the trigger a few more times. Now, it was time to shoot the gun for real.

———

Diamond packed up three guns, boxes of ammo, and protective gear and drove to the headquarters of the NRA in Fairfax, Virginia, so I could use their shooting range. Andrew Arulanandam, the NRA's director of public affairs, met us at the front door of the building, where there is a giant stuffed bear.

Arulanandam took us upstairs to say hello to Chris Cox, executive director of the NRA's Institute for Legislative Action. I had known Cox since I worked on Capitol Hill as a press secretary and he was a mid-level lobbyist for the NRA.

"Well, look who's here," Cox said when I came in.

"I'm going to shoot for the first time!" I said, smiling.

"First time?" he asked. I nodded.

Diamond said, "She will think all shooting ranges are like this one."

Arulanandam then took us to the new, state-of-the-art shooting range, which is under a parking garage. I had nothing to compare it to, but it was so sleek and modern that I thought it looked like a set for *Homeland*. Arulanandam wished me good luck and turned me over to a media staffer and range safety instructor, both female.

They put me in a room by myself to take the written test on the NRA safety rules. Even though it said you could bring in a copy of the rules, I wanted to see if I could pass the test without looking at them. It was multiple choice. I didn't look at the answers and got 100 percent. I held my test up in victory after the range officer graded it.

"Two days ago she didn't know which way was down range," Diamond told the women.

"So it's that way?" I asked, pointing toward the end of the long lanes.

"Yes," they all responded in unison.

The range safety officer gave me protective glasses and earmuffs, which she told me to put on before we walked through the double glass doors. Arulanandam had arranged for me to shoot in a closed range. I would learn later what an advantage this was—the noise in a live range can be frightening for first-time shooters.

Each booth had a touch pad to control the target. The fifty-yard range ended on a special slope designed to slow down the bullets and then hold them for recycling. A climate-controlled air unit took out the gunpowder smell. Now that I've shot in ordinary shooting ranges, I know how nice it is to breathe air that is not full of gunpowder.

Diamond gave me a .22 caliber Browning Buck Mark to start. I wasn't thrilled because it didn't look as cool as the other guns I'd seen at his house. But he insisted I learn with it. He clipped a paper target above my head, then pushed the touch screen to send the target away from me in the lane.

He handed me a full magazine to load in the gun. I had to look at it awhile to figure out how to fit it into the gun. "It only fits one way," he said. "Remember, don't put your finger on the trigger until you are ready to shoot."

Since Diamond's hands were so much bigger than mine, I asked a female NRA aide who was about my size for help with my grip. She showed me how she held it—with the palms of her hands pressing against each other on the left side of the gun.

When I felt ready, I held the gun up to the target and closed my left eye to line up the sights. I was nervous and took a deep breath. But I didn't have to struggle to pull the trigger. POP!

"I did it!" I yelled excitedly, turning around slightly.

"Don't turn around," Diamond ordered. "Keep shooting until the magazine is empty." Pop. Pop. I pulled the trigger repeatedly, trying to carefully line up the gun every time after it recoiled. After ten rounds, I had hit about half in the red bull's-eye in the middle of the target. I was thrilled.

"Now try to group them," Diamond said. I looked at him quizzically.

"Get the shots as close to each other as you can," he clarified. I shot another ten bullets and my aim improved. This was easier than I had expected.

Diamond then handed me the 9mm Sig Sauer P226. I loaded and pulled hard on the trigger. BOOM! This gun was big, heavy, and loud and had a huge kick, but it felt secure in my hands. I kept the gun aimed down range but looked around behind me to see if I should stop.

"Keep going," he said. Boom! Boom! I finished the thirteen rounds and was disappointed that only about three went into the red. Not bad, but not as good as the .22 caliber pistol.

Finally, Diamond handed me the Kahr that I had assumed would be the easiest to shoot because the concealed-carry gun was the smallest. I pulled the trigger and saw a flash of fire. I was scared. "What is this?" I asked, without looking back or moving the gun. No one answered, so I had to finish the rounds.

BAM. BAM. BAM. BAM. I did not like this. My hand hurt. The fiery explosion in front of me on each shot scared me. I shot until there were no more rounds in the gun but didn't get a single shot in the red of the target. I put the gun down.

"That's it, I'm done. I want to go back to the .22," I said. I finished off two more magazines and got good grouping with the last one.

I had shot a gun. It was a powerful feeling. I knew I had a long way to go to feel comfortable ever doing it on my own, but I was excited to shoot again soon. It was fun.

Meanwhile, I was working my way through the seventeen steps to getting my own gun.

CHAPTER 8

THE UNIVERSAL BACKGROUND CHECKS MYTH

"Universal background checks" are the "assault weapons" ban of 2013. The newly invented, vanilla-sounding term is ultimately designed to get public support for a national gun registry. Obama wants you to think it is just common sense to close the "gun show loophole" in order to get the "universal background checks" that everyone is supposed to support—even gun owners, according to the president.

As has been shown in the past, these proposals won't do anything to stop criminals because they don't get their guns through legal means. The only way a mandatory check would work would be if the government could track every one of the 300 million firearms in the United States and then criminals would ask permission before buying them.

Obama's proposal will, however, make it more difficult for law-abiding Americans to protect themselves and their families. That's why it's important to decode the anti-gun politicians' words to understand that their real goal has always been a national registry, so the government will know who has every single gun in this country.

Obama throws around poll numbers to make reasonable people think they're the only ones who don't support his agenda. "These enhanced background checks won't stop all gun crimes, but they will certainly help prevent some. This is common sense," he said at the Minneapolis police department in February. "More than 70 percent of NRA members agree. Ninety percent of the American people agree. So there's no reason we can't do this unless politics is getting in the way."[1]

Obama's national publicity blitz did have a powerful impact on public opinion. A Gallup poll the previous month showed that 91 percent supported "criminal background checks for all gun sales."[2]

I asked Chris Cox how to account for so many polls showing over 90 percent of Americans support universal background checks. He said people are "intentionally misled" by pollsters and gun control advocates into thinking President Obama wants nothing more than a background check system—which we already have. "If you ask people the question, 'Do you support background checks?' Ninety percent of NRA members would say yes. 'Do you support keeping the guns out of the hands of criminals and people who are a danger to themselves and others with mental health problems?' I think close to 100 percent of NRA members would say 'yes.'"[3]

So, when Obama talks about 70 percent of NRA members agreeing with him, he's using a poll paid for by Mike Bloomberg. The survey was conducted by Frank Luntz in July 2012—after the Aurora, Colorado, shooting—and showed 72 percent of "current or lapsed members of the NRA" support "requiring a criminal background check of anyone purchasing a gun."[4] Since Luntz did not have access to the NRA membership list, it is not clear how he found a sampling of the one out of sixty Americans who belong to the organization.

The NRA got fed up with Bloomberg dominating the media with his version of what their members believe, so it did its own poll. The survey of a thousand randomly selected NRA members in January 2013 returned very different results from the poll of supposed "current or lapsed" NRA members Bloomberg had commissioned.

The questions in the NRA poll were phrased so that gun owners knew what was being asked. When the background checks question was whether you favor a new federal law banning the sale of firearms between private citizens, 92 percent said no. 89 percent opposed banning "certain semi-automatic firearms, sometimes referred to as assault rifles," and 82 percent opposed a federal law banning magazines over ten rounds.[5]

NRA members' opinions come from being educated on the facts. Background checks don't do anything to stop the bad guys because they don't get their guns through licensed dealers. If criminals cared about laws, they wouldn't be criminals. The only way a mandatory check would keep a criminal from buying a gun would be for the criminal's buddy selling a gun on the street to insist on calling the FBI before giving him the weapon. Obviously, that is not likely to happen.

When Bloomberg needs a poll to back up his argument, he just pays for it. Bloomberg's Independence USA PAC paid pollster Doug Schoen $491,000 in the 2012 election cycle alone.[6] Schoen is behind all the polls used in MAIG's attack ads in 2013. Schoen polled background checks in all the states and districts targeted by Mayors Against Illegal Guns in February and found support ranging from 79 to 100 percent.[7] Liberal media runs with these poll numbers without explaining their source, as do the anti-gun activists. Mark Kelly, the former astronaut who became a full-time gun control advocate after his wife Gabrielle Giffords was shot, said on *Fox News Sunday*, "I would say to Marco Rubio that 94 percent of his constituents support a universal background check."[8] He was citing Bloomberg-funded Schoen numbers.[9]

But unlike the usual polls that have full transparency, the Bloomberg-funded ones are not put online, so their methodology cannot be known. And some of their results are particularly curious—including one result showing that every single solitary person who was called in the New

Jersey district of Republican Representative Chris Smith supports government intervention in private gun exchanges.[10]

As a society, we have already agreed to certain limits to the right to keep arms. In the Gun Control Act of 1968, certain categories of people were deemed too dangerous to possess firearms.[11]

Felons or those indicted with a crime punishable by over a year in federal prison or two years in state prison lose the right to gun ownership. The dangerous mentally ill, defined as having been adjudicated mentally defective or unable to handle their own affairs, involuntarily committed to a mental institution, or found not guilty by reason of insanity or incompetent to stand trial can't have a legal firearm. Drug offenders cannot have guns until they have been clean for five years.

Other categories of people who cannot own a gun are minors, illegal aliens, fugitives from justice, and those dishonorably discharged from the military. Someone who has a protective order against him for harassing, stalking, or threatening an intimate partner or the child of a partner cannot buy a gun. Also, domestic abusers are banned.[12]

The National Instant Criminal Background Check System—referred to as NICS—was created by the Brady Act of 1993 and implemented in 1998 to help licensed firearm dealers know which buyers are prohibited from owning a gun.[13] Currently, when a buyer goes to a licensed dealer, the seller either calls or uses an online system to put the potential buyer's name in for a review of things such as criminal history, mental health, and restraining orders to determine if the person is prohibited from owning a gun.[14]

When the system is not backlogged, the check takes a couple minutes. If the buyer is cleared, he can take possession of the gun immediately. If the person is denied unfairly, he can appeal the decision. However, if the buyer is rejected because he is a convicted felon or for some other legal reason, the feds are supposed to investigate and prosecute. However, they rarely do.

But Obama now wants to know about private exchanges of guns—the ones done every day by law-abiding people. "It's time for Congress to require a universal background check for anyone trying to buy a gun," Obama said. "The law already requires licensed gun dealers to run background checks, and over the last 14 years that's kept 1.5 million of the wrong people from getting their hands on a gun. But it's hard to enforce that law when as many as 40 percent of all gun purchases are conducted without a background check."[15]

That 40 percent figure is often cited by Obama, Bloomberg, and friends. It comes from a survey done twenty-eight years ago and released by the Justice Department in 1997.[16] There has not been another comprehensive government study looking at gun ownership since then. The study was done before NICS was even put online in 1998.

Even if you take the old study as still relevant today, it breaks down in a way that is a lot less frightening than Obama wants you to believe. Three percent reported getting their firearms "through the mail"—a process that requires a background check from a federally licensed firearms dealer.

That leaves 37 percent of guns not transferred through a licensed dealer. Almost all of these—29 percent—were transfers between family members, friends, or acquaintances. Transfers like these tend not to be dangerous because responsible, law-abiding people are generally not giving or selling guns to a mentally ill neighbor or an ex-con at the office.

So the 40 percent number Obama cites goes down to actually 8 percent of all firearms transactions in the country that may be between strangers who are not dealers. Four percent wouldn't tell the government where they got the gun. That leaves just 4 percent of respondents who said they bought their firearm at a "gun show or flea market."

That is why the "gun show loophole" is a red herring. It is another clever phrase dreamed up by the anti-gun activists who want to give the public the false impression that these conventions are hotbeds of criminal activity. The NRA's Chris Cox pointed out to me, "If you go to a gun show, about 90 percent of the vendors at gun shows are dealers who have a storefront or who have dealers' licenses. They have to do the same background check that you'd have to go through at Wal-Mart."

Criminals just don't go to gun shows for weapons. A Justice Department survey released in May 2013 showed that less than 1 percent of convicts claimed to have gotten their weapon at a gun show.

The statistics come from a survey of state prison inmates on where they got the firearms they used to commit their crimes. Thirty-seven percent of the convicts polled said they got the gun from their own friends and family. Forty percent got the weapons off the streets illegally—over half of those, 25 percent, from drug dealers. Of the remainder of the inmates, 7 percent said their guns were from a retail store, so either they didn't have a criminal record or a friend was able to pass the FBI check and do an illegal straw purchase for them. Finally, 3 percent got their gun from a pawn shop, 0.6 percent from a flea market, and just 0.8 percent from a gun show.[17]

Obama knows this full well. That secret Justice Department memo cited an ATF study that reported 47 percent of criminals acquire guns through straw purchases—which means the bad guy asks a buddy or girlfriend without a record to make the buy. The memo's author, the deputy director of the National Institute of Justice, wrote, "These figures indicate informal transfers dominate the crime gun market."[18]

ATF reported that 26 percent of guns used in crimes were stolen. That's how Adam Lanza got his mother's gun. George Kollitides, CEO of Bushmaster, the weapon used at Newtown, said, "He killed the gun's owner, stole her car, stole her gun, and then went to a school and killed innocent kids. No background check could have prevented that. He illegally obtained the guns."[19]

The ATF reported that 20 percent of guns used in crimes were from an "unregulated private seller"—which would most likely be the family members and friends cited in the Justice survey. Thirteen percent were from a combination of gun shows and flea markets and 8 percent were from "retail diversions."

The NRA's Chris Cox said, "Most people would have you believe that people just buy guns all the time without background checks at gun shows and everywhere else. It's an interesting political statement that's simply not backed up by fact."[20]

Actually, industry insiders estimate that over 90 percent of gun show vendors are fully licensed dealers who must run the NICS check at the time of the sale. Bob Templeton, the president of the National Association of Arms Shows, Inc., told me that the ATF has really stepped up enforcement and oversight in the last three years, so that the number of sellers of firearms without a Federal Firearms License at gun shows has decreased.[21]

"The increased attention which the [Bureau of Alcohol, Tobacco, Firearms, and Explosives] has focused on these non-licensed sellers has had the effect of reducing their numbers to what I estimate is actually fewer than 10 percent of sellers at shows," said Templeton.

Bottom line: there's simply no public threat from a law-abiding citizen occasionally selling a firearm to other collectors at a gun show.

The way the "gun show" loophole deception has been effective in deceiving the public may be explained by cultural differences. Gun shows are more common in Southern and Western states, so those who live in the Northeast or in liberal cities and have never been to one and can be convinced that the conventions are filled with illegal gun running.

———

Once Obama accepted the reality that he couldn't get his beloved gun and magazine bans past the Senate, the White House re-focused its efforts on this background checks issue. The political pressure from 1600 Pennsylvania Avenue on the issue was so intense that the Senate Judiciary

Committee, controlled by Democrats, was forced to pass an expanded background check bill before it had even been written. It was another case of what then-House Speaker Nancy Pelosi said about Obamacare in March of 2009, "We have to pass the bill so you can find out what is in it."[22]

At the markup, Committee Chairman Patrick Leahy of Vermont put forward an old bill sponsored by Senator Chuck Schumer, New York Democrat. The legislation included a section that made it impossible to get the support of the pro-gun senators: "Requiring a Background Check for Every Firearm Sale." The only exception would be exchanges with immediate family.[23]

At the hearing, Schumer announced that he was working on drafting another bill that could pass the Senate, but it would not exist until after the committee voted to send his version to the floor. He later teamed up with Democratic Senator Joe Manchin and Republican Senator Pat Toomey to come up with the legislation the White House demanded.

Schumer said at the hearing that, "The problem, sometimes referred to as the 'gun show loophole,' means that a private seller could set up a tent at a gun show or somewhere else and not have to conduct background checks on his purchasers." He then got dramatic about the small percent of guns that are bought at gun shows and flea markets—which he exaggerated by a factor of more than ten. "Current estimates show because of these loopholes, 48 percent of gun sales are made without a background check. If you're a felon, if you're a gun trafficker, if you're a mentally ill person, you know that you can go to a gun show and not have any check. So of course that's what they do."[24]

Actually, it's about 4 percent of all purchases and less than 1 percent of criminals that get their guns this way, but no one was fact-checking the senior senator from New York.

Wayne LaPierre, CEO of the NRA, views the current battle over guns as the biggest in a generation. That's why he testified on Capitol Hill for the first time in fourteen years at this January hearing. Pressed repeatedly by the Democrats on "universal background checks," LaPierre said, "I just don't think law-abiding people want every gun sale in the country to be under the thumb of the federal government."[25]

America has a history and culture of responsible gun ownership. Now the government wants to get in the middle of normal, everyday trades, gifts, or sales between people who know each other. It is already law that licensed dealers need to do FBI checks.

If you want to buy or sell guns as a business, you have to apply to the ATF to be a Federal Firearms Licensee (FFL). To do that, you send in an application, photo fingerprint cards, and a $200 fee and submit yourself to a qualification inspection by ATF.[26] Once you get the license and can do business, you are required to keep records of all sales in a "bound book"—which I later saw Charles Sykes use—and be subject to an annual inspection by the ATF. There were 58,000 FFLs engaged in business as a dealer or pawnbroker in 2012 according to ATF.[27]

So if a "universal background checks" law wouldn't make us any safer, why is Obama so fixated on it? His real goal is to create a national gun registry to have more control over civilian arms possession. This is not paranoia.

The leaked memo from the Justice Department puts Obama and his allies' plans in context. In it, Greg Ridgeway concluded that the effectiveness of "universal background checks" depends on "the ability to reduce straw purchasing, requiring gun registration and an easy gun transfer process." The Obama administration official wrote that background checks would enable "monitoring of multiple gun purchases in a short period of time" in order to "increase owner responsibility by directly connecting an owner with a gun" and "improve law enforcement's ability to retrieve guns from owners prohibited from possessing firearms."[28] The feds retrieving civilians' firearms is the definition of confiscation.

The Founding Fathers included the right to keep and bear arms as the Second Amendment in the Bill of Rights specifically to prevent government tyranny.

Senator Mike Lee, a member of the Judiciary Committee, told me in an interview after the vote on Schumer's bill, "Universal background checks can't do much of anything unless accompanied by some form of registration. Like a lot of Americans, I am not comfortable with the government keeping track of who bought what gun and when."

If you talk to cops dealing with serious crime problems, they oppose passing laws for "universal background checks" because it wastes their limited resources. Eighty percent said expanding background checks would not decrease crime, according to the PoliceOne poll of fifteen thousand law enforcement officers.[29]

Fifty-two New York sheriffs in New York State sent a letter to Governor Andrew Cuomo to protest the new SAFE Act that New York passed in the wake of the Newtown shooting. On the mandatory NICS check for private sales except between immediate family, they wrote, "We're mainly concerned that this provision will be very difficult to enforce and will likely only affect law abiding citizens."[30]

Obama likes to say that we have to "do something" about gun violence.[31] But he should not get a feeling of accomplishment from infringing on constitutional rights without even making the nation safer. You rarely hear Obama say that NICS is woefully broken right now because that fact doesn't fit into his radical agenda. In order to prevent criminals from getting guns, we would have to have a background check system that actually contains all the records of those who cannot legally own guns, and we would have to prosecute them for trying to get them.

Unfortunately, states aren't submitting mental health and criminal records to the federal government for inclusion in the NICS database, and the Justice Department isn't prosecuting offenders who have broken the law by trying to buy guns.

Ironically, Bloomberg's group, Mayors Against Illegal Guns, which wants more people to go through NICS, also provides the most complete data on how the system doesn't work now because few states have submitted mental health records into the system. In a report released in November 2011, MAIG concluded that "millions of records identifying seriously mentally ill people and drug abusers as prohibited purchasers are missing from the federal background check database because of lax reporting by state agencies."

Twenty-three states and D.C. submitted fewer than one hundred mental health records to the federal database, and seventeen of those states had entered fewer than ten. Four states did not give a single record to the feds. In addition, there are sixty-one agencies that keep mental health data for the FBI, but only nine of them turned over records. And most federal agencies have not submitted any substance abuse records.[32]

While many liberal governors are ramming through legislation to ban guns, they are allowing dangerously mentally ill people to buy guns. For example, Maryland Governor Martin O'Malley spent the 2013 legislative session fixated on passing bans on rifles that aren't used in crimes in his state. Yet Maryland turned in only fifty-eight mental health records to the FBI. Massachusetts has some of the strictest gun-control laws in the country but gave NICS exactly one name of a dangerously mentally ill person.[33]

"Half of the states aren't putting felony convictions, restraining orders, or mental health records into NICS. If they're not in the system, how can the dealer know not to make the sale?" said Lawrence Keane of NSSF, which represents the retailers who do the FBI checks.[34]

Keane also pointed out that the federal government had dropped the ball.

"NICS is broken and needs to be fixed. Congress authorized $125 million for this effort but only appropriated $5 million," he said, referring to the NICS Improvement Amendments Act of 2007, which was passed after the Virginia Tech shooting as lawmakers attempted to prevent other severely mentally ill people from buying guns.

Besides poor reporting from the states and federal agencies, the other critical problem with the background check system is that the bad guys aren't getting caught. Only about 1 percent of those who try to buy a gun are refused through NICS. The FBI conducted over 6 million NICS transfer checks in 2010 and denied over 72,659 applications.[35] Each day the FBI sends NICS denials to an ATF branch with the information on the prohibited person for further investigation. ATF then refers certain cases to field divisions within forty-eight hours. In 2010, ATF received 76,142 NICS denials from the FBI and sent just 6 percent (4,732 cases) to the field.

According to an August 2012 Justice Department study on federal and state investigations and prosecutions of firearm applicants denied by NICS, the remaining 94 percent of denials "did not meet referral guidelines or were overturned or canceled."

Of all the cases investigated by ATF field offices in 2010, only sixty-two charges were referred to prosecutors. Then only thirteen charges resulted in guilty pleas. So from the original denied background checks, basically two out of every ten thousand ended in getting a criminal off the streets.

I spoke with Jeff Reh, general counsel of Beretta USA, at the NRA annual meeting in Houston in May 2013 about why the crimes of perjury on the FBI form should be prosecuted. "Criminals are not that smart," he said, explaining why they may lie on an NICS form and get caught. "You get what you can, even if it's a paperwork violation. It's a deterrent."[36]

Reh gave the analogy of when former New York City Mayor Rudy Giuliani started prosecuting people who jumped the turnstiles in the subways. "He was catching a class of people who showed a willingness to break the law. Once you grab them, you find other criminal activity in their backgrounds. It got them off the streets, and crime decreased."

In February 1997, Virginia launched a very successful program called "Project Exile," in which police were taught how to catch criminals committing gun crimes in a way that could be prosecuted.[37] The program specifically targeted previously convicted felons carrying guns who were involved in drug or violent crimes. Simultaneously the city launched a public relations campaign around the message "An illegal gun will get you five years in federal prison" as a deterrent. The NRA gave $100,000 to help put that message on billboards and buses and in TV and radio ads in Richmond.[38]

The results were remarkable. During the first ten months of 1998 the total number of homicides committed in Richmond was down 36 percent and firearm homicides plummeted 41 percent, compared with the same period in the previous year.[39] Within two years, hundreds of armed criminals were arrested and 317 of them were convicted and sentenced to an average of fifty-six months imprisonment. Fewer bad guys on the streets and more in prison. And probably even criminals who weren't imprisoned were deterred from committing crimes—they knew they would be prosecuted for breaking the gun laws. Many other states followed this model in the years that followed.

The NRA's James J. Baker attempted to explain to Vice President Biden how the Virginia initiative had worked so effectively. Baker was representing the NRA at the Biden meeting, with about a dozen invitees from other pro-gun groups in January. They sat around a table in the Eisenhower Executive Office, and when it came to his turn to speak, Baker focused on changes to the mental health system, school security measures, and prosecutions for violating gun laws, which had decreased during the Obama administration.

"I told him that it didn't make sense to have federal penalties for lying on the form you have to fill out to purchase a firearm if no one is ever prosecuted for it," he recalled in an interview. Baker said that Biden turned to him and said, "Jim, we're not interested in chasing paperwork violations." Baker said, "Well Mr. Vice President, with all due respect, if you're not prosecuting when they lie on the forms, you're not stopping them."[40]

In the first Senate Judiciary Committee hearing on the 2013 gun control legislation, Senator John Cornyn said that it wasn't just the NICS denials that weren't being prosecuted, all firearms crimes were being ignored. "I fail to see how passing additional laws that the Department of Justice will not enforce is going to make America any safer," said the Texas Republican. He pointed out that, under Obama, the Justice Department charged 13 percent fewer total firearms cases from 2007 to 2011. Cornyn added that January 2011 saw the lowest level of federal prosecutions of gun charges (484 in the U.S.) in ten years.[41]

After citing these and other statistics at the January markup, Cornyn asked LaPierre to comment. The NRA leader said that his organization opposes so-called universal background checks because "Even if you turn up someone on an instant check—it's a mentally-ill person or a felon—as long as you let them go, you're not keeping them from getting a gun, and you're not preventing them from getting to the next crime scene. I mean, we have to get in the real world of this discussion."[42]

LaPierre also brought up how Obama is soft on crime when Committee Chairman Leahy pressed him on the "gun show loophole." The NRA executive vice president said, "I think the National Instant Check System, the way it's working now, is a failure because this administration is not prosecuting the people that they catch." He said it was absurd to think that if you don't prosecute, the criminals will just give up trying to get a gun. "We all know that homicidal maniacs, criminals and the insane don't abide by the law."

CHAPTER 9

THE UNSAFE
GUN SAFETY CLASS

S tep two on my list of seventeen to register a gun was to find a
D.C.-certified instructor and sign up for the mandatory gun class.
It turned out to be the biggest barrier to getting a legal firearm.

The course was four hours of classroom instruction and one hour at
the range. It was required whether you have owned guns your whole life
(in another state) or never touched one before, like me. It didn't matter
whether you were registering a rifle or a shotgun, you had to use a handgun at the range. The requirement was complete nonsense, clearly
invented to dissuade people from legal gun ownership in the nation's
capital.

The police don't teach the class. Instead, random people the police
consider "certified firearms instructors" give it. The registration packet
Officer Brown gave me at the firearms registration office included a
rather daunting two-page list of forty-seven instructors, plus a paper
with Xerox copies of business cards. The instructor list was just names
and phone numbers—no addresses, emails, company names, websites,

certifications, or affiliations. It was less informative than an old-fashioned white pages phone book.

The numbers on the list were mostly in D.C.'s 202 area code, which was no help in figuring out where the class would be because the city's laws didn't allow the class to be taught inside D.C. The required hour at the range would violate the city's total ban on carrying a gun. You may wonder how it could be constitutional for D.C. residents to be forced to go to another state to exercise their Second Amendment right to keep and bear arms. It isn't.

As a woman facing the prospect of going alone to this class in a neighboring state, I wanted to know I was dealing with someone legit. From my perspective, I was calling a strange man, who I knew was armed, and telling him that I was unarmed and willing to meet him at an unknown place. Remember, feeling safe was the reason I wanted a gun in the first place.

Setting the intimidating list aside for the time being, I tried the numbers on the Xerox copies of business cards first. At least they had actual addresses and business affiliations for the people.

One of the cards was for Stephen Schneider, the president of Atlantic Guns, with the name "Art Keiser" handwritten and scratched out on it. But neither of these men was also on the list of certified instructors. I called the company and found it was a gun dealership in Maryland. They told me no one affiliated with them taught the class, but they did refer me to a company called Worth-A-Shot, owned by Donna Worthy, which they said might have D.C.-certified instructors. But I noticed that she wasn't on the list of certified instructors either. The other cards were also dead ends.

I turned to attacking the massive phone list and ended up spending a week decoding it.

First, I Googled the names with phone numbers that had the 703 Virginia area code because I live closer to Virginia than Maryland. None of the names turned up results.

A little more looking around on the computer, and I found that the version of the city list on the police department website was different from the printed version Officer Brown had given me at the gun registration office. The online list gave some more information, like a company affiliation, if there was one. I Googled several of the local companies but found no information. The businesses listed either weren't real or mysteriously had zero presence on the internet.

Unfortunately, twenty of the forty-seven instructors were listed as "independent." I would assume most street criminals would have the same affiliation.

My editor wanted to know why my series had suddenly stopped. I told him that I couldn't find an instructor.

"Just take it with anyone. It doesn't matter." Diamond said.

"I really don't want to go to some place with some random guy," I said. "You don't have to worry about the things I do with strange men or unsafe places. Look at you. No one would hurt you."

He paused a while. "I never thought of it that way."

"Neither did the city council when it came up with this law," I said.

Finally, for the sake of the investigation, I decided to call all forty-seven names on the list to figure out what the city was doing.

The list had never been updated. It was the same one that was written when the law went into effect after *Heller* in September 2009. By the time I was making my calls two years later, seven of the numbers were out of service. And over half of the phone numbers went straight to voicemail. Most were individual cell phones rather than a company where you could set up the appointment. For the voicemails that were corporate-sounding, none gave an option to get in touch with the instructor listed on the D.C. list.

Two instructors who did answer, Michael Morgan and John Cutler, both told me that they no longer taught the course and shouldn't still be listed on the form. Three people told me they didn't have a class scheduled for the next few months.

The most absurd conversation I had was with instructor Stuart Asay, whose cell phone number begins with a Colorado area code. He said that his company taught the class in the Rocky Mountain State and Atlanta, but he had no plans to teach the class in D.C. any time soon.

"I don't get it," I said to him. "Why would you teach a class for only Washington residents in Georgia and Colorado and not in D.C.?"

"There's a lot of demand for the classes in those places," he insisted. Since only about seventeen hundred guns are registered in D.C. every year, there is no way that there's any significant demand for the gun safety class in remote Georgia and Colorado. I asked Asay repeatedly to explain his rationale to me, but he never strayed from his original story. We ended the call with the agreement that if I happen to visit Georgia or Colorado in the next few weeks, I could take the class from him for a bargain $150. To this day, I wonder what his real business was.

I finally found four instructors—all in Maryland—who were willing to teach the gun class. I would have to drive anywhere from thirty minutes to an hour each way to take the class. I never found a class offered near a stop on the Metro, which is what we call the subway in D.C. I don't know what any of the many D.C. residents without cars would do to take the class.

All of these four instructors told me that they teach the course out of their own houses. One even clarified that he would be teaching me alone "in my basement."

I'd seen *The Silence of the Lambs*. I was not going to meet some dude with a gun in his basement.

Anyway, who were these guys? I had no idea. At the top of the page of names, I noticed this clarification: "It should be noted that these individuals do not work for, nor do they represent the Metropolitan Police Department." Not reassuring.

I decided to check back in with the officers in the firearms registration office. That day, Office Harper answered the phone. He told me, "At some point, there was a criminal background check done on them." That was good news.

The police officer claimed that it didn't matter that the instructors' addresses weren't on the list because they would be teaching the class at a shooting range. Then why did they all say I had to meet at their houses? He didn't know.

What's the appropriate price range for the class? "That I don't know," Officer Harper replied, before correcting himself. "Well, I can't say that I don't know. I don't give the information out."

Well, the teachers knew they had a monopoly. Of the four I found willing to teach the course, the cheapest one was $130. The others ranged from $200 to $250 for an individual lesson or a $175 group rate.

Considering the small number of legal gun applications in the District of Columbia every year, it would take months to get a group together. So the individual class was the only option if I wanted to get a gun in any reasonable time. Two hundred dollars or more seemed like a lot of money to me, but it would be prohibitively expensive for most of the underprivileged in the city. That's yet another reason Washington residents get guns and don't register them.

While I was glad to learn that these men had been given a criminal background check at some point as of 2009, I still didn't feel safe going alone to any of their houses.

In the whole four months that I went through the gun registration process, this was the one time that I wanted to give up on the idea. I couldn't find any way to take this mandatory class in a way that didn't scare me.

If I hadn't been doing this so publicly in our newspaper, I would have waved the white flag and given Washington politicians the win—and stayed just another unarmed, vulnerable person in a city with increasing violent crime.

It was time to call in the big guns. When I was at the NRA to learn to shoot, I mentioned the so-called safety class hurdle to Chris Cox. Now I suggested that the NRA offer the D.C.-sanctioned class at the NRA range, a safe location. Cox was surprised to hear what was going on and asked his staff about getting someone certified to teach the course, possibly free of charge. That was good for a long-term plan, but I wanted to take the class now, without waiting for someone else to be certified to teach it.

As a last-ditch idea, I swung back to the referral from Atlantic Guns, for Donna Worthy, even though her name wasn't on the list of approved instructors. At least I had found a woman, and I understood from the person I talked to at Atlantic Guns that she had a legitimate company.

I spoke with Worthy and found out that she actually was D.C.-certified after all, but the police refused to put her on the list. "The registration office said they were adding me on the next update, that was last year," she told me. She had called repeatedly to ask to be included, to no avail.

Once I heard Worthy's background, I decided to take the class with her. She is a retired Baltimore police officer—a firearms training instructor no less—who opened Worth-A-Shot (a play on her last name) as a training facility. Her company is in Millersville, Maryland. It took me about forty-five minutes to drive there in no traffic. She charged $225 for the D.C. course.

I asked Diamond for a day off from writing my editorial so I could take the class. I count this as the second day D.C. residents have to take a day off from work to register a gun.

When I pulled up to Worth-A-Shot, I immediately liked that it had a bright and clearly marked storefront. I felt safe there.

Worthy led me to her large classroom, with rows of desks and the course lesson on an overhead projector. We started with the mandatory part of the course, which was reading over the gun ownership rules, restrictions, and laws. Worthy read through the same twenty-two-page packet that I got at the police station. I don't know why the city makes the instructor read it out loud and review it with me like fourth grade grammar class, but it does.

It was about an hour's worth of material, but we had to be in this classroom for four hours for me to get the certification. Worthy offered me a Diet Coke, and I accepted. I needed the caffeine to stay awake. I'm quite sure that most instructors sign the forms and let you off with less time, but Worthy used the extra time to throw in a firearms fundamentals course, for which she normally charges $200.

She lined up five guns on the table: a Glock 17 9mm, a plastic model of the Glock 17, a Glock 26 9mm, an old Smith & Wesson .38 caliber revolver, and her own pink concealed-carry weapon—a Ruger LCP in .380 caliber. Worthy pointed out that her guns did not have the D.C.-mandated ten-round magazines that mine would have to have.

I had learned some of this from Diamond, but it was good to get more training, even though D.C. didn't mandate it. First Worthy taught me how to load and unload the gun. She corrected me repeatedly when I picked up the magazine on the floor after releasing it from the gun. "What you're trained to do is what you will do under a high-stress situation," she explained. "We've had police officers on duty who stopped to pick up their shell casings because that was their habit from the range."

She then taught me to rack the slide three times to make sure there was no round in the chamber. The second time is to make sure a second bullet isn't stuck. The third time is in case you mistakenly thought you saw a bullet flying out. I never went back to this three-time model, but it only took an extra second and could be a good safety practice.

Worthy taught me to load the gun while holding it upright in front of me. "No one can see if the slide is open from in front of you. So if you're caught with an unloaded gun, the bad guy doesn't know it until you have loaded," she explained.

Then she focused on my grip. She showed me how to push the sides of my palms together on the left side of the gun to make a straight line. Worthy had me practice not holding all the pressure in my dominant right hand, but instead balancing it evenly. "Let me see your right hand," she said. I held out my palm, and she laughed at the telltale red waffle marks from the Glock's grip. "That shows me you are holding the gun too tightly on one side, which will make it shoot at that angle."

Next we worked on my stance. She had me stand with feet parallel, shoulders straight, chin up (that was the hardest part, I kept lowering my chin later at the range), arms straight from the shoulder. She taught me to shoot higher or lower by moving my wrists, not my arms. I practiced this over and over by aiming at a bull's-eye on the projector screen.

"Your eyes can only focus on one thing at a time. Keep focused on the white dot on the front sight. The rear sight and the target should be out of focus," she said. "And when you're at the range, don't stop to look at your target, just keep focusing on the front sight and shooting." After four long hours in the classroom, we had finally finished our required time and could go for the hour at the range.

Worthy packed up the guns on the class table. We drove our cars about fifteen minutes to Maryland Small Arms Range, which is in a strip mall.

Inside the range, she explained that D.C. police tell the instructors that they need to verify that the resident can safely shoot the gun. "That means you can basically hit the paper," she told me of the huge paper target just a few yards away. "But, I want more for the people I teach. I want you hitting bull's-eyes."

She got just that, though not right away. The target was five yards away and at first I was hitting a lot of white. Worthy had me switch guns between every five rounds or so to help figure out what kind of gun I wanted to buy. Like the Kahr, the small pink carry gun had a strong kick, which I hated. I was terrible with the revolver, barely hitting the silhouette at all.

After going back and forth between the two Glocks, I was much improved. By the time I had shot all the rounds in the box, I decided that I liked the full-size Glock best because it was easiest to control and gave me the best results. (This was the second cop directing me to a Glock.) Worthy recommended that gun for me because it doesn't have a safety switch that I might forget how to use in the middle of the night.

Worthy filled out the D.C. safety class form, copied it, and put it in a red Worth-A-Shot folder. I felt like I'd just graduated from...well, a long bureaucratic test. At least I hadn't yet given up the fight to get a gun. I had made real progress.

CHAPTER 10

GUN CONTROL THWARTED ON CAPITOL HILL

T he kind of gun control laws that were making it so ridiculously difficult for me to get a gun for self-defense in D.C. have been out of reach for the anti-gun politicians on the national level since 1994.

Capitol Hill has been pro-gun since the Republican takeover of the House that year, in the wake of President Clinton signing the "assault weapons" ban. No major anti-Second Amendment legislation has passed Congress in twenty years.

President Obama may have thought he finally had his chance after the horrific tragedy at Sandy Hook Elementary School, but the will of the people blocked him, for now.

Senate Majority Leader Harry Reid never seemed to believe the legislation could pass, but he was pressured by the White House to bring it up for a vote. Sources familiar with the machinations behind the failed anti-gun bills in April 2013 believe Obama, Biden, and Bloomberg were in a rush to push the issue before the memory of Sandy Hook faded.

Politically, Obama wanted to appease his base by showing he was doing something on an issue that is a high priority for them. He also wanted to force Republicans to be on the record voting against his "common sense" gun control proposals—so he could use those votes against them to elect more Democrats to Congress in 2014.

The president also genuinely believes in limiting gun rights and didn't want to pass up an opportunity—even if it was a long shot—to achieve it on the federal level. The publicity surrounding the push for federal gun control laws only helped their anti-gun campaigns in the states, where they had a better shot at actually getting legislation passed.

After the Senate Judiciary Committee passed the final of four gun control bills on March 14, Reid announced a floor vote. The next three weeks were a battle over the Democrats from rural and pro-gun states. While Democrats have the majority in the Senate, their members are split on gun issues. Those from Western and Southern states that have a gun culture tend to vote in support of the Second Amendment.

Reid attempted to give the package a better chance of passing by putting the more radical provisions—Feinstein's "assault weapon" ban and Lautenberg's provisions that would outlaw "high-capacity magazines"—as amendments. The three main bills were for gun trafficking, straw purchases, and background checks. Obama and Bloomberg decided to throw all their political weight and money behind just the background checks bill as the one most likely to pass. Never mind that none of these bills could possibly get past the Republican House.

While Schumer's drastic "universal background check" bill was the placeholder, he, Manchin, and Toomey drafted an expansion of the broken background check system, which they hoped could get the sixty votes needed for passage. They overshot the mark.

The text of Manchin-Toomey was finally revealed on April 11. Under the bill, anyone but family members would have to go to a licensed dealer to do the FBI check for all sales or transfers done at a gun show or "pursuant to" an ad on the internet (even Facebook) or a publication.[1]

There is zero evidence that the people selling guns online are engaging in illegal sales. And it is already federal law that handgun sales across state lines have to go through a dealer and an NICS check, whether private or commercial.

Honest gun owners are the only ones likely to drive to a dealer before selling or giving a gun to a friend. Also the bill didn't address how rural Americans would have access to dealers who can do the NICS check, nor how to limit fees if one dealer—someone less scrupulous than Charles Sykes—had a monopoly.

Manchin and Toomey attempted to get support for their legislation by including a few provisions that pro-Second Amendment senators would like. Of these provisions, the one that would affect the most Americans was to clarify the federal firearms transport law. The bill made clear that it is legal to stop for food, gas, medical treatment, vehicle maintenance, emergencies, and even to stay overnight when transporting a legal firearm.

This is crucial because law-abiding gun owners who do something as innocuous as stop for gas are often charged in anti-gun states. The burden is then on the gun owner to pay for a legal defense—in another state—to prove that federal law trumps the state law. Unfortunately, politicians bank on the reality that many people can't afford to hire a lawyer, so will take a plea deal for financial reasons. First Lieutenant Augustine Kim, whose true story I tell later in this book, was one American war hero who fell into their trap as he was legally transporting his firearms through D.C.

The pro-gun provisions, however, weren't enough. Senators who value Second Amendment rights weren't going to agree to give up some constitutional rights in order to regain others.

Obama knew full well that the bill would not make America safer. The secret Justice Department memo acquired by the NRA had said that broader "universal background checks" could only possibly work if there was a national gun registry[2]—which the overwhelming majority of Americans oppose. The Manchin-Toomey bill expressly denied the federal government the authority to register guns.

Even so, government officials can always do what they want until they get caught. The NRA's Cox pointed out, "There's a distrust. When you look at the recent issues with the IRS and all these current stories and you're asking gun owners to be a little more confident in the Justice Department? To let them have a little more of your information?"[3]

Gun owners have every reason to fear the government knowing what firearms they own, which is the ultimate goal of Obama and Bloomberg's push for "universal background checks."

Bloomberg put his enormous fortune behind Obama's grandstand on Capitol Hill. The New York City Mayor blew through $12 million of political ads to try to buy votes in just the two weeks before the floor vote—which coincided with the Senate recess when members were in their home states. Mayors Against Illegal Guns (MAIG) announced in a press release that two TV ads would run in thirteen states "where they can most influence the upcoming Senate vote."[4]

Democratic senators targeted for their vote were: Mark Pryor of Arkansas, Joe Donnelly of Indiana, Mary Landrieu of Louisiana, Kay Hagan of North Carolina, and Heidi Heitkamp of North Dakota. The GOP senators Bloomberg shot at were: Jeff Flake of Arizona, Dan Coats of Indiana, Chuck Grassley of Iowa, Susan Collins of Maine, Kelly Ayotte of New Hampshire, Dean Heller of Nevada, Rob Portman of Ohio, Pat Toomey of Pennsylvania, and Saxby Chambliss and Johnny Isakson of Georgia.

In addition, the anti-gun group hired organizers and opened campaign offices in ten key states to plan protests outside the senators' offices, get signatures on petitions, and generally make it difficult for legislators to oppose the gun control bill.

When MAIG released the two ads, I was taken aback—the man featured in both of them appeared to be breaking the most basic gun safety rules. Both commercials featured a man holding a shotgun, wearing plaid flannel with a camouflage cap, and sitting on the tailgate of a pickup truck. While a child swings on a tire in the background, the man says, "I support comprehensive background checks so criminals and the dangerously mentally ill can't buy guns."

But the man was setting a dangerous example to the millions of people who would see the ads, breaking the most basic safety rules I had learned that first day on the NRA range.

The first rule is always to keep the gun pointed in a safe direction. In the ad, there were children playing in the yard. Although the viewers can't see if there is a child to the side of the truck, the man on TV should be pointing the muzzle in the air or at the ground.

The second rule is always keep your finger off the trigger until ready to shoot. In the ironically titled ad "Responsibility," the man appears to have his finger on the trigger as if ready to shoot. He says, "I believe in the Second Amendment, and I'll fight to protect it. But with rights come responsibilities." To demonstrate responsible gun handling, the man should put a straight forefinger above the trigger guard so TV viewers would know he wouldn't accidentally touch the trigger. Look at how I am holding my finger in the picture on the cover of this book in order to show that I'm clearly abiding by that safety rule.

Mayors Against Illegal Guns also invented a "National Day to Demand Action" on March 28 with 120 events across the country to advocate for these gun control laws. Obama held a "gun safety" event at the White House featuring twenty-one mothers of gun violence victims. "Shame on us if we've forgotten," he said of Sandy Hook. He called on the Senate to pass "universal background checks" and to "keep weapons of war and high-capacity ammunition magazines that facilitate these mass killings off our streets."[5]

The Manchin-Toomey bill itself may have been at least in part a result of one of Bloomberg's attack ads. On April 8, Bloomberg aired an ad targeting Toomey in order to pressure him to join Democratic Senator Joe Manchin in writing a bipartisan background checks bill. Once Toomey did exactly that, Mayors Against Illegal Guns pulled the attack ad and replaced it with one thanking him.[6]

By April 12, Mayors Against Illegal Guns was running ads specifically to push the "compromise" deal that was coming together. The commercials aired in D.C., Georgia, Indiana, Louisiana, Nevada, New Hampshire, North Dakota, and Tennessee. Three days later, the political assault intensified. Full-page ads ran in D.C. newspapers supposedly demonstrating that the MAIG advertising campaign had caused Senator Jeff Flake's approval ratings to fall in Arizona.[7] All the polling was done by Bloomberg's guy, Doug Schoen.

Mayors Against Illegal Guns has a set group of victims and relatives of victims of high-profile mass shootings that it brings to Washington to stand behind politicians at press conferences and give media interviews. This group included parents of victims from Tucson, Aurora, Virginia Tech, and Newtown. Their faces became familiar to those of us who covered gun policy events in 2013.

At one event at the Capitol, I sat in a chair that had been used by one of these family members. On the chair was a minute-by-minute schedule for her time in Washington, including transportation to and from every event. It appeared that Bloomberg paid for their travel and controlled their every move.

The Senate vote on the Manchin-Toomey bill was delayed a few days because of the Boston Marathon bombing. (Interestingly, after one alleged bomber was dead and the other was in custody, Fox polled on whether people would want a gun in their homes during a manhunt. Sixty-nine percent said they would rather protect themselves with a firearm, and only 28 percent would prefer to be unarmed.)[8]

On Wednesday, April 17, the Senate began debating the amendments to the legislation. The votes showed that the split in the upper chamber on gun control was not clearly defined by party. The Senate GOP largely stuck together in voting against four anti-gun amendments to the bill— except in a few notable cases—and Democrats lost up to fifteen members at a time on the Big Brother–like proposals.

Bloomberg and Obama's priority legislation on background checks went down in flames, 54 to 46, falling short of the sixty needed for passage. This was a huge blow to the White House and money down the drain for the New York City mayor.

When it became clear that the background check amendment vote was going to fail, Reid switched his vote to a "no." That maneuver would allow him to bring the amendment back to the floor under a motion to reconsider. Obama, using Bloomberg's money, hoped to pressure senators to change their votes and bring it back up before the end of the 2013 session.

At 5:30 p.m. on the day of the vote, President Obama held a drama-filled press conference in the Rose Garden with families of victims of gun violence. A father of one of the children killed at Sandy Hook Elementary School spoke. Former Representative Gabrielle Giffords, the victim of a gun attack by someone with apparent mental health issues, stood to Obama's right side. Vice President Biden stood to his left side with his arms crossed, first scowling and then crying.[9]

Obama, who once served in the Senate, bizarrely blamed the normal procedural rules of the upper chamber of our legislature for the failed vote. "A majority of senators voted 'yes' to protecting more of our citizens with smarter background checks, but by this continuing distortion of Senate rules, a minority was able to block it from moving forward." There was no "distortion." The U.S. Senate was created to be a deliberative body. To avoid filibusters, while still moving business along, the Senate normally agrees to require sixty votes for bills to pass.

The most shocking moment in the Rose Garden was when the President of the United States called the millions of law-abiding, honest citizens who are members of pro-gun organizations liars for opposing this infringement on their rights. "Instead of supporting this compromise, the gun lobby and its allies willfully lied about the bill. They claimed that it would create some sort of 'big brother' gun registry, even though the bill did the opposite," Obama said. "This pattern of spreading untruths about this legislation served a purpose because those lies upset an intense minority of gun owners, and that in turn intimidated a lot of senators." Can you imagine any other president making that kind of accusation against honest citizens just for opposing his agenda?

The morning of the vote, Senator Chuck Grassley, Iowa Republican and ranking member of the Judiciary Committee, along with Senator Ted Cruz, Texas Republican, offered an alternative amendment to the central anti-gun legislation.[10] They addressed the lack of prosecutions under existing law by shifting funding to help law enforcement enforce the gun laws we already have. The GOP plan increased funding for school safety and mental health resources and treatment. It incentivized states to put mental health records into NICS. The bill criminalized straw purchases, but did so in a way that didn't ensnare the law-abiding. It went after gun trafficking by serious offenders.

Grassley-Cruz also included pro-gun provisions such as allowing interstate handgun sales and letting members of the military buy guns in their state of residence or where they are stationed. The bill clarified that the interstate transport law trumped state laws. It also required the executive branch to report to Congress on things such as the number of federal records submitted to NICS, gun prosecutions, and ammunition purchases.

To prevent another operation such as Fast and Furious, in which ATF sales of guns to Mexican gangs was supposedly the work of rogue agents, the legislation would have required a top official at the Justice Department to personally approve any other gun-running operations. It also clarified that ATF cannot collect information on purchases of certain rifles in Southwest border states. Despite support from seven Democrats, Grassley-Cruz failed 52 to 48.

Of the amendments voted on that day, arguably the most important for gun owners was one sponsored by Senator John Cornyn, Texas Republican, for national reciprocity on concealed carry. This common sense legislation would make carry permits transferable between states, just like driver's licenses.[11] It passed the House in 2011, but Reid has stubbornly refused to allow a vote on it in the Senate, wisely for the anti-gun side of the issue, as became clear when the Cornyn amendment came within three votes of passage.

Of the ten gun amendments voted on, only two passed. Republican Senator John Barrasso of Wyoming's legislation would have blocked the government from publicly releasing any information about gun owners.[12] The Barrasso amendment got enormous bipartisan support and passed 67 to 30.

This vote was largely in reaction to a New York newspaper publishing an interactive map with the names and addresses of law-abiding handgun permit holders' homes just two weeks after the Newtown tragedy. The *Journal News* used the New York Freedom of Information Law to get the information from Westchester and Rockland counties.[13] Either deliberately or carelessly, the newspaper set up innocent people to be targets of theft and violence in a piece called, "The gun owner next door: What you don't know about the weapons in your neighborhood."

The amendment that got almost every single vote in the Senate was sponsored by Democratic Senator Tom Harkin of Iowa. It required mental health, felony, and other records be put into NICS so truly dangerous people are prevented from legally buying a firearm.[14]

———

After the Senate votes, the president was enraged. Obama disregarded the possibility that pro-gun senators may simply believe in the Bill of Rights. Defiant, the president said it was a "pretty shameful day for Washington" and promised "this effort is not over."[15]

RNC Chairman Reince Priebus explained that, "He overreached and overplayed his hand. Democrats in his own party sitting in red states weren't going to walk off a plank on a flawed bill that wouldn't even do what it said. The bill doesn't even match up to his rhetoric." The GOP leader added that, "The whole thing was a complete disaster from beginning to end for him politically. In reality, the public doesn't support it, that's why it couldn't get passed."

However, Priebus said that Obama's drama in the Rose Garden and swearing up and down that the legislation would save lives affected public sentiment. "He has mastered the art of having people judge him by the things he says, rather than what he does. And he's good at it, and that's our problem. We have to be better at pointing out those things."[16]

On Thursday, Reid pulled the entire legislation from a vote. "I have spoken with the President. He and I agree that the best way to keep working toward passing a background check bill is to hit pause and freeze the background check bill where it is," Reid said on the Senate floor.[17] "President Obama said it was a shameful day for the Senate, and it probably was, I agree. But we should make no mistake; this debate is not over. In fact, this fight is just beginning."

The NRA views the background checks vote as a clear victory but believes that Obama and Reid are serious when they say the fight is not over.

"The Senate win was an important battle in a much longer war, and we fully expect them to make another run," Cox told me. "They are either going to tweak the language slightly to try to secure additional votes or they're going to wait until the next tragedy—like they did with this one—to try to ram it through."

Cox continued, "What's unfortunate about all of this is that they are doing nothing for the overall goal of all Americans of making sure that criminals and people with mental health disorders who are dangers to themselves and others don't have access to a firearm."[18]

Donald Trump told me in an interview that the president has been successful in energizing his base with gun control efforts. "There are a lot of people who believe in what Obama is saying," Donald Trump, the billionaire real estate mogul who is considering a run for president in 2016, said. "I happen to be a Second Amendment person for the very simple reason that the bad guys are not giving up their guns, but the good guys would give up their guns if laws were passed. It doesn't work."[19]

CHAPTER 11

HOW TO BUY A GUN IN A CITY WITHOUT A GUN SHOP

After going to the registration office, taking the five-hour class, and meeting with Sykes, I had finished all the steps that I could complete before giving the city the serial number of my new gun. I was excited about the prospect of doing something I thought would be fun and easy—choosing a gun—following the weeks of frustration over finding an instructor for the gun class. But like everything in Washington's gun registration process, the maze of laws made this step a lot more difficult than I expected.

I decided on a few parameters for my first gun. Washington is the last place in the country where the courts have yet to overturn the unconstitutional carry ban, so you can't bear arms. Since I couldn't take a gun outside my home, I wanted a full-size model. Since concealment wasn't an issue, I had learned from shooting smaller guns that the large models had less recoil in my hands. Also, I wanted to find a gun that was manufactured in America since I was going to be giving some free publicity to one company.

Although I had shot a few of Diamond's guns and Donna Worthy's, I had no idea how to choose a make and model. Keep in mind that Sykes, the city's only legal gun dealer, doesn't sell guns. Diamond suggested I go to a range and rent different guns to see how they fit in my hand and shot. But there are no gun ranges in the District. The nearest one was Sharpshooters Small Arms Range in Lorton, Virginia, which is about a twenty-five-minute drive from home.

I was intimidated by the prospect of going to a shooting range alone, so Diamond agreed to go with me. We decided to go before work one Friday. It was not easy to find. There were no signs from the main road. It was at the very end of an industrial park, across from a redi-mix concrete plant.

When I pulled up to the store, I was surprised that the parking lot was full on a work day. Many of the cars had military and police stickers. Clearly, Sharpshooters didn't need to advertise for customers to find them.

The glass front door was covered in gun-related stickers. Inside, there was one large room with guns both lining the walls and inside glass cases. Diamond took over and led me to the counter.

"We'll need a lane, rental, and eyes and ears," Diamond said to the friendly looking middle-aged man with a mustache working there. I didn't know what that all meant.

"All right. Let's just see some I.D., and we'll get it lined up," the man said. I handed him my driver's license. He started to fill out a form, but then stopped and looked up at me. He looked down again at the card. His eyebrows furrowed a bit.

"Oh yeah," he said, suddenly smiling. "You're the one writing about getting a gun in D.C. I've been following your stories. You need to move to Virginia!" I laughed and stuck out my hand. He introduced himself as Mike Collins.

Another man behind the counter was listening. "Oh you're Emily Miller!" he said. "I heard you were at the Maryland range already." Apparently word spread quickly in the gun community.

Collins explained that for $10, I could try out as many guns as I wanted from three shelves packed with pistols behind him.

Donna Worthy had strongly advised me to buy a Glock. After the range time, she took me back to the store to point out the case of plain black Glocks lining the glass shelves for sale. I thought they all looked just like the plastic version she used for teaching.

I have gotten a lot of flak from people for wanting a cool-looking gun. I understand that they believe I should only care about the function of the gun. I agree that a gun has to fit well in your hand and function reliably. But once you get into the quality handguns, why not choose one that looks good, too?

"So far, I've had the best experience with the Glock 17 in 9mm," I told Collins about the gun I shot well with Worthy. I looked around before continuing. "But I don't want it because, well, frankly, it just doesn't look very cool. And I want to like the gun I buy."

To my surprise, Collins agreed with me. "The Glock looks like a brick," he said, laughing. "And life's too short to carry an ugly gun."

I had already ruled out pink guns solely on appearance, but for a different reason. I'm a small woman, and bad guys who enter my home aren't going to expect me to be armed and dangerous. If a criminal breaks in to rape or murder me, I don't want there to be any doubt that he's looking down the barrel of a lethal weapon.

This is just my personal opinion and not based on any data, but I think a pink gun could give the impression that it is not real, and therefore that I'm not a threat. That illusion might change the outcome of the encounter.

I told Collins I wanted a full-size gun, but didn't know which one. He and Diamond conferred on the various options, then picked a bunch for me to try. They were all in 9mm. Diamond pointed at the paper targets high on the wall and asked which one I wanted to use. That was an easy decision. I pointed to the bright pink one. In that case, a girly color was just fine.

Collins told me to put on the plastic glasses and earmuffs and directed us to the doors in the back of the store. Some of the men on the range had rifles and others were shooting at rapid speeds. The noise was jarring, so I was relieved that Collins had put us on lane one, so that there was only one man shooting next to me.

I first tried out the gun I had had my eye on since I started—the Sig Sauer P229. It was smaller than Diamond's P226, and the new E2 version with slimmer grips made it easier to control. It was also a good-looking gun. But mostly, I wanted the Sig because I had heard that it was one of the guns that SEALs use. I imagined they were carrying Sigs when they killed Osama bin Laden. It was just a really cool gun.

Diamond and Collins went back and forth between the store and the range to exchange the guns as I tried them. After the Sig, I shot the Smith & Wesson M&P9c. I liked the gun, except the grip was short, so it felt harder to control. Collins went back and found an extended grip model, and that shot much better. I also tried the Kahr K9, which was the best-looking one, but it had a very heavy recoil. I got through about seven rounds and knew that it wasn't the one for me.

Then I tried the Springfield Armory XD(M) 3.8 and found I had great control and accuracy with it. I liked the way it felt in my hand, and it looked great. The Springfield would definitely be a top contender. I tried a Beretta PX4 Storm, too, which was a heavier gun. The weight helped me with accuracy, but it was more difficult to keep control of this gun when it kicked. Still, I liked the way it looked and thought the name sounded like the hero's weapon in a spy movie.

After I had tried every 9mm available for rent, Diamond came to the lane with an enormous revolver. "You've gotta be kidding me," I said, looking at a Taurus Raging Bull pistol, which was longer than my thigh.

"Nope, you're going to shoot this next," he said. "I'll go first to warm it up." He put five .454 Casull bullets into the cylinder. He held it up and went BAM. BAM. BAM. BAM. Even wearing earmuffs, I couldn't help but jump every time he shot.

"You're next, but you only get one round," he said. "I want to be sure you don't throw it."

I looked behind the glass into the range and saw Collins and the two other range guys smiling and pointing at me holding the massive gun. I thought, I'll be damned if I'm going to let those men see me intimidated. I picked up the loaded revolver and struggled to hold it straight because the long barrel was so heavy. I focused on the front sight, kept still and pulled the trigger. BOOM.

I looked up and saw a hole right in the bull's-eye. I kept the revolver aiming down range but looked over my shoulder to see four men with shocked expressions.

"I want five of those bullets now," I said to Diamond, trying not to smile in pride. I shot them all and tried not to flinch. I looked up to see that this big gun gave me my best grouping of the day, all within the X and the 9 ring. Of course, I wouldn't ever buy this gun for protection because I could barely hold it up, but I felt a boost of confidence after firing something that powerful and keeping control of it.

———

After about an hour and a half, I had narrowed down my choices to the Beretta, Springfield Armory, Smith & Wesson, and the Sig Sauer. I wasn't sure how to choose among these, so we decided to put up a poll on the *Washington Times* website and let the readers choose for me.[1]

The Glock 17 went back onto the list because we wanted to see if gun owners were less superficial than I am. We wanted to give one revolver option and so added the Smith & Wesson 686 .357 Magnum. Then Diamond suggested putting in one as a joke. He added the Hi-Point 9mm, a cheap pistol sometimes called a "Saturday-night special," which ended up coming in dead last, with just two votes.

The poll was up for a week. The Sig Sauer won with 27 percent of the vote. The Springfield was a close second with 23 percent.[2] Thankfully, the ugly Glock came in a distant third at 15 percent.

I looked through the Sig online catalog and got my heart set on the gun in a two-tone, with the slide made of stainless steel and the rest of the gun black. It was manufactured in Exeter, New Hampshire, so it fit my qualification of being made in the U.S.A. If I lived in a normal place in America, I would then have started shopping around for the best price. But in Washington, D.C., I first had to be sure the gun I had chosen was legal to register.

Under the District's "assault weapons" ban, certain makes and models of standard semiautomatic guns are arbitrarily classed as illegal. While Senator Dianne Feinstein's national list gave weapons that would be banned, D.C. does the opposite, listing specific models that are allowed. There was a three-page list of these guns in the registration packet—including weapons that were already highly regulated by the ATF and hardly ever used in crimes, such as sawed-off shotguns, short-barreled rifles, and automatic firearms. At the end, the document said that guns eligible for registration in D.C. must be on the California Roster of Handguns Certified for Sale. That list was conspicuously missing from the registration packet.

I looked on the registration office website and found a list of approved makes and models, which appeared to be the California roster with the D.C. logo stuck on the top. One of the requirements for getting a gun registered is proving you have good eyesight. The city must be testing that by posting a thirteen-page list of guns online in about six-point font.

Squinting at my laptop screen, I scrolled down to the Sig Sauer models and found my gun listed: "P229 (Two-Tone)/Stainless Steel, Alloy, P, 3.9, 9m." On the Sig website, I saw the exact model P229 came in a tan "earth" color called the P229 Scorpion. This was exactly the same as the gun I wanted, only a different color. It was not on the list. While I didn't want a gun in earth tones, I thought it was bizarre that the District of Columbia approved guns based on their color scheme.

I was still nervous about making a purchase without being 100 percent sure it was legal. I called Sykes to ask. He had some news since we last spoke. "Remember I told you that you could buy any gun on the three state lists—Maryland, Massachusetts, and California—but only ones that had been on the lists since 2009?" This sounded a little familiar. "Well they upgraded it, now you can buy any gun that is on those lists as of today."

"Really? I'm surprised D.C. would do something like that. When did this happen? Did they tell you?" I asked.

"Nope," he replied and was silent for a moment. "Why would they be informative to me? What time? When? How this happened? I have no idea. It just happened."

I told him the gun I chose, and he reassured me the make, model, and color were fine. He added, "You know to make sure they only send the ten-round magazine and keep the 'high-capacity' at the store, right?"

Uh oh. The Sig I wanted came with a standard magazine that holds thirteen rounds.

I quickly thumbed through the three pages of guns that are illegal in D.C. and saw no reference to the limit on magazine size. But near the front of the twenty-two-page packet there was one line that said, "Please note that it is illegal to possess a magazine that holds more than ten rounds of ammunition in the District of Columbia."

I didn't know what to do because I really had my heart set on the two-tone Sig, so I tried to find one with a smaller magazine that would be legal in the District.

Up to this point, I hadn't looked into the prices of guns. I had a vague sense a gun would cost about $400. I was surprised to learn that quality-made handguns are expensive, ranging in cost from about $600 to $1,200.

I called two local gun stores, Atlantic Guns in Maryland and Virginia Arms, but neither had my gun in stock. Sharpshooters could get it in a couple days, but the price was higher than the prices I saw with online dealers.

I asked around for suggestions of dependable online stores with good prices and also Googled the model number. I looked at about eighteen dealers and found the best prices at Bud's Gun Shop, Cheaper Than Dirt, and Grab a Gun—all sold the gun for about $750. The problem was that all came in the original factory box with the standard thirteen-round magazine. I called the stores to find out if they had the gun in the lower-capacity magazine. A man at Cheaper Than Dirt said, "We don't ship to D.C." I explained that it's legal to send guns to Sykes, but he still refused.

I called Grab a Gun twice in two days, but kept getting voicemail. They contacted me later to explain they had been at the NSSF's annual SHOT—Shooting, Hunting, Outdoor Trade—Show, which is the industry's premier annual convention.

A nice man at Bud's Gun Shop checked the Sig Sauer model list and explained to me that the manufacturer doesn't make the two-tone model with a lower-round magazine. He had an all-black model in a nine-round capacity—marked "California legal"—for $833.

I pulled up the websites of eight online stores to look for the ten-round version of the P229 in black. It seemed I'd have to pay anywhere from $50 to $75 more to get a gun with a magazine holding three fewer rounds. And I couldn't buy the two-tone style I preferred.

I was so frustrated at this point, I considered giving up on buying American and just getting one of the other guns, but I wanted to figure this out for other D.C. residents who had hit this same wall.

I called Sig Sauer's customer service number to ask for help finding a dealer who had the model I wanted in the lower-capacity magazine. At this point, I was still under the mistaken impression that the gun itself came manufactured with lower-capacity magazines. The customer service agent, Andy, said that he could not help me find a dealer. I asked if the P229 was made with the ten-round magazine or could be switched out to it. He said, "No." It turned out that Andy was wrong, and many people following my story called the company to complain about the incorrect information.

Since the week I was searching for my gun happened to coincide with the SHOT show, gun enthusiasts at the Las Vegas gun convention discussed my plight, talked to dealers, and sent advice. Through comments on our website, Facebook, and Twitter, I was assured that the low- and regular-capacity magazines were interchangeable on this model.

The two different magazines are almost impossible to tell apart unless you look inside and see that one has a metal slot stuck into it to block off the last three spaces for ammunition. While the best prices for guns were available from online dealers, I learned that they often just ship the guns in their original packaging from warehouses and so can't do any kind of modifications to an order, even something as simple as switching out a magazine.

I called Sykes to see if I could get the gun sent from one dealer and the magazines sent to him separately from another. He said no. "Make sure they don't send me a gun with a high-capacity magazine because you can't register it," he replied. The city's one gun dealer didn't want to risk even briefly possessing the illicit empty metal case in the city and so wouldn't accept it.

During this public search, three enterprising dealers approached me through my Facebook page to offer to swap the magazines to make the sale—Kyle's Gunshop in Cincinnati and two Virginia stores, Guns & Ammo Warehouse in Manassas and Immortal Arms in Culpeper. I decided to go with Immortal Arms because the price was the best, at $781, which included switching the thirteen-round magazines for ten-round ones and shipping the gun.

The owner, Mark Attanasio, is a disabled U.S. Army veteran who started the appointment-only business in 2010. Attanasio said he'd have the gun in two days. He apparently assumed that speed of delivery would be a selling point—as it would be for most Americans—but it doesn't matter much for a D.C. resident who has several more hoops to jump through before taking possession of the gun.

Now I finally understood Sykes's key role in this whole system. Under federal law, legal handgun transfers can only be done within states. If you buy your gun in another state, the seller has to send it to a dealer in your own state to deliver to you. (D.C. of course is never a state—and should never be—but is treated as one by this law.)

Since you can't buy a gun in D.C. at all, Sykes's transfer business is the only thing allowing Washington residents to buy handguns. When he was zoned out the previous summer, the whole city lost its Second Amendment rights.

When I last talked to Sykes, I asked him what I needed to do to get an online dealer to send and legally transfer a gun to him. "Ask if they have my new address," Sykes instructed. "Make sure they have my license on file. If not, get their name and fax number for me to send it." What about which shipper to use? "Try to get them to send UPS or, second, FedEx, but not the postal service because they don't deliver at police headquarters, and I want my guns passing through as few hands as possible." The post office doesn't deliver to the police department? The fact that this city operates at all is a miracle.

Attanasio kindly offered to deliver my gun by hand to Sykes to try to save me the $125 transfer fee. Initially he believed that, as a Federal Firearms Licensee, he would be able to do this. But after sorting through the D.C. gun laws, Attanasio called me back. "I'm an FFL, and I can't drive it into the city to Sykes, another licensed dealer," he told me, astounded. "But I can send it to him and pass through who-knows-how-many unlicensed hands." Yes, that is Washington logic for you.

So he switched the standard thirteen-round magazines in my gun for D.C.-legal ten-round ones. Then he sent the gun to Sykes through UPS—just seventy miles away—at a cost of $43. Under federal law, guns have to be sent overnight delivery and require an "adult signature."

I was worried about what would happen if Attanasio somehow failed to send the gun with ten-round magazines, which would mean it couldn't pass registration. I had paid $781 for a gun, and generally such purchases are non-refundable. Even after my gun was transferred, I would still need to pass a written test, get paperwork filled out and signed, get approved for the registration, and bite the bullet during a ten-day waiting period. It was illegal for Sykes to release the gun to me before all of these steps had been completed. What if any of these things didn't work out?

Sykes has seen this happen before. "Registration is not 100 percent. The FBI may say yes, but D.C. says no. Or D.C. says yes, and the FBI says no," the long-time gun dealer explained of the various background checks and hoops. "I just send it back to where it came from. Then it's up to you to work it out to get your money. But I'll tell you, the average company is not going to want to talk about returning a gun that's been out of their possession for three or four months." So if you fail anywhere along the line in the registration process, you're out hundreds of dollars—and the right to keep arms.

When I first went to the gun registration office and was told about the written test on the laws, I asked Officer Brown what happens to the gun if you don't pass the written test. "That doesn't happen very often," she said. "And we let you take it over once without paying." This was not very reassuring.

I had put a lot of thought and effort into making sure my gun was exactly what I wanted because it would be a permanent decision. District law says you can't pawn a gun or sell it to anyone who isn't a licensed dealer. That sounds like standard practice until you realize that the only licensed gun dealer in the city is Sykes, and he doesn't buy guns, he only transfers them. This Sig Sauer would be with me until I die or move to a normal place.

I would have always had the impression that this was the way all Americans bought their guns if I hadn't happened to come across Diamond one day in the office during this period. It was a few minutes before our weekly staff meeting at 11:00 a.m. on Monday. He was working on his computer. "Whatcha doin'?" I asked.

"Buying a gun," he said without looking at me. Since he was always a man of few words, I didn't know if he was joking.

"Seriously?" I asked.

"Yes. I'm doing it before the meeting. Look at this," he said, pointing at his screen. I peered over his shoulder at a website called Gallery of Guns. "You just put the gun you want in this box and it pulls up all the options." He selected a Kahr PM9.

"Why are you getting another Kahr?" I asked.

"I've had that one since 1997 and want a smaller one for carry. This one weighs half as much. And I'm keeping the same brand for consistency," he explained. (Disclosure: I found out weeks into writing this gun series that the *Washington Times* and Kahr Arms are owned by the same family. No one at work ever told me to mention this gun company, nor was I offered a discount or freebie. Unfortunately.)

Diamond continued, "I just type in my name, address, and credit card number to order it."

"Don't you have to put in your concealed carry permit number?" I asked.

"Nope. The most annoying thing is remembering my password for the website," he said. He entered his zip code and got a list of gun stores to transfer the gun into Virginia. "Just pick the one nearest to me and go get it. That's it." Unlike in D.C., there was competition for dealers who transfer in Virginia, so he paid only $20, while I would pay Sykes's $125 fee.

"That's it? No tests? No registration? No waiting?" I asked.

"Nope," he said as he hit the submit button and headed to our staff meeting.

The next day at 3:00 p.m., I got an email from Diamond with the subject line: "America Rocks." I clicked it open and his message said, "Just got a call. My gun is ready for pick up."

On Wednesday morning he went to a store in Woodbridge, Virginia. He showed his driver's license and a second form of I.D. (he chose his concealed-carry permit) and filled out two forms. The federal background check form asked for the basics for the NICS check. The one-page Virginia state form asked mostly the same questions, more briefly. The store did the FBI's computerized instant background check. He paid with a credit card and was out the door with his new Kahr PM9 in ten minutes.

Thirteen states do their own background checks.[3] The Brady Act allowed alternatives such as the pre-1993 instant checks in a few states (such as Virginia, that's why Diamond filled out an extra form) or the older purchase permits in some other states. States that have kept their so-called point-of-contact status will give buyers an extra state form to fill out in order to have their own additional prohibited classes of people who are now allowed to own.[4]

I had been working on buying a gun in Washington for over two months at this point, yet one short bridge span away, Diamond got a legal firearm overnight. The contrast was striking.

No one could argue with a straight face that Virginia's reasonable gun laws are making it a more dangerous place than high-crime Washington.

So why do Obama and the other gun-grabbers want to make the rest of the country into a place like D.C.—where there are exasperating, costly, and irrational barriers to getting a gun? They want to disarm the populace and have more control of the citizens.

CHAPTER 12

THE BLOOMBERG FACTOR

New York City Mayor Michael Bloomberg is a very successful businessman who thinks his wealth and success give him the right to be the country's nanny.

Already he has used his money and power to force New Yorkers to drink smaller sodas, breastfeed, eat less salt and saturated fat, and give up the right to keep and bear arms. Having driven the citizens of New York City into submission, Hizzoner turned his focus to bossing around the rest of America.

Bloomberg spent $12 million to try to get U.S. senators to vote his way on expanding background checks for gun purchases and was infuriated when they refused to obey. After Senator Harry Reid was forced to pull the gun control bill, Bloomberg went ballistic. His shocking rhetoric indicated the type of attack ads he would be funding leading up to the 2014 election. "Children lost. They are going to die and the criminals won. I think that's the only way to phrase it. This is a disgrace," he told reporters on April 18.[1]

Actually, the failure of Manchin-Toomey in the Senate was a win for citizens who don't want to see their representatives vote out of fear that attack ads will cost them future elections.

"Mayor Bloomberg has shown a willingness to spend a significant amount of money trying to use his wealth, mostly to influence the representatives of other states," said the NRA's Chris Cox. "But what he's finding is that people—whether a United States senator or the constituents that they represent—don't want to be told by a billionaire from New York City how to live their lives."[2]

Bloomberg pounced immediately after the Senate vote. By the weekend, his group Mayors Against Illegal Guns (MAIG), had organized protests with the theme "Shame on You" at the congressional offices of the senators it determined to be vulnerable for voting against the expanded background checks amendment.

Within weeks, Bloomberg had produced particularly vicious attack ads against senators of both parties. He first went after Republican Kelly Ayotte of New Hampshire. He believed she would be the easiest to turn because she is the only senator from the Northeast not to vote for Manchin-Toomey.

He reportedly spent over $2 million on TV ads in New Hampshire and the expensive neighboring Boston TV market in just the six weeks after the vote. In the first ad, the announcer voices over, "Eighty-nine percent of New Hampshire supports background checks." Then an unidentified woman says, "But Senator Ayotte voted against them."[3] The 89 percent is from a poll by Doug Schoen, paid for by Bloomberg.[4]

Meanwhile, Gabrielle Giffords's group, Americans for Responsible Solutions, launched radio ads in late April in New Hampshire in order to "find the five votes we were short last time."[5] The advertisement, titled "Ignored," featured two women talking over the background sounds of a coffee shop about how Ayotte had "gone Washington" and ignored 89 percent of her constituents.[6] This was clearly coordinated with Bloomberg, who had a new TV ad on the air at the same time about Ayotte called "Gone Washington."[7]

Ayotte refused to bow to the pressure. "Out-of-state special interests are running false ads attacking me and even lying about my efforts to prevent gun-related violence," she wrote in a May 6 op-ed in the local paper. "I want to set the record straight: I support effective background checks and in fact voted recently to improve the National Instant Criminal Background Check System."[8] She was referring to her vote on the Grassley-Cruz alternative.

Second Amendment and conservative groups jumped in to provide suppressive fire for Ayotte. The American Future Fund spent $1.5 million in three weeks in May to go toe-to-toe with Bloomberg in New Hampshire. Their TV ad was on networks statewide and on cable in Boston.[9] The NRA bought $25,000 worth of TV time on WMUR to run a spot called "Stand with Ayotte." In it, a female announcer says, "Seen this TV ad paid for by New York Mayor Michael Bloomberg? Don't believe it. Kelly Ayotte voted for a bipartisan plan to make background checks more effective."[10] The NSSF ran radio ads in support of Ayotte as well. Senator Marco Rubio's PAC spent $100,000 on an ad in May defending his colleague's position on law enforcement.[11]

The battle escalated. In early June, Bloomberg put up a new ad featuring one of the anti-gun groups' pet go-to police chiefs, Scott Knight. "Senator Ayotte uses this vote as an alibi to claim she is tough on crime. Don't be fooled. She voted to kill comprehensive background checks, making us less safe," he says, wearing a police dress uniform but only identified by his name and title. He's actually the police chief of Chaska, Minnesota, far from New Hampshire.[12]

While Ayotte's poll numbers dipped in the immediate aftermath of the ads airing, they rose back up soon after. "I don't see any effect on Kelly," GOP party chairman, Reince Priebus, told me in mid-June. "What is the state motto? 'Live free or die.'"[13]

Bloomberg's air assault was too much for one New Hampshire member of Mayors Against Illegal Guns. Republican Mayor Donnalee Lozeau of Nashua left the group, telling the local paper that the treatment of Ayotte was beyond the pale. "I simply cannot be part of an organization that chooses this course of action, instead of cooperatively working with those who have proven over a lifetime of work their true intentions."[14]

———

Bloomberg also set his sights on newly elected Arizona Republican Senator Jeff Flake with three new TV ads in April and May after the Senate vote.[15] Flake was in a precarious political position because the senior senator from Arizona, John McCain, voted in favor of Manchin-Toomey.[16]

The liberal pollster Public Policy Polling released a survey on April 29 on the impact of the background checks vote on the targets of Bloomberg's attacks. It reported that Flake had an approval rating of just 32 percent and a disapproval rating of 51 percent. It concluded that "nineteen net approval rating makes him the most unpopular sitting senator we've polled on, taking that label from Mitch McConnell."[17]

Flake responded coolly, "Nothing like waking up to a poll saying you're the nation's least popular senator. Given the public's dim view of Congress in general, that probably puts me somewhere just below pond scum."[18]

Mayors Against Illegal Guns went for blood with the third anti-Flake ad, "My Son." It accused him of not keeping his word to Arizonan Caren Teves, whose son Alex was killed in the Aurora shooting. Teves says to the camera, "We wrote Senator Flake, urging him to support background checks. Senator Flake wrote, 'I am truly sorry for your deep loss, strengthening background checks is something we agree on.' One month later, Senator Flake voted against strengthening background checks. The issue isn't just background checks, it's keeping your promise."[19]

A spokesman for Senator Flake said that he actually handwrote the letter to Teves around March 8, and the Manchin-Toomey amendment wasn't even drafted until mid-April. There was no promise made that the senator did not keep.

Nevertheless, Flake replied to the ad by pointing out that his vote for Grassley-Cruz would have strengthened the background check system. "Mayor Bloomberg can spend millions trying to get me to support his view of background checks. That's his call. But we Arizonans aren't easily bullied," the senator posted on his Facebook page.[20]

The nonpartisan FactCheck.org agreed with Flake that the Republican alternative would strengthen background checks, just not expand them. "Voters can make up their own minds about which, if either, bill they prefer. But the fact is Flake never promised to support the Manchin-Toomey bill specifically, nor more generally an expansion of background checks to gun shows and Internet sales."[21]

Bloomberg also took aim at Democrats. Mark Pryor of Arkansas, who is up for reelection in a state that voted for Romney in 2012, faced a wave of ads that insinuated his vote made him complicit in murder. Mayors Against Illegal Guns ran a TV spot featuring Angela Bradford-Barnes, an Arkansas woman who was working for State Democratic Party Chair Bill Gwatney when he was murdered in 2008. The tearful Bradford-Barnes asks people to tell Senator Pryor to "take another look at background checks because we're tired of being disappointed."[22]

Pryor shot back with his own thirty-second ad in late May. "The Mayor of New York City is running ads against me because I opposed President Obama's gun control legislation. Nothing in the Obama plan would have prevented the tragedies like Newtown, Aurora, Tucson, or even Jonesboro. I am committed to finding real solutions to gun violence, while protecting our Second Amendment rights," Pryor said, looking straight into the camera. "No one from New York or Washington tells me what to do. I listen to Arkansas."[23]

On the six-month anniversary of Newtown, Mayors Against Illegal Guns organized rallies in Arkansas, Arizona, Georgia, Montana, and New Hampshire to ask senators to "take a second look" at their vote on background checks. The same day, the group launched a "No More Names" bus tour to send activists to protest at congressional offices in twenty-five states to try to influence votes.[24]

The bus tour was a bust from the start. On the first day in New Hampshire, the organizers included the name of Boston Marathon bomber Tamerlan Tsarnaev when it read aloud the names of people killed by "gun violence" in the six months since Newtown. Mayors Against Illegal Guns was forced to apologize, but its credibility took a big hit.

Then the NRA went through the list and found that 345 of the 5,061 killings cited since Newtown were of alleged criminals by the police or security guards or by armed citizens acting in self-defense.[25] Not exactly the types of people who deserve public sympathy.

Bloomberg's attacks on Democrats for being weak on gun control are actually hurting the party's chances of keeping majority control of the Senate in 2014. Chuck Schumer, the number three Democrat in the Senate, tried to stop Bloomberg from going after his guys. "I am trying to persuade—in whatever way I'm allowed to—the gun groups to put out different ads," Schumer, who was the lead cosponsor of Manchin-Toomey, told *Time* magazine in June 2013. "The mayor of New York City putting ads against people in red states is not going to be effective."[26]

Making matters worse for Obama and the Democratic Senate leadership, Bloomberg sent a personal letter to a thousand of the biggest donors in New York to pressure them to stop giving money to the four Democrats who voted against expanding background checks.[27]

Republican National Committee Chairman Reince Priebus was bemused by the infighting. "Bloomberg is pounding on Democrats in red states. We'll let him do it," he said in an interview.[28]

Unlike most elected officials, Bloomberg doesn't even pretend that there's a wall between his official and political activities. At the top of the home page of the mayor's official website is a box that links directly to Mayors Against Illegal Guns.[29] The chief policy advisor of the mayor's office, John Feinblatt, is also the chairman of Mayors Against Illegal Guns.[30] The city taxpayers even pay for the anti-gun group's emails and websites. A blogger who goes by "Ace of Spades" uncovered that the Mayors Against Illegal Guns website is hosted on the city's servers.[31]

New York City Hall employees have been caught lobbying for gun control in other states. In May, Bloomberg began running TV ads in Nevada to push the Democrat-controlled state legislature to pass a bill to require background checks for private transfers.[32] NRA's lobbyist for Nevada, Daniel Reid, had noticed several lobbyists for Mayors Against Illegal Guns had been added to the official list in the weeks before the vote.

During a Judiciary Committee hearing on the bill, Carrie Herbertson, a former NRA lobbyist in Nevada and now a filmmaker, noticed that Christopher Kocher and Colin Weaver were now lobbying on behalf of MAIG. Kocher is Special Counsel at the Office of the Mayor of New York City.[33] Weaver, who used to work in the mayor's office, is now deputy executive director at New Yorkers Against Gun Violence.[34]

When Herbertson saw their names on the list of registered lobbyists on Nevada's Legislative Counsel Bureau website, she noticed that both men used official New York City government emails and contact information.[35] She took a screenshot of Kocher's page, which showed his email: ckocher@cityhall.nyc.gov. She emailed it to Reid, who then gave the information to two reporters who tweeted out the screenshot.

Ten minutes later, Herbertson went back on the website to get a screenshot of Weaver's information and found that both men's contact information had already been removed.[36] Reid went to the Legislative

Counsel's office to ask how information can be taken off the lobbyist list. He was told that someone else had frantically called the office a few minutes earlier and asked the same question. According to Reid, the counsel's office said that caller had already sent an email to request the contact email addresses for Weaver and Kocher be removed from the website.[37]

Despite the shenanigans, the New York City mayor failed to push his agenda on the citizens of the Silver State. Governor Sandoval vetoed the measure.[38]

Before the bodies are buried or the families have grieved, Bloomberg pounces to exploit the tragic murders of innocent people to advance his political agenda. So, one of the job duties of the mayor's taxpayer-funded staff is to jump all over a shooting anywhere in the country as a publicity hook to call for more restrictions on Second Amendment rights.

Jesse Hathaway of Media Trackers Ohio uncovered emails between Bloomberg's mayoral staff and gun control organizations seemingly trying to exploit the deaths of three high school students in Chardon, Ohio, in February 2012.[39] One hour after that shooting, MAIG director Mark Glaze emailed a CNN story about it to the official government email addresses of three city staffers and other anti-gun activists. Minutes later, William Swenson, one of the mayor's aides,[40] updated the whole group with a note "four injured." An hour later, Lance Orchid, national organizing director of Gun Violence Prevention, emailed, "Perhaps this is the perfect time to push out the new micro-site petition around guns on campus."[41]

That afternoon, Janey Rountree, whose official New York City government title is Firearms Policy Coordinator, Office of the Mayor, asked the group to find out how shooter T. J. Lane got his gun and asked, "Are reporters working on this or planning to push the question?" She later wrote, "It may still make sense to talk about guns on college campus in the wake of this shooting."[42]

The anti-gun activists also used the shooting to build their membership list. The mayor's aide Christopher Kocher, who was later discovered lobbying for MAIG in Nevada,[43] replied to everyone about "membership outreach," pointing out that a group called ProgressOhio had created a website for condolence notes from which "email acquisitions will be shared" with MAIG and a "small subset of these names" will be provided to a group called Ohio Coalition to Stop Gun Violence.[44]

After extraordinary amounts of runaround by the mayor's office, I was able to confirm that Janey Rountree worked there, and that William Swenson had done so. I asked Marc Lavorgna, a spokesman for the mayor, for comment about the mayor's office's coordinating the exploitation of shooting deaths across the country, but he refused.

Brian Rothenberg of ProgressOhio was irate over my questions. "It's ridiculous to say we aren't sincere about the condolence page—that is outrageous! How can you question our sincerity?" he asked me when I called.

"I just did," I replied, pointing out that this email said they were gathering future mailing list names from the condolence page. Rothenberg and I were going back and forth over the facts from the Media Tracker emails when he said abruptly, "We are a nonprofit so we are nonpolitical." Apparently he had suddenly realized that the group could lose its tax-exempt status for what appeared to be political activity.[45]

Bloomberg's staff is a quick draw after a tragic shooting. Longtime gun-rights activists have told me that they had never seen the media turn so fast to blame guns, rather than the criminal, until after Aurora and Newtown. It used to take days or weeks for the national grief over a terrible crime to turn to a political debate about guns, but that gap has turned into hours. This is due to Bloomberg's ability to quickly jump on a tragedy, divert attention from the victims, and redirect the blame on the weapon, rather than the criminal.

Crisis communications is a branch of public relations that has to do with professionals handling a media onslaught to defend someone from unexpected negative press. Bloomberg has created a whole new branch of crisis communications, in which he uses a crisis to drive his political agenda.

Hours after the horrific Aurora movie theater shooting, Bloomberg was in full political mode. According to a report in the *New York Observer*, Bloomberg and aides came up with a strategic plan to spend millions on a media blitz right after initial reports of the tragedy.[46] By 8:00 a.m. the morning after the shooting, he was on WOR radio, saying, "If it was one of your kids yesterday in Aurora, maybe you'd stand up and say I'm not going to take this anymore."[47]

In contrast with gun control groups, the NRA has a policy of not making any public comments until after the funerals and memorials out of respect for the victims and their families.

When it comes to good news about gun-related crimes decreasing, Bloomberg goes silent. The Justice Department released a study in May 2013 that showed gun-related murders in the U.S. had decreased almost 40 percent in the last twenty years.

I noticed that Obama and Bloomberg were mum about the good news. I emailed MAIG spokeswoman Erika Soto Lamb. "Do you have a comment from Mayor Bloomberg or anyone at MAIG on the Bureau of Justice Statistics news that gun-related homicides have been declining since 1993? Does this affect the mayor's belief that there needs to be more gun-control laws?" I asked.

She replied that, "The latest studies should not be taken as 'proof' that this country does not have a gun violence epidemic. We do." She argued, "More people are being shot in America but fewer people are dying. A number of factors are believed to have contributed to this but mostly improved medical care is helping to save more lives."

It's true that the study showed the number of non-fatal shootings increased from 2009 to 2011, but it was still 70 percent lower than 1993. And non-fatal shootings were down 17 percent in the most recent ten years.[48] These are good things, but these facts hurt the gun-grabbers' ability to scare people and pass more restrictions on the Second Amendment, so they disregard them.

Bloomberg's group has quickly overshadowed the Brady Campaign, which was once the anti-gun powerhouse in Washington, credited with passage of the 1993 "assault weapon" ban. The New York City billionaire does not have to spend money to fundraise, nor pull strings to get access to the president and vice president. In an attempt to get a voice in the legislative battles, Brady hired the powerful Democratic lobby firm Elmendorf, Ryan in 2013. The firm has helped the Brady Campaign gain more relevance and direct contact with Biden's gun control policy staff.

But the money the Brady Campaign has spent on lobbying in Washington, D.C., is dwarfed by the tens of millions Bloomberg has spent in 2012 and 2013 to push his agenda, much of it to push gun control in the states. During the 2012 election, Bloomberg started his own super PAC which he used to spend $15 million to counter the NRA's grassroots efforts. Through Independence USA PAC, Bloomberg spent over $2.2 million in just one congressional race in Chicago to prevent pro-gun rights former Representative Deborah Halvorson from replacing Representative Jesse Jackson Jr.[49]

What the gun-grabbers don't understand is that all the Bloomberg billions can't buy Americans' values. "I've been trying to figure out the power of the NRA," Democrat Chuck Schumer said. "It's not the money they give out: they give out $3 million, $4 million a year. There are many groups that give much more. It's not even their membership. They say 5 million—let's say it is. There are tons of groups with more than 5 million members. It's that they have a core group of active members who translate what's going on to the average person—who are sympathetic to them because they're part of their milieu."[50]

What Schumer can't understand is citizens believe strongly in the principle of freedom. "While the financial dynamic has changed significantly—nobody would argue with that—the support of the American people for freedom hasn't changed," said the NRA's Chris Cox. "We'll never match Bloomberg dollar for dollar, but we don't have to. The hearts and minds of the American people certainly aren't for sale to a billionaire mayor from New York City."[51]

Gun control has never been about public safety, just politics. In Governor Rick Perry's view, Bloomberg's gun control effort is part of a larger effort being led by Obama to grow the power of the federal government. "At the end of the day, Mike Bloomberg's money is not going to sway elections," the Texas Republican told me, "This is a new phenomenon that the left is trying to control government. It really has nothing to do with a thoughtful approach to making sure that children aren't killed in schools."[52]

After Bill Clinton lost the House in 1994, he looked at the political map and realized Democrats couldn't win with just large cities. To get more voters, Clinton was determined to get soccer moms in the suburbs, and he thought gun control was a topic that would appeal to them. He was wrong. After 9/11, those soccer moms became "security moms" who preferred protecting their families to going after law-abiding American gun owners.

"Gun control as a political issue has been a loser time and time again, which is why Obama didn't want to touch it in his first term," explained Cox. "We've said all along they were going to do it in their second term. The other side said, 'Oh, he's never done anything. He's expanded gun rights.' Well, how long did it take him?"[53]

The Republican Party chairman explained why the president went after guns in late 2012. "Unfortunately, Obama decided that he was going to take a position after the horrific tragedy in Newtown to score political points," said Reince Priebus. "Gun control is the one issue—flaws and all—that their hardcore base can rally around. What else do they have?"[54]

After the nightmare at Sandy Hook, everyone wanted to find a way to protect our children and prevent such a horror from happening again. The rush to "do something" was understandable, but it's not how public laws should be made. And even if Bloomberg spends every dollar he's earned, the American people aren't going to be tricked into giving up their rights to keep and bear arms.

CHAPTER 13

WASHINGTON'S GUN BUREAUCRATS

Mark Attanasio, my dealer, had given me the UPS tracking number of my package, so I knew that my Sig was being delivered to Charles Sykes on January 25, 2012. Now that I had purchased and transferred it, I had the serial number, so I could proceed with steps eight through fourteen on my registration to-do list.

Step eight was to take and pass a written test. There is no other constitutional right that requires American citizens to pass tests to exercise it. As a newspaper journalist, no one asked me to take a written test before utilizing my First Amendment right to free speech.

Nevertheless, D.C. requires you to pass a twenty-question test in order to exercise your Second Amendment right. The sole purpose of the four hours in a classroom for the District's "safety class" was to memorize the laws in order to pass the test. I felt well prepared from those tedious hours memorizing in Donna Worthy's classroom, but I still studied the registration packet on the Metro on the way to police headquarters to be sure I knew the more obscure rules (step seven, check). I got off

at the Judiciary Square stop and walked two blocks to the Metropolitan
Police Department headquarters.

When I arrived at the Firearms Registration Section, I saw that I was
once again the only person there. Officer Brown was at her regular desk.
I hadn't seen her since I first came to the office back in October. I stood
at the high counter. "Hi, I've bought a gun now, but it hasn't come in
yet to Sykes. So I want to take the written test while I'm waiting," I told
her.

"You get your paperwork from him, and then you come up and start
the process," Officer Brown responded.

"I can't take the test in the meantime?" I asked. I had gone straight
down steps one through seven on my to-do list and was determined to
make more progress.

"You can't do anything until that 219 is filled out by him," she said
holding up a paper about ten feet away from me.

"I called yesterday and talked to an officer, and he said come in any-
time between 9:00 a.m. and 5:00 p.m.," I protested.

"Did he know you didn't fill out your 219 yet?" she asked. She never
explained what form 219 was, but I assumed it was the "Application for
Firearms Registration Certificate" because it had the telltale different
color copy pages when she waved it. This form was the one that Sykes
had to fill out one column of when my gun arrived.

"No, as I told you, I don't have the gun yet," I said.

"You're not going to do anything until I get the 219 from Charles
Sykes. He needs to fill this out to start the process," she answered.

"Why?" I asked, exasperated.

"That's the process," she said.

I pulled out the registration packet's list of instructions and held it up
in front of me. "It doesn't say that in here. It doesn't say you have to do
these things in order."

"But it's the process," she replied.

"But it doesn't say that anywhere," I insisted.

"You're going to go to Sykes and get this all filled out," she said, as if I'd said nothing. "Because I need to check your gun to be sure we can approve your weapon."

Approve my weapon? That was the first I'd heard of that step. "Why do you need to check my gun before anything else?"

"The process," she repeated. "We may not approve it. I have to look at it and be sure it's on the list."

"What if it's not? I just wasted $250 on a safety class?" I was now worried about how much money I could lose in this so-called process. "I was required to do that to get the form signed before coming in here, isn't that right?"

"At this time, I'm not trying to fuss over the issue," she said, ignoring my point. "Before you spend any money with us, I have to be sure the weapon…"

"… I already spent $250…"

"…Not with us, that's not my part of it. I'm talking about the process."

She picked up the phone and asked someone to come talk to me. If she hadn't been an armed cop, I might have started yelling, as the months of frustration hit me. Instead, I just angrily said, "That's fine, I'll leave."

"That is the process," she called out at my back as I walked out the glass doors.

I learned later that the police officers working in the Firearms Registration Section are not an accurate reflection of the force. They enjoy working weekdays, leaving at 5:00 p.m., and not being out on the streets fighting criminals.

However, there's a more insidious reason the office is staffed with people who don't know the gun laws. According to police sources, the police chief and politicians deliberately assign officers to the registration office that lack the training, skills, and knowledge regarding the District's firearms regulations and registration procedures. The goal is to frustrate applicants and to make the process of getting a legal gun seem impossible to the average citizen. It has been an effective tactic.

———

Since I couldn't take the test, there was nothing else I could do until my gun arrived. I decided to try to track it down. I went back outside and looked for UPS trucks on Indiana Avenue but saw none.

I walked a block south to C Street, but found no delivery truck there either. Even though I hadn't made an appointment with Sykes—since my gun hadn't yet been delivered, according to the UPS tracking system—I thought I'd take a shot at finding out if it had actually arrived without yet being marked in UPS tracking.

Sykes's office is down one floor and on the opposite side of the enormous building from the gun registration office. I walked outside, instead of using the internal stairs, so I had to go back through magnetometers. When I got to the C Street entrance, which is the door closest to the DMV, there were about twenty people in line, and it was moving slowly. Finally I got through and walked down the hallway to the door marked "CS Exchange."

I didn't know if Sykes was there or not, but I rang the buzzer.

After a moment, he opened the door and recognized me. "Don't you ever make an appointment?" he said, shaking his head while smiling. "Well you might as well come in if you're here."

We stood in his front office talking awhile. The buzzer rang again.

Sykes opened the door. I spied a man in the telltale UPS uniform of brown pants and a brown shirt. His back to me, he was pulling a hand truck of boxes. "Is it my gun? Is it my gun?" I asked excitedly.

"Hush, let the man in the door," Sykes said, holding the door open. The delivery man handed a box to the gun dealer. I reached for it, but Sykes pulled it back from me. "Hold it now, let's see what we have here. Slow down, come back to the office and let me see what this is."

We walked back to his small office. Sykes sat down at his desk. He carefully and slowly opened the package. I saw a black Sig Sauer box.

My heart rate quickened. This was the first time in three months that it felt real that I would soon be a gun owner. Sykes slowly opened the black case. He looked inside and pulled out the magazines and confirmed that both were the D.C.-legal, ten-round ones. I couldn't check anything off my to-do list since I hadn't known to put "find legal magazines" on it at the beginning, but I felt like I was finally getting somewhere.

Sykes put the magazines back in the box and pulled out an inch-thick, worn, black hardback book, and started writing notes by hand. This was part of ATF's requirement that FFLs record every transaction in a "bound book."[1] The system seems antiquated to me.

Then he pulled out my shiny new gun. It was wrapped and had an orange piece of plastic sticking out of the top.

"Oh, c'mon. Let me hold it," I pleaded, as he wrote down the serial number and other details. "Please, I've only seen photos. Just for a second. I'll give it right back. Please?"

Sykes handed me my new gun for the first time. I was in love.

I gripped it with both hands and aimed it at the firearms safe to feel the weight and grip. I took a picture of my hand holding the gun as a memento. Then I handed the Sig back to him.

Sykes gave me a couple of papers to complete. One was the 219 that Officer Brown wanted so much. At the bottom of the form in bold capital letters it said: "THIS IS NOT A LICENSE TO CARRY A CON-CEALED FIREARM." No mistaking that the nation's capital does not recognize the constitutional right to bear arms. Once Sykes filled out his half of the form, that meant I could check step nine off my to-do list.

I was also finally completing step one, which was filling out the eligibility form, because it needed to be notarized. Sykes signed and stamped it.

Then he picked up the phone to call the FBI to do the NICS background check. It took less than five minutes. He hung up and told me I passed. He handed me the receipt for the gun from the box.

After filling out the papers, it was time to pay him $125. I took out my checkbook, but Sykes stopped me to say he only accepts cash and money orders. Thankfully, there was an ATM machine in the hallway outside for parking ticket payments, so I was able to pay him cash on the spot. It was almost 3:00 p.m.

With my completed forms in hand, I headed back to the police station. This time I took the inside route, up one floor and circle the building, to avoid the lines at the metal detectors.

═══════

Officer Brown was gone when I got back, replaced by Sergeant Hall. Evidently the boss had been called down to deal with me. There was also a woman in civilian clothes. (I learned later that sometimes an officer on a limited duty assignment staffs the registration office, not necessarily in uniform.)

The woman was extremely polite and clearly new to her job. Sergeant Hall directed her every move. She walked up to the counter when I came in. "How has the registration process been for you? Is it as easy as you like?" she asked me, without any sarcasm.

I felt bad hurting her feelings, but I said, "It's been horrible. So much worse than I expected."

"Are you from another state where it's easier?" she asked innocently, not realizing that D.C. and Chicago are the only jurisdictions in the country that require every single gun to be registered with the government. (Hawaii has the requirement for new purchases.)[2]

Instead, I just told her that I'd never owned a gun before, so I couldn't compare.

I handed her the eligibility form and 219 that Sykes had filled out downstairs, which completed step fourteen—take all the documents to the registration office. I did not have to take a vision test—step four—because my driver's license sufficed. Non-drivers had to take a test. Step five was also easy, just showing my license proved I was a D.C. resident.

Now I could finally do step eight, which is to take the written test. The woman handed me a clipboard and told me to sit down in one of the two chairs facing the high counter to take the test. There were twenty multiple-choice questions covering the District's firearm laws.

Since no one could see me behind the counter, I took a quick photo of the front and back page of the test so I could remember the questions when I wrote my article later. Most of the questions were easy. Sawed-off shotguns and machine guns are illegal in the District. Yes, I know not to shoot anyone who is in my home but not threatening my life and not to fire a gun just to scare away car thieves.

To transport a gun, it has to be unloaded and inaccessible and—obviously—not "loaded in open view." Only the thugs who held up my neighbor were allowed to do that.

The registration packet said ammunition had to be in a separate location, out of reach, and specifically not in the glove compartment or console. I wasn't sure how that worked, but I would figure it out when I wanted to go to the range.

Most of the questions were about the city's unique firearm laws. Some of the answers were amusing in their absurdity. One question was: "When can a District of Columbia resident possess a firearm in a public space? (A) When traveling to or from any lawful firearm related activity, (B) When traveling to and from a bank to deposit large sums of money, or

(C) For personal protection." The answer was A, meaning you can't take your gun outside the home unless you're taking it to a shooting range in another state. My father's reason for needing a carry permit for bank drops back in the day wouldn't fly in D.C. Also, the answer to when you can discharge a firearm in public was definitely not while "Waiting for the official New Years [sic] celebration."

It makes no sense that merely possessing a bullet without a gun is a danger to society, but nevertheless two of the twenty questions hammered that restriction home. There are real-life consequences of falling afoul of D.C.'s ammunition registration law. Adam Meckler, a former Army Specialist whose experiences I report later in the book, is one American hero who suffered those consequences. It's also illegal to buy ammunition in the city from anyone other than a licensed firearms dealer—but our only dealer, Sykes, doesn't sell it.

The most difficult questions were obscure facets of the regulations totally unrelated to public safety. It asked for the exact year of manufacture that made a firearm "antique" and thus not subject to registration in D.C.: (A) 1900, (B) 1910, or (C) 1898. I hadn't memorized this law because it seemed so pointless.

I checked all the boxes on the test and turned it in to the woman, only to be handed yet more forms. I signed the "Background Investigation Release Form," even though Sykes had just done a national FBI check on me. I also had to sign the "Notification of Fingerprinting Services Fee," which turned out to be a pricey $35.

While I was sitting out of sight behind the counter filling out the papers, I overheard a phone conversation between Sergeant Hall and another District resident who was apparently frustrated with the gun registration process. The police officer was trying to calm the person down, but clearly having the opposite effect. "Some states are even tougher than D.C.—California I believe," he told the caller.

I wanted to yell out—"No, we're worse!"—but I held my tongue. I kept signing my name on forms while Sergeant Hall continued politely listening to the caller and answering his questions, but ceded no ground regarding the difficulty of the process.

After he hung up, he said to the woman in the office, "I always say, 'When in Rome, do what the Romans do. And if you don't like Rome, move somewhere else.'"

Move. That's the city's answer to American citizens not having their constitutional rights respected in the nation's capital.

Since I couldn't fight with a police officer—especially one who still had power to decide if I get to keep my gun—I stood up so they remembered that I was there. I held out the forms and called out, "All done, now what?" The woman came over and took the forms. None of those documents were on my to-do list, so I hadn't made much progress checking steps off in the last half hour.

I waited, stewing over Sergeant Hall's comments. The woman in civilian clothes came back with good news.

"You passed your test," she told me. "You got one wrong, so that's a 95 percent. Good job." That one question was about antique guns.

Sergeant Hall came back to the front of the room and handed me a small form of multi-sheet paper. "Here are your fees. Take it to room 1157 and pay this and bring back the receipt to get your fingerprints done." The form was four by six inches. He had checked off the boxes: $35 for the fingerprints, $13 for gun registration, and $12 for ballistics—$60 total.

Room 1157 was the DMV, which is oddly the only place where you can pay your city fees to register a gun. Once again, I walked around the building on the inside and down a flight of stairs. It was about 3:30 p.m. and the line at the entrance to the DMV for the purpose of sorting through who was there for what reason was long and slow. When I got to the front of the line, I was directed to get in another line for the cashier who would accept my payment.

I walked to the back of the huge room to the cashier line where I had been directed. There was no one at the desk. I was fourth in line. After ten minutes, I asked the teller next to the empty desk if anyone was working there.

She said that he was on break and would be back "soon." Others in line with me were mumbling, looking around irritably, pacing.

I got out of line and found someone at the front of the DMV who looked to be a manager. I told her the problem. She went to the back, and suddenly a man appeared at the desk to take our money. When it was my turn, I handed him the slip of paper in triplicate and $60 in cash (the DMV also doesn't take credit cards or checks). He kept the white copy and gave me the pink and yellow as a receipt for payment. I could check off step ten now.

For the third time in one day, I headed back around the building to the police department.

Entering the Registration Section at 4:30 p.m., I was worried that they wouldn't finish the process before the office closed at 5:00 p.m. As I was still the only person in the office, Sergeant Hall knew exactly where I was in the process. "Got the receipt now?" he asked. I handed him the yellow paper, which left me with the pink receipt, and he told me to follow him into the back of the office to complete step nine, getting fingerprinted.

I had never before been allowed around the Registration Section's desk counter. In the back of the office, past a Keurig coffee maker and a police jacket on a hook, was a computer with a foot pedal. Sergeant Hall held my right thumb onto the computer and slid it side-to-side until my thumbprint was clear on the screen. The machine dinged "good print" and he tapped the foot pedal and put my right index finger to the screen. We did this for all my individual fingers plus all four fingers at once.

Once I had finished, Sergeant Hall led me back to the front. The staffer in civilian dress was sorting through my papers. "Do you have your passport photos?" she asked.

Oh no. I forgot step six. I was so worn down, I felt like I was about to cry. I didn't want them to reject my whole application. I apologized and explained I had forgotten to get the photos. To my surprise, Sergeant Hall said it was okay and to just bring the photos when I came back.

Relieved, I asked him what to do next.

"Now we have the 'cool down law,'" said the police officer. I'd been working on getting a gun for almost four months? If I cooled down any further, I would go into hibernation for the winter months. "You have ten days for us to approve your registration." I had thought the two five-day periods meant I had to do something in between, so lumping them together meant I could check off step fifteen.

I started to gather up the papers to leave when Sergeant Hall suddenly started speaking again. "But if you have your receipt and it shows you bought your gun earlier, we can count those days to the cool down," he said. Now I understood why Sykes had given me the receipt for my Sig earlier that afternoon rather than leaving it in the box. I showed the receipt to Sergeant Hall.

"Says here you bought it on Monday, so that means your period ends, the twenty-sixth, twenty-seventh...February third," he said. "So you have eight days. You can call on the second and find out if we approved your registration, but don't come back until the third."

A little before 5:00 p.m., I left police headquarters with less paper but no gun. The eight days remaining for me to supposedly cool off just made me more fired up about D.C.'s gun control laws.

And there were still three steps left to go.

CHAPTER 14

BARACK OBAMA, THE MOST SUCCESSFUL GUN SALESMAN IN HISTORY

Barack Obama's election in 2008 and ensuing attack on the Second Amendment has resulted in the biggest increase in gun sales and gun ownership in history.

Americans have stocked up on firearms and ammo out of fear he may take their guns. That upward trend went almost directly vertical in 2013 when Obama overtly talked about outright bans on certain guns on the federal level. Obama has inadvertently made the country safer—with record-high levels of gun ownership and carry permits for the good guys.

There's no way to know the exact percentage of Americans who own guns because most don't have to register with the government. And many don't want to tell a random pollster who calls. However, there is no question that there are more gun owners and firearms in America today than at any time in history.

One hundred million gun owners own 300 million firearms in our nation. Forty-seven percent of Americans self-report having a gun in the home, according to a Gallup poll released in October 2011. That number was up from 41 percent a year earlier and the highest Gallup has recorded since 1993. The survey found that one in three Americans (34 percent) personally owns a gun.[1]

Along with gun ownership, the number of Americans who have a permit to carry a gun is also at a record high. There are at least 8 million active permits to carry concealed handguns in the U.S.[2] Twenty-five years ago, twenty-one states prohibited all carry rights.[3] Today, every state in the nation recognizes the right to bear arms outside the home. Illinois was forced to overturn its carry ban in 2012, leaving the District of Columbia as the only place where you can't defend yourself with a gun outside your home.

In 1987 Florida created a model "shall issue" state law, which means a citizen only has to meet some uniform standard—such as undergoing a background check and taking a class—to be granted a permit. A "may issue" state is one in which a gun owner has to give the government a reason for needing to carry a handgun, such as a dangerous job, like my dad did in Maryland. There are now a remarkable forty-one states that have "shall issue" carry laws.

———

Typically gun companies do well when the economy does badly, as has been the case since the end of 2008. "We are countercyclical to the economy, and we've been in a sustained downturn, so that accounts for part of the sales increase," explained Lawrence Keane, the senior vice president and general counsel for the NSSF, which is the trade association for the firearms industry. "Our industry has good times in down periods because of concern about crime and instability. And when the economy is not doing well, more people go hunting to put meat in their freezer."

The rest of the sharp uptick can be chalked up to having a gun-grabber in the White House. "The other driver for sales is the legislative concern," said Keane. "Everyone knew Obama was anti-gun—despite the claims he wasn't, nobody bought it."[4]

The firearms industry is one of the few that has been growing and investing during the Obama economic malaise. The companies in the U.S. that manufacture, distribute, and sell firearms, ammunition, and hunting equipment had a direct economic impact of $14 billion in 2012, according to NSSF.[5] When you take into account the supplier and ancillary industries, the total economic activity was a whopping $33 billion. In comparison, in the last year of the Bush administration, the direct economic impact was only $6.7 billion and the total economic activity was only $19 billion.[6]

According to NSSF, Americans imported 2.6 million handguns in 2012, a 77 percent increase from 2008. One million rifles were bought from overseas that year, which is an amazing 93 percent increase since Bush was in the White House. Shotgun imports rose 31 percent in 2012 to 700,000. Ammunition purchases from overseas have gone up 21 percent during the Obama presidency to 2.2 billion cartridges in 2012.[7]

There is a two-year lag for ATF's release of manufacturing numbers, but in 2011, there were 6,540,0000, guns made in America. The bulk of those were 2.6 million pistols and 2.3 million rifles.[8]

NICS is another way to evaluate gun sales. While FBI background checks have steadily increased every year since 2000 (except for 2010) the number skyrocketed after Obama was reelected.[9] During Obama's first year in office, NICS checks went up 10 percent from President George W. Bush's last year as president.

While not every FBI check means the person ultimately bought a gun, the data shows patterns. After Obama used the Newtown tragedy to declare war on the Second Amendment, NICS checks hit historic levels. They were up a startling 49 percent in December 2012 over the same month in 2012. An ATF newsletter to Federal Firearm Licensees in March 2013 reported that December 2012 was the highest volume month ever for NICS background checks.[10] Nearly 1 million checks were received during the third week alone. Eight of the top ten highest volume days NICS had ever recorded occurred that month.

Demand went through the roof in January 2013 when Obama announced mid-month that his top legislative agenda included bans on "assault weapons" and "high-capacity" magazines. NICS checks were up a staggering 81 percent over the first month of 2012. The FBI report of the highest weeks of NICS checks showed that since 1998, all the top ten have occurred between December 3, 2012, and March 3, 2013.[11]

The NSSF releases adjusted NICS figures monthly that exclude checks done for determining carry permits or renewing them. While the adjusted figure is also not an exact number of gun sales, it does give a more accurate picture of the market than the total numbers do. The NSSF-adjusted figures, as of May 2013, showed monthly checks had increased for thirty-six straight months compared to the same period in the previous year.[12]

Gun companies contribute significantly to tax revenue—$4.6 billion in state and business taxes and $460 million in excise taxes a year.[13] On the federal level, the Firearms and Ammunition Excise Tax for manufacturers is 11 percent on ammunition and long guns and 10 percent for handguns.

The Treasury Department gives all the revenue to fish and game agencies in the states for wildlife and habitat conservation, public shooting ranges, and hunter education courses. Over the years, the firearms manufacturers have contributed $7 billion for such things as restoration of wild turkey, bald eagle, duck, elk, and antelope populations. "Hunters were the first conservationists," said NSSF's Keane. "They're the original green movement."

You'd think Obama would be pleased with how the environment benefits from the firearms industry. The federal tax revenue from manufacturers has increased 83 percent since 2008—perhaps the only place in the budget that was in the black during Obama's presidency. In 2012, the gun industry paid $644 million for these hunting and outdoor upkeep efforts, according to NSSF. The 2012 taxes translates into sales of $2.1 billion worth of long guns, $2 billion in handguns, and $1.9 billion of ammo.

The two publicly traded firearms manufacturers in the U.S. have experienced a rapid increase in share price since Obama came to 1600 Pennsylvania Avenue. Sturm, Ruger & Co.'s stock was 5.29 on the day Obama was elected in 2008. It steadily increased throughout his presidency and into the second term. When I checked it on June 3, 2013, the Ruger stock was at 51.02. That is a jaw-dropping 864 percent increase. Don't you wish you'd bought that stock?

The company had a remarkable 2012. In the first quarter, it had orders for 1.2 million units, more than the total for all of 2011.[14] The steep jump forced Sturm, Ruger & Co. to temporarily stop accepting new orders from March to May to catch up with demand for its products. At the end of 2012, the company announced net sales of $492 million, a 50 percent increase over 2011.[15] Things kept going upward into 2013 for the Connecticut-based firearms manufacturer. The first quarter report showed a 39 percent growth in sales over the previous year.[16]

Smith & Wesson stock closed at 2.06 on November 3, 2008. On election day four years later, it closed at 9.46. That's a 359 percent increase. It has stayed high, closing at 9.22 on June 3, 2013. The company ended its 2013 fiscal year on April 30 with net sales of a record $588 million, a 43 percent increase over the previous year. Even though firearm production for the year increased by 40 percent, the company reported to shareholders in late June that it was "unable to meet the ongoing demand across most of its firearm product lines, resulting in additional growth in the company's order backlog."[17]

Freedom Group, the world's largest privately owned gun and ammunitions manufacturer, is the umbrella over sixteen brands including Remington, Bushmaster, DPMS, Marlin, AAC, and TAPCO. It employs over four thousand Americans and is valued at $1 billion. (Freedom Group was up for sale when this book went to print.) The company sold 1.4 million long guns and 2 billion rounds of ammunition in 2012, raking in $932 million, a 20 percent increase over the previous year. Revenue for the first quarter of 2013 was $320 million, a 50 percent increase from the same period last year.[18]

Since 2011, the company has had a dramatic increase in sales of modern sporting rifles (MSRs)—what Feinstein calls "assault weapons." Freedom Group's CEO Kollitides is bullish on this style of firearm. "The MSR may replace most of the guns on the market. Bolt action and lever action markets will decline because the younger generation likes the MSR product. It's easy to handle. You can modify it, dress it up, customize to your own uses and special needs," said Kollitides. "I see that product as having incredible longevity."[19]

Colt Defense entered the commercial market for the modern sporting rifle as sales took off in 2011. Until then, the company was at capacity making the M4 carbine, which the military used in the Afghanistan and Iraq wars. The Colt version of the MSR was, as Obama would say, "military-style" because it was based on the M4 platform, but of course it is only semiautomatic.

Colt's Roger Smith told me that the transition into the commercial market for rifles has been successful for the Connecticut-based company because of its well-known brand and reputation for providing quality rifles to the military, as well as the timing with the Obama gun control agenda.[20]

The five-hundred-year-old Beretta Company is still owned by the original Italian family and does not release financial data. Jeff Reh, general counsel of Beretta USA, would only say that the manufacturer, based in southern Maryland, has "had significant increase in sales after Obama was elected."

Reh has been with Beretta since 1983 and gave interesting insights into market patterns. "At the end of Bush, the industry as a whole was going through a good period. Post September 11, people had more of a sense of approval of owning guns, and they bought them as an exhibition of American independence and strength. Also, servicemen and women returning from the wars were buying guns."

The longtime firearms executive said, "What was extraordinary was that when Obama was elected, sales skyrocketed and continued to for four more years. Then Obama was reelected at the tail end of what was then an eight-year pattern of good sales, and sales went up even further after Newtown. Handgun purchases are driven by threats of government restrictions or confiscations."[21]

───

Of course a gun isn't of any use without ammunition. Gun owners have been frustrated in 2013 because of the massive ammo shortages in stores and online. Supply was low at the end of 2012 because it was such a big year for sellers, and then demand increased dramatically in December and through the first quarter of 2013. Manufacturers have struggled to backfill and get supplies back up to pre-2012 levels.

In a regular year, there are 10 billion cartridges manufactured in the U.S. or imported annually, according to the NSSF.[22] The major manufacturers crank out millions of rounds a day. To try to meet demand in 2013, the large companies have added extra shifts at the plants, up to twenty-four hours a day, seven days a week at the biggest factories.

"It's basic economics. Demand exceeds supply, which leads to shortages," explained NSSF's Keane. "The reason that demand is so high is a combination of gun control legislation and organically, more people are hunting and shooting, a lot of first-time buyers. Also the concern about Homeland Security allegedly buying up all the ammunition—though not well founded—adds to demand."

The industry spokesman said that government purchases in 2012 and 2013 have not been out of line of previous levels, but the conspiracy theories have led to more buying. "The public sees the shelves are empty. So, they buy more than they need and stockpile because they are afraid that they won't be able to get it in the future—because of Obama, or state laws, or the prices will increase."

―――――

You can also see the impact of Obama on the firearms industry at the retail level. The NSSF puts out an annual retail report to its members tracking products sold, sales trends, inventory, consumer behavior, and profit margins. The report is compiled for the previous calendar year from online surveys of retailers in the spring.[23]

The 2013 edition includes responses from seven hundred firearm retail dealers. The data showed that 84 percent of retailers had more sales in 2012 than the previous year. The category of firearms that the most retailers (77 percent) said increased was AR-style modern sporting rifles.

Interestingly, retailers reported that one out of four customers was a first-time gun buyer. Also, the number of women customers increased for the third year in a row, with three-quarters of retailers reporting more women came into their stores in 2012. Women most often bought semi-automatic handguns followed by revolvers, AR-style rifles, shotguns, and traditional rifles.

Iowa-based Brownells is the world's largest supplier of gun parts, ammunition, and gunsmithing tools. The company's CEO, Pete Brownell, does not release financial information about the seventy-five-year-old family company, but he gave me some insights into how the political changes in Washington have resonated in his business.

"Since President Obama was elected, there's been this political elasticity of demand. The more there is a perceived threat, the more demand increases. And it's been a very specific demand for components that would fall under an 'assault weapon' ban—AR-15 components, thirty-round magazines for the ARs, any magazine for concealed-carry pistols."

He said sales of these items slowed significantly after April. "They had the quickest drop-off after the Senate vote. The immediate threat was gone," he said in an interview.

"That's the political elasticity. As political pressure decreased on those components, the demand did too." Since his company sells accessories and components, the demand lags behind firearms purchases, which are estimated from FBI checks. "We're seeing significantly greater growth than the NICS checks suggest," Brownell said in early June. "People are maintaining their weapons and personalizing them, adding components to make the gun fit their needs better."

Brownell said that more than the political bump, he has seen a surge in new types of gun owners. "There is a much more sustainable market in the new urban protection-minded individual. That market, which is half women, has become very strong since 9/11 as they are waking up to the fact that the world isn't as safe as it once was. They had a lot of faith that the government could handle a threat, but it was a false sense of security. Even with natural disasters—floods, fires, tornados—when the support structure isn't to the highest standards, we have to protect ourselves."

He said this new market is buying concealed-carry pistols, shotguns, and accessory items that help aim a firearm in dangerous situations. "The industry has done well because people are saying, 'Give me the choice to protect myself and own these weapons,'" said the businessman. "Look, the polls are right here. America is voting—just look what they are buying. They are buying AR-15s."[24]

I also spoke to a few independent retailers around the country about their experiences. At H&H Shooting Sports Complex in Oklahoma City, gun sales and range attendance have gone gangbusters. According to owner Miles Hall, revenue was $15 million in 2009. It went down slightly in 2010 and 2011, then hit $23 million in 2012. He expects revenue of $25 million in 2013. The company was founded in 1981, employs 117 people, and has an economic impact of $128 million on the local economy.

Hall is a meticulous record keeper. He counts the number of people who come to his 82,000-square-foot complex to buy a gun or shoot at his sixty-one-position indoor range. He said that 187,000 people came into H&H in 2009, but that skyrocketed to 740,000 by 2012. "Last year, thousands showed up, people we had never seen before. That's a lot of daggone people," he remarked. "Oklahoma only has 4.2 million people and over 700,000 of them came through my door." He expects to see over a million customers this year.

As high as the numbers were leading up to Obama's reelection, Hall saw a spike after Newtown. "When the tragedy struck Sandy Hook, the initial buying push was not guns but safes. People said, 'I don't want irresponsible folks getting my stuff, and I don't want thieves getting them either,'" Hall told me.

"It was not until the administration made the statements about banning guns did the buying binge start. It was off the charts. We sold as much in a week as we did in an entire year, only a few years back." He said people were lined up forty deep to buy whatever gun they could find in stock. "First thing that went out the door was platform guns, the so-called assault weapons, you know, basic semiauto rifle with a rail. And then went the handguns and shotguns. As long as we had it, we could sell it. We went from three thousand guns in the building to fewer than a hundred in one week in December."

Hall has noticed a significant change in the type of customers in recent years, which he attributed to a "fear of safety in their own homes" as well as Obama's push for gun bans. "Everyone back East thinks it's just old, white men getting guns," said Hall. "That's not this new breed at all. They are in their mid-thirties, ethnically across the board, almost 50/50 women, and understand the value of guns."[25]

In Yuma, Arizona, Sprague's Sports had a 42 percent increase in sales from 2008 to 2012. The owner, Richard Sprague, attributes the boom in business to Obama's election, which "got people off the fence and into the store." Then sales pushed up 56 percent during the first six months of Obama's second term. With demand so high, he's had trouble filling the holes in the inventory of his fifty-six-year-old family business. Sprague told me in an interview in June 2013 that he recently met with a distributor who listed 950 different handguns in his selection, but only twelve models were available.

Sprague echoed what Hall said about the changing customer base. He said that after the 2012 election, these buyers who are new to the shooting world had a wakeup call. "They faced—for the very first time— their newfound interest and freedoms being challenged with pending legislation. This fired up the masses stronger this time than the first election," said Sprague, comparing Obama's reelection to the 2008 election. He said attendees for classes in concealed carry and basic introduction to gun safety have doubled in 2013.[26]

―――――――

It is clear from government data, public corporate financials, and industry and retail reports that Obama and his policies have caused the spike in gun sales and ownership, but his allies can't believe it. Instead they blame the NRA and gun-rights advocates of fearmongering in order to drive up sales. They know that the NSSF, not the NRA, represents the manufacturers. The NRA is just bigger and better known because of its 5 million members, so has a larger target on its back.

"The NRA leadership's top priority is to make sure the corporations that make guns and ammunition continue to turn huge profits," wrote Gabrielle Giffords's husband Mark Kelly in an op-ed in the *Houston Chronicle* on the day the NRA annual meeting began in the city.[27]

"Guns fly off the shelves after tragedies because [Wayne] LaPierre and the gun manufacturers he represents exploit people's fears. In return, gun manufacturers gave LaPierre and the NRA tens of millions of dollars last year alone." There is not a shred of evidence that the manufacturers give the NRA "tens of millions of dollars." Captain Kelly, while a very nice man, is not keen on facts. For example, Chris Wallace asked him on *Fox News Sunday* about the reality that the "assault weapons" ban was in place for ten years and didn't work to reduce crime. "Well, I don't know if it worked or not. I mean, I haven't looked at all of the statistics," replied Captain Kelly, who co-chairs a gun-control advocacy group with his wife.[28]

"The NRA is basically helping to make sure the gun industry can increase sales," New York Representative Carolyn McCarthy told the Huffington Post in January.[29] McCarthy, a Democrat, is the sponsor of the House bill to ban magazines over ten rounds, which she says have the "sole purpose" to "to kill as many people as possible."[30]

"The NRA primarily wants to sell guns. They represent gun manufacturers," Democratic Representative John Yarmuth of Kentucky said on MSNBC. "They want to create the fear that the government is actually going to come after guns, because that helps sell more guns."[31]

The gun-grabbers have it backwards. Obama and his cohort's efforts have had the unintended effect of arming more Americans. The good people of America are buying up guns and ammo because these politicians and activists want to take their Second Amendment rights away from them.

Industry leaders and corporate and independent retailers who I spoke to all separately reported a significant new type of demand that defies common stereotypes. More women, urban-dwellers, and younger people have entered what was largely a rural, male, and Southern culture.

Keane, who has been in the industry since 1996, attributes some of this cultural shift to the Supreme Court's rulings in *Heller* (2008) and *McDonald* (2010). "Part of why we are seeing so many first-time buyers is the burgeoning awakening upon the American public that, in fact, what they have always believed is true: that the Second Amendment is a fundamental, individual, constitutional right."

That is exactly why I set out to become a first-time gun owner. The *Heller* ruling gave me the legal ability to own a gun, and I learned first-hand that I had to defend myself when the police aren't there.

CHAPTER 15

EMILY GOT HER GUN...
AND TOOK IT HOME
ON THE METRO

I was waiting out what Officer Hall had called the "cool down law"—the ten-day waiting period that the city's politicians created supposedly to stop criminals from buying guns in anger and shooting someone. While I was officially cooling off, the $762 Sig was sitting in a locked safe in Sykes's office at police headquarters.

One of the problems with these mandatory waiting periods is that people often get a gun because they're in immediate danger. And I can't imagine that someone crazy and evil enough to murder would change his mind because the government didn't approve his gun application right away.

After a couple days, I called the firearms registration office to be sure I hadn't missed an obscure detail in "the process." The first woman who answered the phone put me on hold. A second woman then picked up. I asked if everything on my application was okay. She put me on hold again.

"Yes ma'am," she said when she picked up again. "You need to call Sykes and see when you can meet up with him. And once you meet up with him, he'll send you upstairs to the gun registration office to wait for your ballistics."

There seemed to be some missing pieces in this explanation. How do I get the registration certificate to Sykes so he can release the gun? How does my gun get to wherever the ballistics test is done?

"Once you come to our office, an officer will go down to Sykes's office and pick it up and take it down to the ballistics office," she said.

I wondered why I needed a police escort to bring an unloaded gun up one floor. Were the police afraid I'd take my nearly legal gun and make a break for it without the final test? Or did they think I'd hit someone over the head with my gun in the elevator?

"You'll sit in gun registry, Room 2169, until the ballistics test has been completed," she told me.

"And then I can just leave with my gun?" I asked, having become all too familiar with the fact that not all the gun regulations the District government expects you to follow are actually in the law or the official paperwork.

"That's correct," she answered.

"Are there any regulations about my leaving? I mean, do I need to use any kind of transportation?" I asked. She replied that she didn't understand my question. "Can I just walk out and down the street with my gun? Are there any rules on how I leave?"

"You can leave any way you want as long as it's in a lock box. We'll give you the registration forms, which will be notarized," she responded. Wait, a lock box? I didn't have a "lock box," and this was the first I'd heard about needing one.

"I read the entire registration packet and didn't see anything about a lock box. Does it say it in there?" I asked.

"Well, I don't know it verbatim," said the woman, whose full-time job was to enforce the details of the gun laws.

"Is this the law?" I asked.

"I'm not going to say it's the law to have a box," said the police officer. "But normally when you are transporting, it has to be in some kind of locked container—a box or a back pack."

Ah, I got it. Buried in the packet—in Part IV, Section 9, the third bullet point, to be exact—it says, "When transporting a firearm in a manner other than in a vehicle, it must be unloaded, inside a locked container, and separate from any ammunition."

"The weapons usually come in a box," she told me. I said mine did. "We'll give you a lock." I thanked her for being helpful, and said I'd be there next week.

As an added precaution, I called Sykes for his advice. He said my Sig Sauer came with a lock in the box. He explained that he keeps some lock boxes for sale in his office in "emergency situations," when a customer's gun comes in a cardboard box.

Problem solved. I just needed to spend yet another weekday at police headquarters. I asked Diamond to be relieved from writing one of my daily political editorials. We decided the following Wednesday—day nine of my "cooling off"—would be "gun day." By this point in the process, a resident who wanted to legally register a gun would have taken off most or all of four work days.

Criminals get their guns off the streets within minutes as part of their day jobs. Five minutes and no fees for an illegal gun, versus weeks and over $400 in fees for a legal gun. Which option do you think most people in this city are choosing?

The final day at police headquarters turned out to be as much of a waste of city resources and my time as the rest of the registration process had been. The day before "gun day," I called the registration office again to find out if my application had been approved. It had. Whew. I made an appointment for 11:00 a.m. Wednesday with Sykes, in order to give him the approved form so he could release my gun.

I took the Metro and got to the police station at 10:30 a.m. to pick up the forms. Once again, I was the only city resident in the registration office. "Hi, Officer Brown," I said with much friendliness, knowing this would probably be the last time I had to talk to her. "I'm Emily Miller. I'm here to pick up my gun registration." There was also a male uniformed officer behind the counter.

"Did you bring your two passport photos?" Officer Brown asked. Apparently so few people are registering their guns that the officers know by heart the exact status of each individual application. I handed over the $20 worth of photos I had to buy.

"Sign this," she said pushing a piece of paper over the high desk. It was a form that said that, under the 2008 law, the police department had "initiated an expiration date for all registrations approved as of June 21, 2010." She had filled in the block to say that my gun registration would expire on February 2, 2015. Apparently, this would not, after all, be the last time I'd have to deal with Officer Brown.

I signed the expiration date form and then waited about fifteen minutes. Officer Brown came back to the desk with the application—the top white sheet had been ripped off. My photo was now stapled to the thin yellow and pink copies underneath. "Is this my certificate?" I asked. "Do I have to carry all these papers with my gun?"

The male police officer, whose name tag said Officer Harper, answered. "Just this top sheet. But if you want to add photos to the other pink sheet, you can use that too." I could not believe that the city gave D.C. gun owners just a piece of thin paper instead of a laminated I.D. like a driver's license that could not be easily altered. And we had to carry around the flimsy sheet of yellow paper for three years until our registration expired.

I sat back down and waited. No one told me what was happening. After ten minutes the phone rang, and Officer Brown answered. When she hung up she said, "Officer Harper called from Sykes's office. He's waiting for you."

"He didn't tell me he was leaving, or that I was supposed to go with him," I said. She didn't care. I grabbed my papers and headed down one floor and around the enormous building to the gun dealer's office next to the DMV.

Officer Harper was sitting in a chair. Sykes was on the phone explaining the registration process to a potential gun owner. Clearly, most people use Sykes, rather than the bureaucrats staffing the Registration Section, as their resource for navigating the registration system. Plus, Sykes always offers his customers beef jerky, Twizzlers, and a bottle of cold water from a small refrigerator. I grabbed a licorice and waited.

Sykes hung up, shook hands and took my registration certificate to use to fill out more forms. Then he pulled my gun out of the Sig Sauer box and told me to check the serial number against the one on his form. I loved holding my gun, just for a moment.

Officer Harper then took my gun and put it in a black envelope. "What exactly do you do with it now?" I asked.

"We take a photo of it. Then we shoot two rounds and keep those as like fingerprints for the gun," he said. I'd heard from one D.C. gun owner that he believed his pistol was shot up to fifty rounds during the test. Another resident told me that he thought the police broke his gun. None of these people have filed a report, so I wanted to follow up on the rumors.

How long does the test take? "Twenty or thirty minutes," said Officer Harper. Can I watch? "No." Can I listen? "Not unless you have super-power hearing." Is it done in the basement? "Yes." I had no choice but to let him walk off with my brand new gun.

After the police officer left, I thanked Sykes for getting me from the girl who thought carry permits were legal in D.C. to an actual gun owner.

I walked back upstairs to the registration office, where all was still quiet. Office Brown looked to be doing paperwork. True to his word, Officer Harper was back in a short time with my gun. He held open the case, and I could see the Sig was no longer wrapped and the orange plastic piece was gone. My brand new gun was now a used gun, but I had never fired it.

I reached out to check my gun to see if he had damaged it. Officer Brown started. "Not out here, you can't. Come to the back of the office," she said leading me to the back by the fingerprint area.

I can understand this precaution. If I was walking by a D.C. government office and saw someone pull out a full-sized 9mm and rack it, I'd probably scream and duck.

Officer Brown pointed out a metal container at a forty-five degree angle to the floor and about knee high. She told me to hold the gun inside the metal thing and then rack it. I did, and the gun worked fine.

Back out front, I had to show that the firearm was being taken home in a locked box. I pulled out the gun lock provided with my new Sig and looped it through the handles of the plastic box. I put the key in my bag.

As soon as I did, Officer Brown took the box away from me. She wrapped it in a brown plastic bag and walked out the door. She didn't say why, so I just followed. People coming through the magnetometers at the police station stared as Officer Brown carried my bagged gun box in front of her like she was passing a tray of hors d'oeuvres.

After she went through the turnstiles, she took the Sig out of the brown bag and handed it to me. I thanked her.

I pushed open the glass doors of the police department for the last time. Outside, I held my gun—in its case—above my head in absolute delight. Victory!

Four months and $435 in fees later, I was a legal gun owner in Washington, D.C.

While it is against the law in D.C. to have a gun outside the home, there is an exception for going to and from the registration office, as long as the gun is unloaded and locked for the trip. Since there's no parking around the police station, I always take the Metro.

I held my plastic Sig box in one hand and headed down the escalator. I put the Metro card through the machine, and passed through the turnstile with my gun. The train came quickly, and I jumped on it. I was a little worried about being robbed, so I sat down with my black box on my lap, holding it close. One woman stared at the lock on the box, but it seemed more out of curiosity, as if she wondered whether I was carrying diamonds or CIA secrets.

I took my gun straight home, where I practiced my stance and grip. "Drop the gun!" I yelled into my bedroom mirror, while pointing my unloaded gun. "Get down on the floor! I will shoot!"

I loved having a gun at home, but without ammunition, it was just a very expensive paper weight.

One of the most bizarre of all the gun laws District politicians have come up with is that it is illegal to possess ammunition without a registered gun. There's no rationale for this law. What is the worst I could have done with, say, a box of 9mm at home and no gun? Throw it hard at my neighbor and leave a red mark?

The penalty is the same as having an unregistered gun—a $1,000 fine and up to a year in jail.[1] (And people really have gotten into very serious legal trouble in D.C. for this, such as former Army Specialist Adam Meckler, who I profile later in the book.) So I was very careful not to buy ammunition before I had my legally registered gun at home.

I didn't know where to buy ammunition—although this was well before the shortages, so it should not have been difficult. I started by consulting my well-worn registration packet for the laws.

A bullet that is capable of penetrating more than eighteen layers of Kevlar® from a barrel of five inches or less is prohibited.[2] Of all the gun-control laws, this one has the highest penalty: ten years in jail. But how would you know what a bullet can penetrate? The guide also said the sale and transfer of ammo is prohibited unless the seller is a licensed firearms dealer. But Sykes is the only dealer, and he doesn't sell ammo.

I had heard from friends that the cheapest ammunition was from online stores. This option turned out to be impossible for D.C. residents. Bass Pro's website says it does not ship to D.C., Illinois, Massachusetts, New Jersey, and New York City. Cabelas and The Sportman's Guide also don't sell to these places.

Cheaper than Dirt's website will not let you order from a D.C. address, nor will Bud's Gun Shop. Midway USA does not post any restrictions on its site, but I called customer service and was told they won't ship ammo to the District. The appropriately named AmmoMan says on its homepage that it does not ship to Alaska, Hawaii, Massachusetts, or New Jersey. I called and was informed that Washington is also on their no-sell list.

It's not against the law for retailers to send ammunition through the mail to D.C. residents, but it seems these stores are all afraid of running afoul of the jurisdictions with the stiffest gun-control laws. What will happen if Bloomberg and Obama succeed in spreading those laws to more and more states? A gun without a bullet is the same as disarmament.

I tried asking the police at the registration office. Office Harper, who I'd last seen when he returned my gun to me after shooting it to keep a casing for ballistics, answered the phone. I asked where to get ammunition legally.

"Any licensed gun store or dealer," he told me, not needing to state the obvious—that these options were both available only outside the District. So I can go to any gun store in Maryland or Virginia? "The only thing you need to take with you is your registration certificate and driver's license," he said. A friend told me that, after online purchases, the second-best prices were from retailers like Wal-Mart. Gun stores and shooting ranges had the highest prices.

I asked Officer Harper how I could legally go to a store and buy ammunition before going to shoot. "The only time you should be separated from your weapon is in your home. Once you put it in your vehicle, you shouldn't be leaving your vehicle," he told me.

Well then, how do I go into a store to buy ammo? "As far as going to purchase ammunition, if it were me, I wouldn't care what the law was in that state, as far as leaving my weapon in the vehicle, because to me, that's crazy," he said.

So should I bring the gun in the box with me into the store? "That's your option if that's what you want to do. That's a whole lotta carrying around a weapon that someone could snatch out of your hand while you're going to the gun store," he said. I hadn't worried about getting robbed on my ammunition-shopping trip before he said that.

I asked if there was anything else I should know. He repeated that I should have my D.C. registration certificate handy in neighboring Virginia. I protested, "No one in Virginia needs to see the registration."

"If you're going to purchase ammunition they do," he replied.

"They do? I didn't know that," I said.

"Yes!" he exclaimed loudly. "You don't have a Virginia state driver's license, do you?"

Of course I didn't.

"To purchase ammunition, you need a valid registration certificate and your driver's license in order to prove you're the person who that weapon is legally registered to," he explained.

I had a feeling that Virginia retail stores wouldn't care if my gun was registered in D.C. since Virginia has no registration requirement and no law against owning ammunition. But I couldn't get a word of common sense in during Officer Harper's lecture on Virginia's firearms laws.

"If I'm a gun dealer, and you come into my shop, and you want to buy ammo, first of all you need to be able to identify yourself," said Officer Harper, taking on the role of a Virginian shop owner. "If you show me just your driver's license, I can't sell you ammo unless you have a valid D.C. registration certificate. If you can show me that, you have a picture of you on there and a picture on your driver's license, and the license says you live at such and such an address. Everything matches up the way it's supposed to, then I feel comfortable selling you ammunition. Other than that, you're not getting ammo from me."

He paused, then added definitively, "You gotta have the valid registration certificate with you in order to purchase ammunition. Period."

The police officer wasn't done with his legal lesson. He wanted to get the gun dealer in trouble with the law too. "If you go somewhere and they sell you ammunition without that, then there's a problem," said Officer Harper. "It's not necessarily on you. But if you happen to get stopped and you don't have the registration certificate with you, then you shouldn't have the gun or the ammunition."

I switched topics. Even though I had passed the written test at the police station, I was still confused about the logistics of lawfully transporting a gun somewhere to practice shooting. Owning a firearm is a big responsibility. I have been told repeatedly of the importance of regular training, but D.C.'s politicians do not encourage residents to do that.

There are no shooting ranges in the District, and it would be virtually impossible to open one. In addition to the zoning laws, it is illegal to discharge a gun within the city limits. Also, it is against the law to have a gun in a public space—which means anywhere but your home. Thus responsible gun owners who live in Washington have to go to Virginia or Maryland for target practice, which means figuring out the interstate transport laws.

The District's twenty-two-page handgun registration packet offers only four bullet points for guidance on legal transport. These same transport laws also apply to any U.S. citizen who is driving through the nation's capital with a firearm.

According to the police registration packet, a gun can only be transported when going directly to or from "hunting, shooting at practice range, etc." The same information on transport was on the police website. The gun had to be unloaded. Neither the firearm nor the ammunition could be directly accessible from the passenger compartment of the vehicle. If the vehicle does not have a compartment separate from the driver's compartment, the firearm or ammunition must be in a locked container.

These points left me with many unanswered questions. I was most worried about interactions with the police and other unforeseen circumstances. If I got pulled over, how would I prove to the police that I was on my way to a shooting range? What if I needed to stop for gas? (This is a common occurrence for me because I drive until the last drop, now that gas is over $4 a gallon in D.C.)

Since the packet didn't explain, I asked Officer Harper for help—though I should have known better after getting the ridiculous answers about ammunition laws. He said I had to have the gun in a locked box—I knew that—and the "registration certificate with the picture on it."

But how did I prove that I was transporting a gun to a shooting range? (I was sounding paranoid, but the fact is, some really terrible things have happened to otherwise perfectly innocent, responsible people who have accidentally fallen afoul of the District's irrational gun laws. You can read those people's stories later in this book.)

Officer Harper replied, "When the officer says, 'May I have your driver's license and registration? Ma'am, is there anything in your car I need to be concerned about?' You advise him, 'I've got my weapon in the trunk of my vehicle, and I'm on the way to the range, or I've been to the range. Here's my receipt. And if you're on your way to the range, that's all you can tell him, 'I'm on my way to the range.'"

They will just take my word for it? "What choice does he have? I mean it's optional whether he wants to take your word for it or not," he answered.

Now I was really concerned. The District is basing whether I go to jail for a year on whether the cop takes my word? Optional is not a good thing when it comes to law enforcement.

"You say, 'I'm on my way to the range,'" the police officer told me. "He's not likely to get on his cell phone and call, 'Do you have a reservation for this young lady here I have stopped at a traffic stop?' I doubt very seriously they are going to do that."

Yeah, right. I should just depend on the police to be reasonable—like the time I got pulled over and held for thirty minutes outside my church for "driving with coffee cup"?

Officer Harper had more unsettling news. "Most ranges close—for the sake of argument—at 9:00 p.m. And say you're riding around in your car at 11:30 or 12:00 o'clock at night with your weapon in your car. And you get pulled over and say that you're going to the range. Then he'd have probable cause to believe you weren't doing what you say you're doing. And at the least, he can take the weapon for safe keeping."

In Washington, that means confiscation. (Read later about what the police did with Lieutenant Kim and Sergeant Corrigan's guns while holding them for years for "safe-keeping.")

What if I have to go to the bathroom on the way in or out of town? "The only thing I can tell you is don't do any more than you can stand," answered Office Harper. Now the police are telling law-abiding citizens to "hold it."

What if I run out of gas? "Then you're going to have to get someone to come bring you some," he answered. That seemed to me about the

ABOVE: Emily got her gun! After four months, I finally registered my first gun. Here I am standing outside Washington, D.C., police headquarters after the ten-day waiting period ended. (February 8, 2012)

RIGHT: The *Washington Times* put rack cards all over D.C. on our newspaper racks for my coverage of Second Amendment issues.

This is the photo Richard Diamond took to use as the logo for my series in the *Washington Times*. Gun people complained that I shouldn't pose like *Charlie's Angels*, but it is very difficult to get a close enough shot for a newspaper showing someone holding a gun in a natural way.

Officer Brown posted this "Out of Office" sign (with no return time) as she left at 3:30 p.m. on the first day I went to the D.C. firearms registration office.

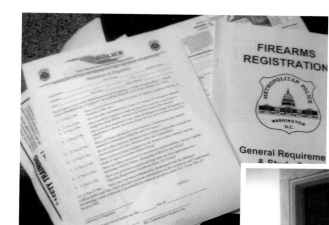

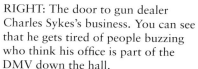

LEFT: Here's the firearm registration packet along with the massive stack of papers Officer Brown gave me that first day.

RIGHT: The door to gun dealer Charles Sykes's business. You can see that he gets tired of people buzzing who think his office is part of the DMV down the hall.

This is the very first time I shot a gun. I'm at the NRA range in Fairfax, Virginia, and using all Richard Diamond's guns. The good target is from the .22.

ABOVE: Donna Worthy, right, and I are reading over the D.C. registration packet during the four hours of class-room instruction required to get a legal gun.

RIGHT: Outside Maryland Small Arms Range after Worthy signed the certification that I had completed the mandatory five-hour gun class for D.C.

This is when I rented guns at Sharpshooters to decide what to buy. Halfway through the test shots, Diamond replaced my pink target with his choice color.

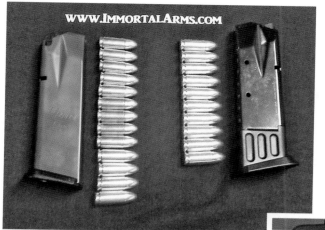

WWW.IMMORTALARMS.COM

LEFT: My gun dealer, Mark Attanasio, sent me a photo of the thirteen-round magazine that came standard in my Sig next to the ten-round one he had to swap in it to make it legal under D.C.'s "high-capacity" magazine ban. You can see they are exactly the same, but the one on the right has a metal block on the end to prevent the last three rounds from being loaded.

RIGHT: This is what I saw when Charles Sykes opened the box of my brand new Sig Sauer P229. I was in love.

BELOW: I'm showing all the calibers of ammo I shot with the friendly North Carolinians at the Wake County Firearms Education and Training Center. Just one of these casings could land a tourist in D.C. in jail.

Army Specialist Adam Meckler in a village near the Arghandab River Valley, Afghanistan.

Army First Lieutenant Augustine Kim during his second tour in Afghanistan, before he was injured.

Army Sergeant Matt Corrigan in Virginia in June 2012, the month after all charges against him in D.C. were dropped.

LEFT: Attorney Richard Gardiner is investigating the bizarre statue *Guns Into Plowshares* that sits outside the D.C. police evidence department where Lieutenant Augustine Kim's guns disappeared for over two years.

BELOW: Gardiner points to a piece of history destroyed by the D.C. government. The Polish Radom Vis pistol was carried by the Polish Underground when they fought the Germans during World War II.

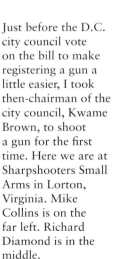

Just before the D.C. city council vote on the bill to make registering a gun a little easier, I took then-chairman of the city council, Kwame Brown, to shoot a gun for the first time. Here we are at Sharpshooters Small Arms in Lorton, Virginia. Mike Collins is on the far left. Richard Diamond is in the middle.

I am at the Beretta USA factory in Accokeek, Maryland, shooting the ARX-160 rifle in 5.56 mm. It is a weapon manufactured for the military so it can be switched into automatic mode, but they only let me shoot in semiautomatic mode.

LEFT: This was the first time I shot an AR-style rifle. Trainer Rob Pincus, at left, taught me at Winchester. I was shooting balloons flying around on the ground. It was a blast.

RIGHT: This is an event at Tampa Bay Sporting Clays during the Republican National convention in August 2012. I love shooting clay, but it's so much harder than shooting a handgun in a range.

most absurd possible solution. Wouldn't it be better for gun safety to just pull into a gas station? "Well if you are going in a gas station, if you lock your car, how long does it take to get gas? Especially if you have a credit card. You're right there at your vehicle," he said, making it seem like he was approving of this quick stop. "You take your keys out and if you feel the need to, you lock the car up so no one can get in it. And um, well, hopefully you don't get carjacked."

Robberies at Wal-Marts and carjackings at Exxons. This police officer was making me very anxious.

What do I tell the cop if I need to get gas? "You have to just explain what happened. Only thing is he'll ask, 'Why didn't you get gas before going to the range?'" said Officer Harper.

I never get gas before doing anything. I just drive until the light turns yellow. (I know men reading this are shaking their heads. I'll also confess that my dad still calls to remind me to change my oil.)

"Then you need to explain that to whoever you need to convince," he answered. Convince? These laws are so far from black and white, they might as well be invisible. "If I know I'm going to the range, and my car was almost on 'E,' I think I'd fill up before I made that trip so you don't have that problem," he said, sounding like, well, my father. I said thank you and hung up.

By now I'd had my new, legally registered Sig Sauer at home for ten days and wanted to use it. Even after all of Officer Harper's frightening warnings, I packed my gun in a locked box and put it in the back of my SUV and set out for a shooting range.

I had just started out for Sharpshooters, which is twenty miles away in Virginia, when—as if on cue—the yellow gas light lit up on my console. I had two choices. Go to a D.C. gas station and risk getting pulled over for something else and getting into a mess. Or, drive the three miles to Virginia and get gas there. From what I was told, by doing the latter, I would be violating the letter of the D.C. law by not going directly to a shooting range. But it seemed the better option, since Virginia cops wouldn't be enforcing District laws.

With gas and a gun, I arrived at Sharpshooters. Mike Collins immediately recognized me from my first visit. "Well look who's here," he said smiling. I felt like I was in a safe place now, with people who weren't looking to make me into a criminal.

I signed up for a lane, then said, "And I need a box of 9mm caliber."

Collins smiled, "Just say, 'A box of 9mm.' You don't need to say 'caliber.'" We emailed regularly, and he'd been patiently working on teaching me how to "speak like a gun owner."

"At least I didn't say a box of 'bullets.' I just learned that a couple weeks ago," I said, laughing. He reached behind him and put a white box on the counter.

"Don't you need to see my driver's license?" I asked.

"Nope."

"What about my gun registration certificate?" I said, holding up the flimsy yellow sheet of paper with my picture on it.

"Nope," said Collins.

"The D.C. firearms registration office said you need both those things to sell me ammo, or the store will be breaking the law," I said.

"That's not true," he said, shaking his head. "Emily, you don't need to show me anything to buy ammo."

Later I emailed Virginia-based firearms attorneys Dan Peterson and Richard Gardiner about the law as interpreted by Officer Harper. They confirmed what Collins said—that the Virginia dealers do not need to see D.C. identification or registration certificates to sell ammunition. (Although they may ask for identification to confirm that a person is not under age. Clearly, Collins wouldn't mistake me for a teenager.) They confirmed that Officer Harper was wrong in saying retail stores would get in trouble for not doing these checks.

There is also no law in Virginia against leaving a firearm in a locked box in the car. If I needed to bring the pistol into a dealer's store, the lawyers told me that "cased and unloaded" would be the best way to do that. Gardiner and Peterson said that a D.C. resident driving with the gun in a locked box in the trunk on the "way back" would be fine after crossing the Potomac, as long as it was unloaded and inaccessible to anyone in the car.

Before I left target practice at Sharpshooters, I carefully saved some rounds in the box. Officer Harper told me that ammunition had to be transported in a container separate from the locked gun and out of reach of the passenger seat. I put the ammo in a bag in the way back of my truck. I was still concerned about correctly following D.C. laws, but I needed to save a few rounds to take home, so that my gun could actually function for self-defense.

CHAPTER 16

LIBERAL MEDIA DISTORTION

I am a member of the mainstream media, but I'm also pro-Second Amendment. There are few in the journalism profession who share my beliefs.

The public, therefore, gets a heavily biased view of firearm ownership and gun violence in America.

The anti-gun media bias has had a serious impact on the public's understanding of the issues. Most tellingly, the majority of Americans don't know that gun violence has been going down every year.

Firearm-related homicides in the U.S. have declined 39 percent in the last thirty years—from 18,253 in 1993 to 11,101 in 2011—according to a Justice Department study released in May 2013. Non-fatal firearm crimes decreased 69 percent from 1.5 million to 467,300 in that time-frame. The sharpest downturn in gun violence was in the mid-1990s, but it has steadily decreased since.[1]

This government study was not breaking news to those of us who cover firearms issues. Every year, the FBI's Uniform Crime Records comes out showing violent crime, including gun-related homicides, decreasing in America.[2] The annual report is almost entirely ignored by most media outlets. It took the federal government specifically putting the three decades of data together into a special report to get the media's attention.

The network evening news anchors merely read short briefs on the crime report, according to the watchdog Media Research Center.[3] Scott Pelley, the anchor of CBS News, apparently never reads the annual crime reports: "You know we've seen so many high-profile murders involving guns we were surprised today when the Justice Department reported that gun violence has declined sharply in the past two decades," he said. Brian Williams of NBC News said, "In light of the post-Newtown gun debate in this country, some new stats from the Justice Department show that, on the whole, gun related crime is actually much lower than it was two decades ago."

When the people whose job it is to know current events are so ignorant about crime trends, it's no wonder the rest of America does not know they are safer now than in the past.

The same day as the Department of Justice study, Pew Research Center released a poll that showed 56 percent of Americans believed gun violence was higher than twenty years ago, and 26 percent thought it was the same.[4] Only 12 percent knew that firearm-related crimes were lower. Asked about trends in firearms crimes "in recent years," 45 percent thought the number had gone up and 39 percent thought it was the same. Just 10 percent correctly said that it has gone down. In fact, gun crimes are down 13 percent in the most recent five years.

This public misconception affects legislating. A Rasmussen survey that same week showed 64 percent of the people who want more gun control also think crime is up.[5]

"Obama, his friends and their allies in the media are counting on a phony narrative to fool people long enough to force through their 'solutions' to 'an epidemic of violence' that simply doesn't exist," David Keene told me when he was NRA president about why the public is so misinformed about crime trends.[6] (The day before this book went to print in July 2013, Keene was named editorial page editor of the *Washington Times*. I was stunned and delighted by the news. A highly respected intellectual, Keene will assuredly expand our conservative opinion pages to an even wider audience.)

I agree that the media is largely to blame for this misconception. There are two main reasons for the media distortion of the facts. "If it bleeds, it leads" is a saying that originally described local TV stations that started their news broadcasts with stories about violent-crime victims, but it also applies equally to the national media after a mass shooting.

The Sandy Hook massacre was particularly horrific because the victims were innocent school children, but it was a rare event, not a sign of an increase in mass shootings. Nevertheless, the media went wall to wall with coverage from Connecticut for weeks. Then Obama and his money man Bloomberg used the terrible crime to launch their plans to bring back the "assault weapon" ban.

But the media distortion goes beyond the fact that shootings and grisly deaths interest viewers and boost ratings. Anti-gun bias also plays a role. Mainstream media outlets are based in New York, Washington, and Los Angeles. Few reporters are gun owners or have any familiarity with firearms. As a result, they are constantly making mistakes about simple gun terminology and functionality.

Their ignorance of basic types of firearms was widely exposed after the White House released a photo of Obama skeet shooting. Major print media outlets, including the *New York Times*, incorrectly labeled the gun a "rifle" instead of a shotgun.[7]

Just to be clear, a rifle shoots a single bullet straight, while a shotgun fires a shell that usually has many pellets that scatter in a wide area. Skeet shooting, which Obama claimed he does "all the time,"[8] is done with a shotgun in order to have a chance at hitting the small, fast-moving clay. Rifles are what the gun-grabbers want to take, not shotguns. At least not yet.

Almost every newspaper uses the term "assault weapons" and "high-capacity" magazine (or frequently "clip") without putting quotation marks around those loaded terms.

Reporters use words such as "stockpile," "arsenal," and "weapons of war" for the kinds of firearms and amounts of ammunition in the average gun-owner's possession. The media is continually astonished at unremarkable quantities of ammunition. A *New York Times* editorial in July 2012 entitled "6,000 Bullets" questioned why bulk internet purchases of ammunition aren't monitored by the government.[9] A *Washington Post* editorial that same month mentioned the "astonishing 3,000 rounds of handgun ammunition" that Aurora shooter James Holmes purchased online and asked, "Should online sales of ammunition be prohibited or more carefully scrutinized?"[10]

Apparently the writers didn't realize that an avid shooter can easily go through over a thousand rounds at the range in a single weekend. So it's very common, perfectly reasonable, and cost-effective to order a large amount at one time. As I wrote this paragraph, I went to my closet to see how much ammunition I have. I'm no gun nut, just a woman who owns a gun for self-defense and goes to the range to practice shooting occasionally. I have fifteen hundred rounds in boxes right now. It takes up about as much space as my TiVo.

––––––––

I am on the editorial board of the *Washington Times*. We are conservative and very strong on the Constitution, including the Second Amendment. Except for the *Wall Street Journal*, most other daily newspapers' editorial boards are liberal and oppose gun rights.

The *New York Times* takes the most extreme anti-gun position. Its editorial board has called for requiring a "new and stronger ban on assault weapons,"[11] record-keeping for ammunition sales,[12] and the "outlawing of magazines of more than 10 bullets."[13] The paper doesn't even pretend that the "background check on every gun sale"[14] it has called for is anything other than the government knowing exactly what firearms every citizen owns: "Requiring background checks at gun shows, parking-lot sales and websites would reduce the cash-and-carry anonymity of millions of gun transactions, putting buyers on notice that their sale is being recorded and can be traced."[15]

The Old Gray Lady is so over the top in its anti-gun views, you have to wonder if anyone on its elitist editorial board lives without an armed guard at work and a doorman at home. This was the editorial after Obama and Reid failed to get sixty votes to pass Manchin-Toomey: "For 45 senators, the carnage at Sandy Hook Elementary School is a forgotten tragedy. The toll of 270 Americans who are shot every day is not a problem requiring action. The easy access to guns on the Internet, and the inevitability of the next massacre, is not worth preventing."[16] The online version of the editorial links the "270" to a Brady Campaign fact sheet.[17]

The *New York Times* wants Congress to pass a federal law to force states to make it more difficult to get concealed-carry permits and "prohibit guns from public places like parks, schools and churches." Of course the *Times* strongly opposed commonsense national concealed-carry reciprocity, saying it would "turn a porous system into a sieve."[18]

And this is how the *New York Times* editorial board described citizens who are pro-Second Amendment: "The gun lobby is a combination of forces that includes manufacturers, hunters and hobbyists, political opportunists, and a fanatically active faction that believes guns are needed to fight off the conquest of freedom by the government."[19] The newspaper has even started a daily blog called "Gun Report" by Joe Nocera that lists every death by firearm, even accidental ones.[20]

If you only follow liberal media and listen to President Obama, it would be easy to believe that gun owners are all bitter clingers, reckless hicks, or criminals. The truth is that the 100 million gun owners in America are among the most responsible, patriotic, family-oriented citizens in our nation. And they use guns millions of times a year to avert crimes.

That's why I asked law-abiding gun owners to send photographs of themselves to be included in this book. We were inundated with hundreds of photos that show Americans—men and women, young and old—exercising their Second Amendment rights.

Along with the photos, many people have written notes explaining why they chose to get firearms and how they use them. I have been so overwhelmed with emotion by these powerful stories that I decided to ask permission from the contributors to publish some in the *Washington Times*. I'm grateful to those who agreed. The series, "The American Gun Owner," helps illuminate the positives of gun ownership, which are rarely seen in the media.

Besides the *Washington Times*, the other daily paper in Washington, D.C., is the *Washington Post*, which is also staunchly anti-gun. The *Post*'s editorial board opined, "A COWARDLY minority of senators blocked a gun background-check proposal on Wednesday, in one vote betraying both the will of the American people and the charge voters gave them to work in their interest."[21] The word "cowardly" was in all capital letters. I've never seen that done in a major newspaper before or since.

In comparison, here's how my paper, the *Washington Times*, led its editorial: "The president raged. The mayor of New York frothed. Joe Biden cried. But at the end of the day, common sense prevailed. The Senate killed the effort to unreasonably expand background checks for buyers of guns."[22] Our editor in chief emeritus who was then the acting editorial page editor, Wes Pruden, wrote that editorial. I high-fived him after I read it.

The *Wall Street Journal*'s editorial began, "President Obama's gun control agenda was routed in the Senate on Wednesday, and Mr. Obama naturally blamed the National Rifle Association. The truth is that Mr. Obama invited this meltdown by assuming he could exploit the Newtown massacre to ram through a liberal wish-list that wouldn't have stopped the next mass murder."[23]

With the exception of Fox News, the TV networks are even more strongly anti-gun rights than the newspapers. The big three broadcast networks—ABC, NBC, and CBS—ran 216 segments on gun policy on their evening and morning shows in the month after the Newtown shooting, according to a Media Research Center study.[24] Of these, the stories advocating more gun control outnumbered stories featuring opposition to new restrictions by a ratio of 8 to 1. CBS was the most biased with a 22 to 1 ratio of gun control to gun-rights stories.

Sound bites on the networks were very skewed. There were twice as many anti-gun comments aired as pro-gun ones. Gun-control advocates were guests on twenty-six segments, but pro-gun people only appeared seven times. The media watchdog group pointed out that, from the day of the Sandy Hook shooting, the supposedly neutral news anchors were actively laying the groundwork for gun control legislation. CBS News's Pelley said the Friday of the shooting, "One wonders if the nature of this crime and the age of the victims might create the debate in Washington that could push legislation along?" Three days later, Jake Tapper, who was then at ABC, reported as fact on *Good Morning America* that the event was "a tipping point for a national conversation about gun violence."

The cable networks are even more extreme. MSNBC's Lawrence O'Donnell essentially called the CEO of the biggest gun manufacturing company in the world a murderer. O'Donnell referred to "George K. Kollitides II, who is chief executive of Freedom Group, the merchants of death who made the Bushmaster military-style assault rifle used to rip up the bodies of the 20 children and six educators inside Sandy Hook Elementary School."

O'Donnell's next action was beyond irresponsible—to the point of putting a life at risk. "We have a picture of him up there. I want people to take a good look at it. Leave it up there for a while. I want this merchant of death to be stared at by a national audience for as long as possible."[25]

Kollitides brushed off the name-calling. "Say I am the 'merchant of death'—that doesn't upset me. It's his constitutional right." What about his safety? He has had to get full-time security for his family since Newtown. For his own safety he has a concealed-carry permit in forty-two states and New York City.[26]

Freedom Group's company Bushmaster has been the target of much liberal media hatred because it was the make used in Newtown and by the D.C. "Beltway snipers" in 2002. A *New York Times* editorial in December 2012 blamed the company's marketing campaign for criminal activities.

"The brand's repeated presence in murderous incidents reflects Bushmaster's enormous popularity in the gun world, the result of a successful marketing campaign aimed at putting military firepower and machismo in the hands of civilians," wrote the *Times* editors. "The effect of these marketing campaigns on fragile minds is all too obvious, allowing deadly power in the wrong hands. But given their financial success, gun makers have apparently decided that the risk of an occasional massacre is part of the cost of doing business."[27]

The Bushmaster CEO said his customers buy his rifles—which range from $500 to $3,000 in price—because they are well made. "It has nothing to do with our marketing campaign. It has everything to do with a reputation for high quality, high performance. Do you race a Ford Pinto or a Ferrari?"

While Kollitides is not worried about personal attacks on himself, he gets angry about media attacks on the quality and safety of his products. "What upsets me is the media doesn't fact check or frankly oftentimes will twist the facts." He's referring to a lengthy story covering allegations of misfires by Remington shotguns and rifles in March 2012 on Brian Williams's NBC now canceled show *Rock Center*.[28]

Williams updated a 2010 CNBC story on accusations about the Remington Model 700 rifle. Correspondent Scott Cohn reported NBC had uncovered 125 incidents of malfunctions of the Common Fire Control—the firing mechanism—since 1973.

Kollitides denies that the issue was with the firearm. "Guns don't misfire. You have to remove a safety, load a round, and pull the trigger. No one—not the defense attorney or the plaintiff's attorneys—has ever been able to replicate a misfire when the gun was properly maintained and not altered."

Even NBC Sports is openly anti-gun. Bob Costas launched into a sermon on banning guns during halftime of *Sunday Night Football* on December 2, 2012.[29] NBC would not respond to my questions about whether its executives pre-approved the monologue or would censor the anchor.

Costas doubled down two days later, saying all semiautomatic guns should be banned. That would leave only revolvers and shotguns allowed in the U.S.[30] Costas then told Bill O'Reilly on Fox News that, "Far more often, bad things happen—including unintentional things—than things where the presence of a gun diminishes or averts danger."[31]

This is patently false. About thirty thousand people are killed by firearms a year—two-thirds are suicides—while guns are used to prevent crimes as often as 2 million times a year.[32] "There have never been more firearms in civilian possession in America than there are today, yet crime is at its lowest level since the early 1960s," NSSF's Keane said. "Firearm accidents are at their lowest level since recordkeeping began in 1903."[33]

There are a few exceptions to the rule of anti-gun bias in the media. The most powerful voices in support of the Second Amendment are TV anchors and gun owners Sean Hannity and Lou Dobbs of Fox News.

Of course the self-appointed czar of the anti-gun media is CNN's Piers Morgan. He likes to compare the U.S. to his home country, England, in gun deaths. Larry Pratt, the executive director of Gun Owners of America, appeared on *Piers Morgan Tonight* the week after Newtown. Pratt explained that while Britain has few gun-related homicides, it actually has a higher violent crime rate than the U.S.

"America is not the Wild West that you are depicting," Pratt told Morgan. "We only have the problems in our cities, and unhappily, in our schools where people like you have been able to get laws put on the books that keep people from being able to defend themselves."

Morgan got so angry that he spurted out to Pratt, "You're an unbelievably stupid man."[34]

Americans don't want a multi-millionaire British TV host lecturing them on their rights. Gun owners launched a petition on the White House website on December 21, 2012, to call for Morgan to be deported for exploiting his position as a national TV host to undermine the Bill of Rights. The petition has over 100,000 signatures.[35] While the former UK tabloid editor openly milked the publicity surrounding the petition, his show remains a distant third in the ratings after Fox News and MSNBC.

Chris Matthews of *Hardball* got frustrated that gun control fever was fading by June 2013. He railed that supporting the Second Amendment was abnormal. "The gun people—they think about nothing else. And they never change their minds, never change their attitudes and never change the fricking subject. How do you keep an interest among normal people that keeps up with that intense, almost, well, obsession that the gun people have?" he asked on MSNBC.[36]

Even CNN's Anderson Cooper, who is supposed to be an unbiased anchor, showed his true beliefs in the course of an interview with me on *AC360*. In a typical bait and switch, the show's producer first told me she wanted me to be comfortable and invited me to Manhattan for a debate on gun control. I thought Cooper was fair and the debate straightforward. It never aired. The next day, the producer said they had to redo the interview, this time remotely from D.C.

Within minutes, I knew I'd been had. Instead of asking questions of both me and Obama pollster Cornell Belcher, Cooper jumped in and took on the role of the gun control activist. I felt like a punching bag. He must have realized he was out of line because he said, "The thing I don't understand, and I've asked the NRA this and I don't take a position on this, I'm not my job. I'm not Piers Morgan here…"

"Thank God," I responded.

"I'm not trying to push an agenda," emphasized Cooper, and then went on to argue even more fiercely for gun control.[37] CNN aired only about twelve minutes of the twenty-five-minute tape, leaving out good points I had managed to make despite the interruptions.

I was very upset about the interview. I emailed the fearless Ted Nugent with my concerns about the show. Nugent could sympathize because he regularly tangles with anti-gun media figures. He had recently been lit into by Piers Morgan demanding to know in the "least inflammatory way possible" why "anybody needs" an AR-15, "outside of hog hunting."

The rock legend defended law-abiding gun owners to the CNN host. "Would you leave us the hell alone? Go after the nut jobs. Go after the murderers. Because I don't know any. We need to lock up the bad guys…. We have a mad man problem in America, where they're running around. We have a felony recidivism problem in America. Let's focus on that together and leave the rest of us alone."[38]

When I emailed Nugent about my run-in with Cooper, he encouraged me. "Do not despair. You do great. I'm sure you witnessed me hand ol' Piers his ass. Erin Burnett last week too, but gentlemanly of course. Carry on."

Carry on, indeed.

CHAPTER 17

HOW GUN CONTROL CREATES A CRIMINALS' PLAYGROUND—AND PUNISHES THE INNOCENT

W hen the Founders chose the swampy marshland along the Potomac River to serve as the home for the federal government, they couldn't have envisioned it would one day become a cesspool of violence. Crime was way up in the District of Columbia in 2012.

D.C. has in place every one of the laws that Obama wants to push through on the federal level and in the states. The fact that crime is rising at a startling rate shows the end result of more gun control laws. Americans should consider whether they also want to live in a city that saw robberies with guns go up 18 percent in just one year.[1]

The city's politicians and Police Chief Cathy Lanier don't want residents to know about the increase in crime in the District.

In a September 2012 column called "D.C.: District of Crime," I highlighted how Chief Lanier was doing her best to make the crime numbers look less bad.[2] At that point in the year, violent crime was up 8 percent after going up 2 percent the year before, according to MPD's own "crime mapping" website, which tracks crimes in real time. But the numbers Chief Lanier filed with the FBI for the 2011 Uniform Crime Report (UCR) showed a 6 percent decrease in violent crime. The difference depends on whether the numbers are counted according to the FBI's methodology, or using the local "crime mapping" system that classifies incidents according to the city's criminal code.

The point I made was that Chief Lanier's opinion on which rating system is best depended on which got her the better results to cite. For the Metropolitan Washington Council of Governments annual report on crime released that month, the police chief cited numbers in the FBI format, which made the police department look more effective.[3] "As the COG report on UCR Part I crime shows, all crime in DC fell in 2011 except larcenies," she emailed through her spokesman, Gwendolyn Crump. "As the 2011 report shows, people in the District are safer than ever."[4]

That seemed a marked shift from a couple years ago. In 2010, she had emailed the *Washington Examiner* about the 2009 numbers, "I don't use the FBI [Uniform Crime Reporting] statistics to draw any conclusions.... They are not reflective of true crime in D.C."[5] She also downplayed FBI numbers for 2008 when it showed violent crime increased.

The difference between the numbers can often be stark. MPD's website shows 4,184 robberies committed with or without a gun in 2011, but the UCR showed only 3,756.[6] That means 428 robberies—more than one a day—vanished from the books. Crump explained that the FBI counts robberies without threat or violence as "larceny."

Kris Baumann, the chairman of the Fraternal Order of Police for D.C., disagreed with how his chief operates. "Chief Lanier has politicized policing by continually misrepresenting crime numbers throughout her tenure," he told me in July 2013. "While it has served her well politically —by ensuring her public popularity and secured her a 34 percent increase in her compensation in just six years—it has done incalculable damage to the District, its residents, and victims of crime."[7]

The police union represents the approximately 3,600 police officers, detectives, and sergeants of the Metropolitan Police Department. "If we are not honest with the public about the level of crime, then it is difficult to force the politicians to accept and confront the problem. The result is less resources, resources not being deployed where they are most needed, and, once discovered, permanent harm to the trust residents place in their police department."[8]

Baumann added that, "Remember, politicians like Lanier come and go, but it is the rank and file police officers that have lifetime commitments to the residents and the city. So, harming our relationship with those we protect is inexcusable."

The police union chief hit on a common misconception that the uniformed police chiefs standing behind Obama at gun control events represent their force. In reality, the rank and file don't support more gun control laws because it means wasting their time going after otherwise law-abiding people instead of real criminals. The police chiefs are appointed by big-city liberal mayors and are doing their bidding. That's also why you see the elected sheriffs in the country refusing to even enforce pointless gun control laws.

The two cities with the stiffest gun control laws—D.C. and Chicago—had increasing crime. Murders in the Windy City were up 16 percent in 2012 to 506 people. And there were 2,460 shooting incidents—a 10 percent increase from the previous year.[9]

There are two reasons tough gun control laws don't stop crime. First, only the good guys follow the laws, the bad guys just get their guns off the streets. Second, gun ownership and carry permits create a deterrent to criminals. When the bad guys know they are the only ones armed, the rest of us are just sitting ducks.

The District's registration laws were deliberately written to discourage civilians from owning guns. The registration process, however, does nothing to reduce violence. No registered gun has ever been used in a crime in D.C.[10]

Meanwhile, the city is swimming in illegal guns. Remember, according to the police department's own data, assaults with a firearm increased 12 percent from 2011 to 2012.[11]

After I got my Sig, I started reporting on what had happened to otherwise law-abiding citizens who had inadvertently run afoul of the District's firearms laws. I profiled veterans of the wars in Afghanistan and Iraq who had been arrested and prosecuted for various firearms offenses. Their stories helped people understand the real-life impact of these laws. Along with my original series about buying a gun in D.C., they also led to a reform of the gun laws in the District.

––––––––

First Lieutenant Augustine Kim, who had served two tours in Afghanistan, was transporting unloaded firearms from his parents' house in New Jersey to his home in Charleston, South Carolina, in June 2010. He stopped along the way in D.C. for a medical appointment at Walter Reed Army Medical Center, was pulled over, arrested, jailed, and charged with possession of unregistered firearms.

I met Lieutenant Kim in May 2012 as he was fighting to get the city to return the $10,000 worth of guns and parts confiscated during his arrest.[12]

Lieutenant Kim had been the liaison officer to a specialized unit in Afghanistan when he was injured in a vehicle crash. The M1A1 Abrams tank platoon leader broke multiple bones on the left side of his face and shattered his right arm. He was medivacked to Germany, where he was treated for two weeks. He spent three months in and out of Walter Reed hospital undergoing the facial surgery necessary to fix his cracked lower orbit.

After his recovery, he wanted to bring his firearms back home. He had one Colt Carbine AR-15 rifle 6920 5.56/.223, a Beretta 92S in 9mm, and a custom Springfield Armory 1911 in .45 caliber. His hobby is building and working on 1911 models, so he also had spare parts, including a frame, barrel, and upper receiver.

After the stop at Walter Reed for a doctor's appointment, Lieutenant Kim got lost driving his two-door Honda Civic in downtown D.C. in the evening. Trying to find his way, he made an illegal turn and was pulled over by police. The police officer told Lieutenant Kim that his driver's license had been suspended. He was unaware of this. He cleared that up the next morning after finding out that his license had been wrongly suspended because of a clerical error from a speeding ticket in North Carolina.

But because of the suspended license, the D.C. police officer called for backup and told Lieutenant Kim that he would have to go to the police station. Then the cops asked him for permission to search his vehicle. The lieutenant agreed because he knew that his guns were unloaded and properly locked in a case in the trunk, in compliance with federal firearms transport laws. During the search, the veteran was handcuffed and told to sit on the curb.

Despite the wacky interpretation of transport laws from Officer Harper and others in the police registration office, the city's law is exactly the same as the federal law. Under the Firearm Owners' Protection Act of 1986, a person can transport a firearm for any lawful purpose to and from any place where he may lawfully possess and carry. During the transport, the gun has to be unloaded and not directly accessible from the passenger compartment of the vehicle. In the case of a truck or SUV that doesn't have a trunk, the weapon has to be in a locked container.[13]

(I eventually got City Council Chairman Mendelson to send a harsh letter telling Chief Lanier to fix all her documents and train her force in the correct transport laws.)

In the case of Lieutenant Kim, he could legally possess and carry his guns at his parents' house and his own home. The firearms were cased in the trunk, under a duffle bag, clothes, books, and other belongings. It was a perfectly legal transport, but D.C. decided to interpret the law incorrectly.

Lieutenant Kim told me that things turned sour during the inspection when the officers got "upset about the fact that I had the AR-15, which D.C. considers to be an 'assault weapon.'" This model of rifle is illegal in the District, but not in South Carolina. The officers told Lieutenant Kim he was violating the District's ban on carrying outside the home—in this case, in his vehicle.

"I told them I had been under the impression that as long as the guns were locked in the back, with the ammunition separate, that I was allowed to transport them," Lieutenant Kim told me in an interview. "They said, 'That may be true, however, since you stopped at Walter Reed, that made you in violation of the registration laws.'"

Actually, the officers were the ones who were wrong about the laws. His attorney, Richard Gardiner, told me that it was perfectly lawful for Lieutenant Kim to stop for a medical appointment while transporting. The federal transport laws would have been the defense had the matter gone to trial.

Gardiner then repeated his common refrain to gun owners. "The mistake Augee made was agreeing to a search of his vehicle," Gardiner explained to me. "If the police ask for consent to search, the answer is 'No.' If they ask, 'Why not?' the answer is, 'No.'"

Whenever I give speeches to gun owners, I repeat Gardiner's advice. I also suggest that when traveling interstate, gun owners bring a copy of the federal transport statute to show local police.

After loading the gun cases into the squad car to be used as evidence, the police took Lieutenant Kim to police headquarters. He was booked on four felony counts of carrying outside the home. The maximum penalty for all these charges would be a $20,000 fine and twenty years imprisonment. He was one of 506 people that year charged with possession of an unregistered firearm in D.C. In 103 of those cases, that was the top charge.[14]

The injured vet spent what he called, a "few hours in the drunk tank" and then was moved to the central jail. It was cold on the steel slab, so he asked the police guard for a blanket. "He was surly with me and sarcastic. He said, 'Oh you want blankets? Well they're back ordered,'" Kim recalled when I interviewed him. "I remember thinking, we treated detainees in Afghanistan better than this." He didn't get much sleep that night.

In the morning, the national guardsman was given a public defender and taken to arraignment. "I knew if I got one felony, my military career would be over," said Lieutenant Kim. He went to the Army JAG office for legal advice, but since the matter was in civil court, the military officer couldn't help him with the charges. "I asked him for his opinion on how this would affect my getting subsequent security clearance," the soldier recalled. The JAG eased his concerns. Lieutenant Kim recalled that he was told, "You got arrested for carrying guns. That's what you get paid for."

He went on the gun forum AR15.com and asked for recommendations for firearms' attorneys in the area. "The posters said, 'Don't accept anyone else but Gardiner,'" he said. (Richard Gardiner was made a judge in June 2013. I am concerned about other veterans finding the best legal counsel without him. Gardiner is a patriot and had great empathy and outrage over how military personnel are treated in the nation's capital.)

Over the next two months, Lieutenant Kim drove back and forth between South Carolina and Washington for hearings and negotiations between Gardiner and the representative for the U.S. attorney. The feds knocked the original felony charges down to four misdemeanors of possession of unregistered firearms. The soldier felt the prosecutor was sympathetic. "Pretty much everyone seemed in agreement on the fact that this had been some crazy misunderstanding. And, unfortunately, we had to go through this whole goat rodeo," he told me, evenly.

Gardiner finally made a deal in which Lieutenant Kim would plead guilty to one misdemeanor charge of one unregistered gun. Then, if he avoided violating the law for nine months, all the charges would be dismissed. Gardiner still insisted that his client was legally transporting, but recommended that his client accept the prosecutor's offer because it meant avoiding the risk of a felony on his record, which would end his military career.

"I have no doubt in my mind that it was legal transport under both D.C. law and the federal law," the longtime firearms attorney told me. "If the cops had known what the law was—and they probably relied on information from the firearms registration bureau, which we know is not correct—they probably wouldn't have even charged him with the violation."[15]

Lieutenant Kim accepted the deal on August 23, 2010. The following May, the charge was dismissed. His record, however, is not expunged. It still shows he was arrested on four firearms charges, which were later dismissed.

Three weeks after the charges were dropped, the U.S. attorney's office sent a form to the Metropolitan Police Department property clerk certifying that Lieutenant Kim's guns were no longer needed for evidence. But the police would not release the guns. After waiting six months, Gardiner wrote to the District's property clerk, Derek Gray, to ask for the property. Neither Gray nor anyone from the police department responded.

"This is legalized theft," Gardiner told me in May 2012. "The charges were dropped, and they don't give you your property back? The Constitution requires that if the government takes your property, it has to do something to keep it. They can't sit around twiddling their thumbs."

Gardiner brought me this story in the hopes that media attention would push the police to return Lieutenant Kim's confiscated firearms.

I asked police spokesperson Gwendolyn Crump about the guns. She said the department "notified the respondent's attorney last week of his right to a hearing concerning the return of weapons."[16] Gardiner never received this supposed letter. I asked Crump for the date the letter was sent, but she did not respond to that question.

Crump also said that the police had sent Lieutenant Kim a letter in March 2012, but it was returned undeliverable from his legal address—which she was unable to provide. The Army lieutenant said that he moved within South Carolina in September 2011 but had the mail forwarded to his new address. In any case, the normal process is to notify the attorney of record, and the police never responded to Gardiner's letter from the previous December.

When I hit a wall that can't be pushed through, I will find a creative way around it. That's what I did to get back our war hero's property.

After I published my first story about Lieutenant Kim, I sent the link and a note to all the Republican members of the South Carolina congressional delegation asking them to help their constituent. Senators Lindsey Graham and Jim DeMint (who has since retired) and Representative Tim Scott (who would later take DeMint's seat) all quickly offered assistance.

Scott told me, "Lieutenant Kim has and continues to serve our country with honor, and it is unfortunate he has been forced into this situation. My staff and I will continue drilling to the core of this matter, and I am hopeful for a quick resolution before the lieutenant leaves to serve our nation once again this summer." Lieutenant Kim deployed to Kosovo in the summer of 2012.

Graham, a gun owner who is the ranking member of the Senate Armed Services Subcommittee on Personnel, wrote a letter to Police Chief Lanier that said he would, "strongly encourage you to return the firearms to Lieutenant Kim's possession as soon as possible." Graham hand wrote in all capital letters at the bottom of this letter: "PLEASE LET US KNOW SOON!" He then personally called her to follow up on the letter.

Once Capitol Hill got involved, Chief Lanier folded fast. After almost two years of radio silence from the police, Gardiner got a call from Inspector Nathan Sims to say the property clerk, Derek Gray, would meet with him the following day for a hearing on the guns. Gardiner called me and said it was unheard of to do it that fast. The standard procedure is to send a snail mail letter to set up the meeting.

"When you get two senior U.S. senators and a member of Congress calling the chief of police, it makes a difference," Gardiner remarked. The lawyer invited me to go with him to the hearing at the Evidence Control Division Warehouse across the Potomac River in Southwest Washington. We wondered if the guns would even be there—and in what condition—after being held so long by the police.

When I drove up, Gardiner was waiting for me outside. "Do you realize what that is?" he asked me pointing to a bizarre, gigantic metal statue in front of the building? I did not. "Come, walk closer to it," he said, leading me to the formation that was sixteen feet high and nineteen feet long. When I got up closer, I realized that the entire structure was made of real guns.

"Look at this one," Gardiner said, pointing at a bronze gun frame. "This is a Polish Radom Vis pistol. This is what the Polish Underground carried when fighting the Germans in World War II." He shook his head. "My father-in-law was in the Polish Underground. It's just unconscionable that the D.C. government would just wantonly destroy a piece of history." We circled around, looking at the thousands of hollowed-out firearms.

"Is this what happened to Augee's guns?" I asked.

"I hope not," said his lawyer. (I later researched the sculpture and learned it was called *Guns Into Plowshares*. Artist Esther Augsburger designed the four-ton structure in 1994 using firearms from a gun "buy-back" program.)[17]

Inspector Sims met us at the front lobby and led us through the empty building. He left us in a tiny windowless room. A few minutes later, the property clerk, Gray, a large man, came in pushing a chair on wheels with an odd-looking metal object on the seat. He sat down and spent seventeen minutes going through the papers in Lieutenant Kim's file with Gardiner.

Finally, he ruled that the police would return the "dangerous articles" because the Army national guardsman fulfilled the plea agreement. The property clerk said the department would transfer the guns to a police department in Charleston "next week." After both Gray and Gardiner signed a document, Gray picked the metal object off the rolling chair and put it on the desk. It was an iron stamp lever to validate the hearing document. It looked like it had been around since about 1850.

Gardiner and I stopped in the lobby on our way out so he could call Lieutenant Kim with the good news. After a short conversation, Gardiner laughed and told me, "Augee is so laconic. All he said was, 'That's good news.'" Lieutenant Kim is a soldier's soldier. However, the battle was not yet won.

By Thursday, May 24—with one day to go until the deadline—Lieutenant Kim reported that his guns had not yet arrived. Gardiner tried unsuccessfully to get either Inspector Sims or Clerk Gray to respond with information on the package. So I called Crump for answers. She responded two hours later that the guns, "will be delivered to the Charleston County Sheriff's Office by Saturday."[18] Once again, the police did nothing until their obstruction was about to be exposed in the press.

In order to make their deadline, the police paid to ship priority over-night for Saturday FedEx delivery. The department might as well have saved the taxpayers' money. The Forensic Services department in the Charleston County Sheriff's office was closed on the weekend. Since Monday was Memorial Day, Lieutenant Kim was not able to pick up his personal weapons until Tuesday.

Since these guns had been missing for two years, everyone was concerned about their condition. At first Lieutenant Kim was pleased when he opened the two large boxes and found all of the items accounted for—the two pistols, the rifle, various parts and accessories, even eleven rounds of .45 caliber ammunition. Most of the items were sealed in moisture-resistant evidence bags and showed little corrosion on the parts.

But then Kim noticed something. "It looked like the property had been very well cared for, then Augee investigated more closely and found markings," Gardiner reported back to me.

When the national guardsman unwrapped the pistols, he found letters engraved on the sides of the frame of each gun. Gardiner emailed Inspector Sims: "Lt. Kim picked up his packages this morning. He noticed that there were what appeared to be initials engraved on all but one of the firearms. Is it departmental policy to mark recovered items with the officer's initials and/or any other markings?"

Inspector Sims wrote back, "Yes, it is our General Order 601.1 policy. Whoever was the recovering officer is required to mark pistols/handguns to allow for easy identification by the member at a later date. Large weapons would have only been tagged."

While it is routine practice for cops to engrave their initials on seized firearms, they are supposed to do it in accordance with their agency's policy, which Inspector Sims referred to as General Order 601.1. It is detailed in an internal police directive and specifies that evidence should be marked "in a manner that does not deface or alter its appearance." The guidelines are very specific on how to do it properly. "All pistols shall be marked by removing the grips from the frame of the weapon and making the appropriate remarks beneath the grips."

Lieutenant Kim's guns were marked on the side of the gun, which is clearly a violation of the policy and diminishes the value of the firearms. Gardiner told his client that he could file a lawsuit over the damaged property, but Lieutenant Kim wanted to put the ordeal behind him before his next overseas deployment.

At the time this book went to print, Lieutenant Kim was working as the officer in charge for the Operations, Plans, and Assessment cell for his unit in Kosovo. He was rarely able to check email, but last we communicated, he said, "I've been working pretty much non-stop twelve to sixteen hour days getting our operations running so we can sustain them for the next several months."

A valiant soldier who proudly serves our country was treated like a criminal by the District. The nation owes him gratitude, not harassment for safely transporting guns through the nation's capital.

The Kim story ruffled a lot of feathers on Capitol Hill. Representative Morgan Griffith has been working to get a hearing on his bill that would add more specifics to federal transport laws so that anti-gun jurisdictions will stop arresting innocent people.[19] The Virginia Republican's legislation would amend the current law to make it clear that individuals who transport their guns from state to state are allowed to stop for food, gas, and vehicle maintenance. They also may tend to an emergency, stay overnight, and seek medical treatment, which the District wrongly claimed made Lieutenant Kim's transport of his guns into the District no longer legal.

This language was similar to what was in Manchin-Toomey and Grassley-Cruz in the Senate a year later, but Griffith's bill had an enforcement mechanism. States and localities would be forced to pay the attorney bills for anyone who is arrested for illegal transport if they are exonerated based on this proposed law.

"The beauty of this is that the fear of having to pay the legal fees will make sure they bring charges that are valid and founded," Griffith explained to me in an interview. Referring to Lieutenant Kim's case, the congressman, who was once a defense attorney, said that a locality would only have to pay the legal fees of the accused one time and "every risk-assessment manager in the United States of America is going to inform their police that you better make sure he's violated the law before you arrest him for having a locked gun in a case in the trunk—because that's going to cost them a lot of money."

Griffin said that he would also have advised Lieutenant Kim to take the plea deal in this case. "This fellow had to risk whether or not he was going to take four felonies—his lawyer did a great job getting him one misdemeanor—but he shouldn't have had to worry about it. He should have been able to say, 'No matter what the risk, no matter what the cost, I'll fight.' But the risks are great. You've got four felonies on your record? If he were my client I would have advised the same thing. I don't like it, it stinks, but take the misdemeanor."[20]

I asked him what Lieutenant Kim would have been able to do differently if his bill had been in law. "He would have something to push back and say, 'Look, I'll pay the fine for driving on a suspended operator's license—whether that's just or not—I'll pay it. And his attorney could say, 'You give his guns back. You drop all the charges. And we won't sue you.'" The Griffith bill even picked up four Democratic co-sponsors in 2012, but never got a hearing in the Judiciary Committee. It was reintroduced in 2013 and now has forty-two co-sponsors.

Clarifying legal transport should be high on the list of pro-gun priorities in Congress. What Lieutenant Kim went through should never have happened to any soldier—any American, for that matter—legally transporting his guns through our nation's capital.

GUN GRAB SUCCESS IN THE STATES

Despite the failure of gun control legislation on Capitol Hill, President Obama did make significant inroads against Americans' Second Amendment rights in 2013. He was successful in exploiting the horrific Newtown shooting to get radical new laws passed in a handful of states.

The president always knew that his gun ban agenda couldn't get fully implemented on the federal level because of the Republican majority in the House of Representatives. So he used the White House bully pulpit and a coast-to-coast barnstorming campaign to support liberal governors' efforts to ram through gun control.

New York's quick-draw Governor Andrew Cuomo was the first to craft a hastily written gun control package.

Six days after the Sandy Hook shooting, Cuomo announced he wanted a new gun ban. "What is an assault weapon? In this state, the 'assault-weapons' ban has more holes than swiss cheese," he told radio host Fred Dicker on Albany's WGDJ-AM. In fact, New York already banned semiautomatic rifles and shotguns that have two cosmetic characteristics such as a folding stock or a pistol grip. Cuomo wanted to make the gun laws in New York even more restrictive. He even told Dicker, "You could say, 'Confiscation could be an option.'"[1]

By early January, the first-term Democratic governor announced gun control was his legislative priority. In his State of the State address on January 9, 2013, Cuomo thundered, "Forget the extremists. It's simple. No one hunts with an assault rifle. No one needs ten bullets to kill a deer. And too many innocent people have died already. End the madness now!"[2] Nowhere in the Constitution does it mention that the right to keep and bear arms is related to hunting.

Cuomo made it clear that the swift passage of a new gun control law in his liberal state would pressure the other blue states. "Set an example for the rest of the nation. Let them look at New York and say, 'This is what you can do, and this is what you should do.' This is New York—the progressive capital. You show them how we lead."[3]

Just one month after Sandy Hook, on January 14, 2013, a backroom deal passed the New York state senate 43 to 18. The Assembly approved it the next day (104 to 43) and put it on the governor's desk. Just twenty-four hours after it was introduced in the legislature, Cuomo signed the gun control measure into law.[4]

The most radical part of the Securing Ammunition and Firearms Enforcement Act (SAFE) was banning ammunition magazines that can hold more than seven rounds, the lowest number in the nation.[5] Current owners of a now-certified "high capacity ammunition feeding devices" were given one year to sell or give them away out of state or face a class A misdemeanor charge.

The state's existing "assault weapon" ban was expanded to grab more guns by reducing from two to one the cosmetic features that make a rifle an assault weapon.[6] A New Yorker who owns a gun that falls under the new ban would have to either sell it or register it with the state police before April 15, 2014. Failure to register an "assault weapon" by the deadline is punishable as a class A misdemeanor and results in confiscation of the weapon.[7]

This statute has nothing to do with public safety. Of the 769 people murdered in New York in 2011, only five were killed by a rifle of any type—that's one fewer than the number of victims who died by strangulation. The top methods of homicide, in order, were handgun, cutting or stabbing, unknown weapon, unknown firearm, blunt instrument, and hands or fist.[8]

The state adopted mandatory registration for every gun purchase, as was already the policy in New York City. Gun retailers have to record long gun sales for the state police, in addition to following the federal law on handguns. The seller has to record the buyer's name, age, occupation, and home address, along with the caliber, make, model, manufacturer's name, and serial number. Counties that granted lifetime gun permits were forced to make the permits renewable every five years (with increasing fees).

A new "universal background check" means even private gun sales have to go through a federal check. The state also instituted mandatory storage laws similar to the ones struck down by the Supreme Court in the *Heller* decision in 2008. And dealers have to record every ammunition sale with the buyer's name, age, occupation, and residence.

The law was written so quickly—reportedly by Bloomberg's staff—that it couldn't even be implemented. Cuomo never checked whether seven-round magazines even existed. So he was forced to amend the law. In doing so, he created an even more ridiculous policy that began April 15, 2013. People could keep their ten-round magazines but only load seven rounds, unless at a shooting range.[9]

As if New York criminals would meticulously count out the rounds and stop at seven.

Cuomo also belatedly realized that he wanted the police to have enough ammunition to fight criminals, so he had changed the law to allow law enforcement to possess "high-capacity" magazines. Law enforcement was also made exempt from the "assault weapons" ban and the law against guns on school campuses.[10]

━━━━━━

Maryland Governor Martin O'Malley has his sights set on running for president, so he didn't want to get outflanked on the left by the ambitious Cuomo.

On the one-month anniversary of the Newtown shooting (and the same day that the New York Assembly passed the SAFE law), O'Malley announced his own legislative agenda to tighten Maryland's already restrictive gun laws. With Bloomberg standing at his side, O'Malley rolled out his agenda at a forum on gun violence at the Johns Hopkins Bloomberg School of Public Health in Baltimore.

"Regulating assault weapons certainly falls within the bounds of the Second Amendment," the mayor said at the event. "These guns and equipment are not designed for sport or home defense. They are designed to kill large numbers of people quickly. That's the only purpose they have. They belong on the battlefield, in the hands of our brave professionally trained soldiers, not on the streets of our cities, suburbs or rural areas."[11]

Actually, we don't send our men and women into war with only semiautomatic rifles.

O'Malley said he would push for Bloomberg's agenda. "Mayor, you will be pleased to hear that in Maryland, we are taking on this issue again in this year's legislative session." O'Malley said the legislation he was introducing "will ban military-style assault weapons that have no place on the streets of Baltimore or in any other neighborhood in our state. And it will also limit the size of magazines to make it harder for criminals to gun down in succession police officers or school children."[12]

O'Malley did not mention that only two of the 390 murders in Maryland in 2011 could be traced to rifles of any style. In comparison, seventy-three homicides were by knife.[13] The facts did not fit his emotional appeal.

A few weeks later, the Democratic governor used creepy big-brother tactics to get public support for this gun grab in the "Free State." Gun owners started reporting in early February that they got an email from O'Malley encouraging them to support his legislative agenda. The email was purportedly about the upcoming Junior Waterfowl Hunting Day.

But O'Malley also wrote, "I also want to take this opportunity to address you directly about the proposal we recently introduced to reduce gun violence. Our goal is to enact common sense proposals to keep guns out of the hands of dangerous criminals, and to try to reduce the risk of a mass shooting like the one that occurred in Newtown. Let me be clear: We are committed to protecting hunters and their traditions. That's why we specifically carved out shotguns and rifles from the licensing requirements of our bill."[14]

That was only half true. O'Malley wasn't proposing a license for long guns, but he did want to ban many of them with scary-looking cosmetic features.

Patrick Shomo, the president of the pro-gun rights organization Maryland Shall Issue, told me that O'Malley "appears to be tapping the state's Department of Natural Resources database for hunting licenses." Shomo added that, "In O'Malley's mind, he can push gun control all he wants as long as he can split off 'the hunters' from the rest of us. It's not working."[15] Many hunters were among the thousands who showed up to a pro-gun rights rally held in Annapolis to protest a hearing on the gun bill.

O'Malley was out of touch with most Marylanders' views. A poll by Susquehanna Polling and Research on February 6 showed that most disagreed with the concept that "one's choice of firearms for personal self-defense should be limited only to those the government allows for hunting" by a 50 to 39 vote. The survey also reported that 83 percent of

Marylanders believed they have a right to use a firearm to protect them-selves and their families.[16]

Nevertheless, O'Malley was able to ram his gun control bill through the state legislature. On February 28, the State Senate approved the pro-posal, 28 to 19. The General Assembly passed an amended bill on April 3, by a vote of 78 to 61. All of the 43 Republicans plus 18 Democrats opposed the measure. The senate passed the amended bill the next day.[17]

Under the new law, the legal magazine size was reduced from twenty to ten rounds starting on October 1, 2013. Law-abiding Marylanders who want to buy a handgun now have to submit to fingerprinting and licensing, which will require taking a four-hour training course.[18] This will be just like the mandatory safety course in D.C.—before the city council reformed the gun registration process—that I wrote about as burdensome to exercising my right to keep arms.

The "assault weapon" ban, however, was secretly watered down before O'Malley signed the bill on May 16. Beretta USA, which is one of the largest employers in southern Maryland, tried to kill the entire bill. When that proved impossible, the firearms manufacturer made an effort to improve the legislation in a backroom meeting with chairman of the House Judiciary Committee before the final vote in the House of Dele-gates.

Beretta's general counsel, Jeff Reh, said he had already asked Joseph Vallario Jr., a Democrat, to eliminate the ban on magazines with more than ten rounds and the fingerprinting requirement for gun owners.[19] Vallario, who had been chairman of the committee for twenty years, was not able to make those concessions, but he agreed to changes so that fewer guns fell into the category of "assault weapon."

O'Malley's gun bill had the two-characteristic test that was used in the 1994 federal ban, which outlaws fewer rifles than the ban passed in New York or the one pushed by Feinstein and Obama in 2013. The key to making it even less restrictive was to reduce the number of possible cosmetic characteristics that would earn a gun the "assault" label.

Vallario crossed out these characteristics: pistol grip that protrudes conspicuously beneath the action of the weapon, thumbhole stock, telescoping stock, and forward pistol grip.

Thus, the only banned features that can combine to make a gun an "assault" rife in Maryland are a folding stock, a grenade launcher, and a flash suppressor. Of these, only the folding stock is common, so few rifles will have two of these traits and thus be banned.

However, the statute still grabs a lot of guns with a list of eighty-one specific pistols, rifles, and shotguns—"or a copy regardless of the producer or manufacturer"—that are illegal in Maryland. The state also made illegal entire manufacturer lines and platforms, including the Avtomat Kalashnikov (AK) semiautomatic rifle in any form, all Bushmaster semiautomatic pistols and rifles, and AR 100 and AR 180 type rifles.[20]

Reh, whose Beretta AR70 type semiauto is on the banned list, said, "The law that finally passed went from being atrocious to simply being bad."[21]

―――――――

Connecticut was obviously hit hard by the terrible shooting in Newtown, but even there, politicians were focused more on political gain than on measures that would actually make children safer in schools. In late January 2013, the state legislature held the first public hearing in Hartford on the gun control plans that were speeding through the legislation. By early April, Governor Dannel Malloy had used "emergency" procedures to get them into law.

Before the Newtown tragedy, the Brady Campaign determined that Connecticut was already the fifth-highest-rated state for restrictive gun control laws, "At the time of Sandy Hook, Connecticut had a pre-existing 'assault weapon' ban, which like all gun bans, was based on cosmetic features," George Kollitides, the CEO of Bushmaster told me. "Any weapon in the hand of a criminal or those bent on destruction is dangerous. Bans don't work. Preventing access and punishment work."

Kollitides does not believe the terrible school shooting involving his company's rifle would have been averted by more gun control laws. "Only two things could have potentially stopped [Lanza]—his mother locking up her guns and an armed guard. Even then, he could have driven his stolen car into a playground full of kids. He was intent on killing, which we know is already illegal."

By mid-February, Malloy was apparently frustrated that his own "Sandy Hook Advisory Commission" and the General Assembly's bipartisan gun control task force weren't moving fast enough to benefit from emotional appeals.

So Vice President Biden made a trip to Connecticut to add to the pressure on the deliberating lawmakers. "Would it be that every governor in the country acted as swiftly, decisively and as courageously as you have," the Veep said to Malloy at an event in Danbury. "I believe the price to be paid politically will be to those who refuse to act, who refuse to step forward because America has changed on this issue."[22] The White House lobbying helped Malloy, a Democrat, ram through legislation that passed the state senate on April 3. It passed the Connecticut House the next day, and the governor immediately signed it into law.

Connecticut lawmakers decided that the state's existing "assault weapons" ban, which had a two-characteristic test, was not severe enough, so all semiautomatic rifles with even one feature such as a folding stock were made illegal. The bill cited one hundred specific makes and models that are also banned.[23] Standard magazines that are "large-capacity"—defined as anything over ten rounds—will be illegal in Connecticut after January 1, 2014. First-time offenders caught with a magazine over ten rounds that was obtained prior to the effective date will be fined $90, but any subsequent offenses will be charged as a class D felony.[24]

The Newtown shooting was an aberration from Connecticut's usual crime patterns. A rifle was the cause of death in just one of the 129 murders in 2011. A shotgun also caused one homicide. In 2010, there were 132 murders—none by rifle and one by shotgun, and twenty-two by knife.[25]

Nevertheless, long guns are now much more heavily regulated. Before buying or transferring a shotgun or rifle, citizens have to get a $35 eligibility certificate from the Commissioner of Emergency Services and Public Protection. There is no statutory time limit on how long the application process can take. All long gun transfers—even a father passing down his shotgun to his son—require a background check and registration.

The category of citizens who are permanently prohibited from having a rifle or shotgun was expanded to include those who have been convicted of misdemeanors. Furthermore, a gun permit or a new "ammunition certificate" will be required to buy ammunition and magazines after October 1, 2013.

The National Sports Shooting Foundation (NSSF), the firearms industry's trade association, is actually based in Newtown, Connecticut. NSSF's Lawrence Keane told me, "We all share the goal of wanting to make our communities safer, but these gun control proposals will not do that."[26]

In Colorado, the White House put the screws to Governor John Hickenlooper to link the Newtown and Aurora shootings in an attempt to create the impression that mass shootings in the suburbs are increasing.

Before Obama started pressuring him, Hickenlooper was much more reasonable about not blaming guns for the movie theater shooting. The governor was on ABC News's *This Week* just two days after the shocking events at a late-night screening of the Batman movie *The Dark Knight Rises*.

Anchor George Stephanopoulos told him, "You probably heard the comments of Mayor Bloomberg of New York, who made headlines on Friday with his calls for tougher gun laws. Other people, several in your state, are saying that perhaps if someone else in that theater had a gun, the killer could have been stopped. Does it make you think at this point that you need to take another look at Colorado's gun laws?"[27]

"This wasn't a Colorado problem, this is a human problem, right? And how we can have such a warped individual and no one around him be aware?" replied Hickenlooper. "I worry that if we got rid of all of the guns—and certainly we have so many guns in this country, we do have a lot more gun violence than many other countries—but even if you didn't have access to guns, this guy was diabolical. Right? He would have found explosives, he would have found something else, some sort of poisonous gas, he would have done something to create this horror."

Unfortunately, Hickenlooper was not able to stand up to Obama and Bloomberg. Six months later, the Democrat in a moderate state pushed through two gun control laws. Starting on July 1, 2013, magazines that could hold over fifteen rounds were banned. The first time a citizen is caught with a "large-capacity magazine," he is charged with a class 2 misdemeanor. The next time, it is a class 1 misdemeanor.

Also, Colorado began "universal background checks," so that any firearms transfer except between immediate family members had to be done by a licensed dealer who did a background check.[28] The state set a limit for how much dealers could charge for this transaction.

"Colorado's federally licensed firearms retailers are being asked to process private-party transfers as if they were selling from their own inventory. They're being told to monitor both seller and buyer through a state-administered check process that can take hours or even days," NSSF's Keane said. "Our retailers won't be able to recoup the actual cost of providing the service—which is capped at $10—but they will be liable for paperwork errors and subject to license revocation."[29]

———

Even though Massachusetts already has some of the strictest gun control laws in the nation, Democratic governor Deval Patrick wants more.

Just one month after Newtown, he sent a fully written bill to the legislature with a note: "Both proactively, and in the wake of too many tragedies, I have filed legislation tackling the problem of gun violence and illegal firearm possession. We can no longer allow gun violence to permeate our communities, and we must cease the incalculable pain it causes families of victims in the Commonwealth and throughout the nation."[30]

Either Patrick read Cuomo's bill or he had the same person in Bloomberg's office draft his legislation because he also proposed the arbitrary seven-round magazine limit. A firearms identification card is already required before residents can purchase a firearm.

However, Patrick wants to tighten the law so that those law-abiding citizens with the card can buy or rent only one firearm every thirty days. The penalty for violating the provision would be up to $1,000 in fines and two and a half years in jail.

Patrick, who is stepping down in January 2015, wants to leave a legacy of requiring gun owners to renew their license every two years and to maintain liability insurance for criminal acts committed with their guns. He also proposed that gun show organizers would have to provide the state with the names and licenses of all attending dealers, who would then be required to submit records of all sales, transfers, or rentals. The governor also wants citizens to surrender magazines capable of holding more than ten rounds.

The Massachusetts governor announced a "universal background checks" system would be put in place with a limit of $25 on how much a dealer can charge for doing the check. The only aspect of his bill that Americans who value their Second Amendment rights can applaud is a requirement that courts transmit mental health adjudications and orders into the NICS system. The Bay State has the second worst record in America—after Rhode Island—on this issue. It put just one mental health record into the federal database in 2011.[31]

Massachusetts lawmakers didn't move as fast on gun control as other states. Then they seemingly got sidetracked by the Boston Marathon bombers who killed three people and injured over 260 with pressure cookers. The state legislature was still holding hearings in the summer of 2013.

New Jersey governor Chris Christie jumped on the gun control band-wagon by January 2013. No matter that New Jersey already had the second most restrictive gun laws in the country, according to the Brady Campaign, Christie wanted more.[32] The Republican created a "SAFE Task Force"—apparently taking the name from the title of New York's law—to look at the "root of violent crime in our society, including but not narrowly limited to gun crime, ownership and trafficking."[33]

Three months later, Christie announced a plan to "responsibly expand New Jersey's strict gun control measures."[34] The New Jersey legislature went along with all of it. The bills that passed the state house and senate in June required a training course—like the one in D.C.—just to get a "firearms purchaser identification card" to buy a gun, and the card was also made into a more intrusive photo identification. The legislation mandated that all private sales go through the government and instituted a seven-day waiting period to buy a handgun.

With such restrictive gun laws already on the books, Christie seemed to be stretching to find anything to add. He asked for and got a ban on the Barrett .50 caliber or any weapon substantially identical to it, even though these types of firearms have not been linked to crime.[35]

As New Jersey ranks thirty-ninth in the number of mental health records put into NICS (they forwarded just seventeen in 2011), the new law would mandate those records be included.

But the true intent of the New Jersey politicians was much more devious.

This was revealed by official audio recording of a Senate Budget Committee hearing on May 9 in which an informal discussion after a hearing was picked up by a hot microphone. Three women, reportedly Democratic senators on the committee, were heard talking after the conclusion of the hearing, and the Association of New Jersey Rifle and Pistol Clubs publicized the exchange.[36]

"We needed a bill that was going to confiscate, confiscate, confiscate," said one woman. "They want to keep the guns out of the hands of the bad guys, but they don't have any regulations to do it."[37]

"They don't care about the bad guys. All they want to do is have their little guns and do whatever they want with them," said another.

This is how gun-grabbers talk when they think we aren't listening.

Fortunately, not all states are jumping on the bandwagon. Mississippi, Vermont, Wyoming, and Oklahoma have either rejected the knee-jerk gun control efforts or adopted even stronger protections for the Second Amendment. And states that respect Americans' gun rights may benefit economically.

═══════

One immediate consequence of these new state gun control laws is that anti-gun governors are putting jobs and tax revenue at risk. Companies whose products have been suddenly banned are packing up and leaving for more gun-friendly parts of the country. While it takes at least five years to move large factories, the firearms industry is under pressure from its customers to get out of the anti-gun states.

Texas governor Rick Perry has been the state executive most aggressive in recruiting companies. His personal use of and appreciation for firearms give him a unique advantage over the other governors competing for the gun businesses. For instance, he went shooting with Remington Defense's George Kollitides in April at Red's Indoor Range in Austin.

The governor started his personal pitch to thirty-four companies nationwide early in 2013. I interviewed Perry at the NRA annual meeting in Houston in May 2013 after he told the enthusiastic audience that he is a "proud lifetime member" of the NRA. He cited Magpul Industries—the firearm accessories manufacturer that said it was leaving Colorado if the new gun control laws passed—as an example of why gun companies should move to Texas.

"What's kickin' them out of Colorado is bad decisions by the Colorado legislature," Perry told me of his discussions with the companies' executives. "Do not get confused—Magpul wouldn't move an inch if the legislature was friendly to them."

Perry said that he especially wanted to see Connecticut-based Colt move to his state because "their value is their name." The original Texas Rangers were outfitted with Colt revolvers. The governor told me that many current Texas Rangers carry Colt 1911 pistols.

The Texas governor traveled to Connecticut on June 17, 2013, to make a personal appeal. He went to the corporate headquarters of Colt, O.F. Mossberg & Sons, and Stag Arms. Then he had lunch at Max's Downtown with executives from those companies, as well as PTR91, Ruger, and NSSF. He told me earlier in Houston that the Connecticut law and similar ones "rushed through" in New York and Maryland are viewed by manufacturers as careless and "underhanded." Connecticut manufacturers of items now forbidden in the state are part of an industry that employs more than seven thousand people and generates $1.8 billion in economic output.[38]

Stag Arms, which makes AR-15 style rifles, is being wooed by gun-friendly states with offers of tax incentives and favorable gun legislation. After Perry's visit to Stag's New Britain-based headquarters to discuss the advantages of moving to Texas, the company's president, Mark Malkowski, told me that he had not yet made a decision. Malkowski went to South Carolina for meetings the following week.

Malkowski said of the new Connecticut law, "It will prevent us from producing our product, cost thousands of jobs, the loss of millions in revenue, and not make the state any safer." The company directly employs two hundred and spent $13 million last year buying supplies and services from local vendors. "We've increased gun production, but we've seen no increase in gun violence. We don't see a connection," Malkowski explained.[39]

Mossberg has been based in the Nutmeg State since the firm was founded in 1919. The company recently invested $4 million in new equipment and hired a hundred new people to meet increased demand. Now the firm is seriously considering shifting its expansion plans to its Texas facility.

In Maryland, O'Malley's singular obsession with passing extreme gun control laws has infuriated the executives at Beretta. "The idea of investing additional funds in Maryland and thus rewarding a government that has insulted our customers and our products is offensive to us," Reh told me.

Reh said that the company is looking to expand production in other states. He told me the "bright-line test to consider any new state for relocation is its consistency in supporting Second Amendment rights—which includes if any of the cities have sued the gun industry for criminal misuse and how its federally elected officials have voted on gun control measures in Washington."[40]

He specifically ruled out Ohio and Pennsylvania because of lawsuits brought on by the liberal cities. He was also inclined to eliminate Louisiana and West Virginia because of how Senators Mary Landrieu and Joe Manchin voted for expanding background checks. Taking into account other considerations such as energy costs, skilled labor, and tax incentives, Beretta is looking with great attention at Texas, Virginia, Kentucky, Tennessee, and North and South Carolina.

All the manufacturers I've spoken to say that moving companies is not as easy as the public imagines. Not only does it require shifting production, building new plants, and finding skilled labor, it also means leaving loyal employees to suffer the consequences.

As Beretta's Reh told me, "It's no small thing to move a factory. We put tens of millions of dollars into building it. You can't just pick up and move in a day. We also have military contracts with tight deadlines, and we won't do anything to delay delivery to our troops." Since 1985, Beretta has supplied the standard-issue M9 pistol to all five branches of the military from its plant in Accokeek.

Like Reh at Beretta, George Kollitides, the CEO of Freedom Group, which owns New York-based Remington, is concerned about his long-time employees, in particular at the Remington plant in Ilion, New York. The union workforce is employed by the only industry in the town of eight thousand.

"Look, I'm a capitalist. We have a skilled labor force up there. They know how to make the products," explained the CEO. "If we were to move, the customer would be furious because we wouldn't get products on time. You can't just pick up and move a million-square-foot factory. That's a five to seven year effort. And what happens if the law is overturned in court or we elect a new governor?"[41] Cuomo, like O'Malley, has his eye on higher office.

CHAPTER 19

THE REAL CONSEQUENCES OF GUN CONTROL: PERSECUTING A HERO

The anti-gun laws in the nation's capital have made criminals of upstanding citizens—and they'll do exactly the same thing in the rest of the country if Mayor Bloomberg, President Obama, and the anti-gun crowd get their way.

I first met Sergeant Matt Corrigan inside a D.C. Superior Courtroom on May 21, 2012. He was there to appear before Judge Michael Ryan for a hearing on the ten charges against him—three for unregistered firearms and seven for possession of ammunition in different calibers. Wearing a blue suit and black-rimmed glasses, he looked nervous next to his lawyer Richard Gardiner at the defense table. The representative from the Office of the Attorney General for the District of Columbia moved to dismiss all the charges.

After the hearing, Gardiner looked more pleased than his client. I expected some sense of vindication or, at least, relief, but the soldier was weighed down by the trauma of his experiences over the last two years.

"For court, I put on a face showing I'm okay," the thirty-five-year-old said. "Overall, this has broken me." As he told me his story from the beginning,[1] his raw pain often brought me to tears.

At 4:00 a.m. on February 3, 2010, Sergeant Corrigan was asleep in his basement apartment in a row house at 2408 North Capitol Street when he heard his name being called on a bullhorn from outside. There was a heavy snow falling—the first storm of what became known that winter as "Snowmageddon." Floodlights glared through the front and back windows of his English basement apartment. "Matt Corrigan, we're here to help you, Matt," the voice said in the darkness. He turned on his cell phone, and a police detective immediately phoned and said, "Matt, don't you think this is a good time to walk your dog?" The SWAT team outside could see the eleven-year-old pit bull, Matrix, a rescue from dog fighting, who had been with Sergeant Corrigan since graduate school in northern California.

"I'll come to the window and show myself," he offered. Sergeant Corrigan still had no idea why his house was surrounded, but he knew exactly what he should do in this situation. "I've been on the other end of that rifle trying to get someone out," he explained.

In 2005, Sergeant Corrigan was an Army reservist in a drill sergeant unit based in Alexandria and a statistician at the Bureau of Labor Statistics during the day. He volunteered to serve in Iraq. Corrigan and nine other soldiers embedded themselves with the Iraqi army to train them to be a functional military force. Among other duties, the sergeant would go out on patrol in Fallujah with the Iraqis and clear routes of improvised explosive devices. He was awarded the bronze star.

His twelve months of service ended without much time to readjust to civilian life. "In twenty days, I went from being shot at to sitting in a cube wearing a suit," he recalled of the difficult transition back to his civilian job as a statistician. "Your body is in America. Your head is in Iraq."

Like many recent war veterans, he was suffering from Post-Traumatic Stress Disorder. Sergeant Corrigan told me that he was still looking for the "IED triggerman" in his daily civilian life. He was having terrible nightmares that left him constantly sleep-deprived. "I kept seeing my own dead body with my friends and family standing over me, looking disappointed. Sometimes I died in Iraq, sometimes here," he recalled of the dreams.

That February night, Sergeant Corrigan had struggled to fall asleep, after four or five nights of sleeplessness in a row. In his Army Reserve job, he was working on preparing a mental health manual for his soldiers on mild traumatic brain injury and suicide prevention. Looking for someone to help him get some sleep a little before midnight, he called the counseling number on the National Veterans Crisis Hotline.

Though it wasn't listed as such, he had inadvertently called a suicide hotline. The woman who answered his call, who said her name was Beth, asked for his name, unit, address, phone number, whether he was active duty, and if he was using alcohol or drugs.

Then she asked if he had any firearms. Sergeant Corrigan had three personal guns for protection in his home. He had a Smith & Wesson 5904 in 9mm that he bought when he turned twenty-one years old. He purchased an M1A Scout Squad rifle from Springfield Armory in 308 cartridge when he was accepted into a fully paid graduate school program. Then he bought a Sig Sauer P226 in .40 caliber when he got his first job after graduate school.

Sergeant Corrigan had recently moved from Virginia to the District, but he had not registered his guns because he thought the process was too risky. "It didn't sound right that I could just carry my guns to the police station and not get arrested," he explained. (I have heard the same thing from many people who move to D.C. When asked, I recommend they pay Sykes $125 to pick up the guns and take them to the police station.)

Sergeant Corrigan answered Beth's question truthfully, admitting that he owned guns. Bizarrely, she took his answer to mean that he was about to kill himself. In fact his guns were locked and cased.

"She kept saying, 'Put down the gun,'" Corrigan recalled. "She talked like I had the gun in one hand and my cell phone in the other." He repeatedly told her that he was not holding a gun, but she insisted that he say the words, "The guns are down." He told me, "I finally got agitated and said, 'I shouldn't have called' and hung up."

He took a sleeping pill that had been prescribed to him by the Veterans Administration hospital and went to bed. Without his permission, however, Beth called 911 and reported that he "has a gun and wants to kill himself." According to a transcript of the 911 recording, the crisis counselor told the cops, "The gun's actually on his lap."[2] The drill sergeant told me he said nothing of the kind, and that his two pistols and rifle were hidden under clothes and in closets, to avoid theft.

While Sergeant Corrigan slept, dozens of SWAT and Explosive Ordnance Disposal (EOD) officers spent hours preparing a full-scale invasion of his residence in the middle of the snowstorm of the century. This was not an operation to protect the public from a terrorist or to stop a crime in progress. It was to rouse a sleeping man over a secondhand report that he might have an unregistered gun.

———

Around 1:00 a.m., the police knocked on the door of Tammie Sommons, Sergeant Corrigan's upstairs neighbor in the row house. Police officers told Sommons that someone had reported the smell of gas coming from Sergeant Corrigan's apartment. "I told them that there was no gas in his apartment—it was all electric," she recalled in an interview. "I said if they smelled something, it's just my roommate, who was cooking chicken parmesan."

The officers asked Sommons whether Sergeant Corrigan owned any guns. "I said, of course he has guns, he's in the military," she replied. Sommons had never seen the sergeant's guns, but she is from a military family, in which gun ownership was the norm. She disclosed this information to the police because she was unaware at the time that the District requires residents to register guns with the city.

Over the next hour, Sommons repeatedly told the police she was sure that Sergeant Corrigan was merely sleeping. She knew he took prescription sleeping pills. But they weren't interested in a simple explanation.

"The cops said we needed to leave our house because Matt was going to shoot through the ceiling," Sommons told me. "They painted this picture like Rambo was downstairs and ready to blow up the place."[3]

At 3:00 a.m., the police called in an EOD unit—the bomb squad. They brought in negotiators. They had the gas company turn off the gas line to the house. A few minutes before 4:00 a.m., they started calling Sergeant Corrigan's cell phone, but they got no answer because he had turned it off before going to bed.

At 4:00 a.m., with the police invasion in place, Sergeant Corrigan was jolted awake by the bullhorn and the bright lights. By phone, the drill sergeant agreed to exit his home. As he walked out his front door, he turned the knob on the handle so that it would lock when he closed it.

When he got outside the door, he saw about twenty-five officers in full body armor and Kevlar® helmets, carrying M4 rifles. SWAT and EOD teams were on all sides. Streets were barricaded for blocks.

Police memos from that night describe the situation as involving a man who is, "threatening to shoot himself," but "doesn't want to hurt anybody." None of the cops' documents indicate a threat that warranted a barricade and the closure of several streets to create "an outer perimeter that prohibited both traffic and pedestrian access." With dozens of cops on the scene, they even created a "staging area" two blocks away.[4]

The veteran knew how to surrender with the least chance of being hurt. He put his hands over his head and turned in a circle so they could see clearly that he was unarmed.

"I looked down and saw ten jiggly red dots all over my chest," he said, referring to the laser targets painted on him by sighting devices on the police officers' weapons. Recalling this, he appeared afraid at just the memory. "I crumbled," he said simply.

Out of the corner of his eye, he saw an officer ready to tackle him, so he dropped to his knees and crossed his ankles to demonstrate complete defenselessness. Officers in full protective gear handcuffed Sergeant Corrigan's hands behind his back and pulled him up from his knees.

"They immediately zip-tied me tighter than I would have been allowed to zip-tie an Iraqi," Sergeant Corrigan said, pulling up his dress shirt cuff to show his wrist. "We had to check to fit two fingers between the tie and the Iraqi's wrist so we weren't cutting off circulation. They tied mine so tight that they hurt."

Once restrained, Sergeant Corrigan was forced into a large tactical command center called the "BEAR" that was parked at the staging area. Without reading him his Miranda rights, he said, officers began questioning the Iraq veteran, trying to get him to admit to owning guns. He remained silent about his three unregistered weapons.

A police commander then jumped into the truck and demanded to know where Sergeant Corrigan put his house key. "I'm not giving you the key. I'm not giving consent to enter my house," Sergeant Corrigan recalled saying.

He said the officer responded, "I don't have time to play this constitutional bullshit with you. We're going to break your door in, and you're going to have to pay for a new door."

"Looks like I'm buying a new door," Sergeant Corrigan replied.

Realizing quickly that his house would get raided without his permission, he asked for one thing from the police. "I said, 'Please don't hurt my dog. He's friendly. He's a good dog. Please don't hurt him.' They said they wouldn't."

Sergeant Corrigan was taken to the Veterans Affairs hospital in restraints. He didn't want to be put in the hospital against his will, so he agreed to sign himself in temporarily. "After having all those guns at me, I was broken," he said, pointing at his chest, where he'd seen the red laser dots from the police rifles. "I hadn't slept in days. I just wanted to sleep."

Once Sergeant Corrigan was out of the area, the police broke down his door, without bothering to seek a search warrant before doing so, according to court documents.[5] "They were all keyed up because they had been there and ready to go all night," said his attorney Gardiner, who represented Corrigan in court.

The first to enter the supposedly dangerous apartment was not the bomb squad, but a team that secured Matrix and handed him off to animal control, according to police reports. Only then did the EOD personnel enter to search using portable X-ray equipment.

During the "explosive threat clearing efforts," police reported finding the sergeant's "hazardous materials," which included two pistols and a rifle, binoculars, and ammunition. The report also details how it took the combined efforts of the police, EOD, and the D.C. Fire Department to seize the "military ammunition can that contained numerous fireworks type devices." These were in fact merely fireworks, left over from the Fourth of July.

The police also took into evidence what is described as a "military smoke grenade" and "military whistler device." This smoke-screen canister and trip wire had been put in Sergeant Corrigan's rucksack by his squad leader back in 1996. Corrigan had forgotten all about them for years. The rest of the materials were handed over to the crime scene search department at 7:30 a.m.

Police Lieutenant Robert T. Glover was pleased with the seven-hour operation, which resulted in securing items commonly found in millions of homes across the country. In his report to Chief Lanier, he concluded, "As a result of this barricade incident, there are no recommendations for improvement with respect to overall tactical operations."[6]

The dry after-action notes give no clue to the property damage done that night. Officers tore apart the 900-square-foot basement apartment. They cut open luggage with knives instead of simply unzipping it. The raiders dumped over bookshelves, emptied closets, and threw clothes on the floor. The guns were seized, along with the locked cases, leaving only broken latches behind. The ammunition, hidden under a sleeping bag in the utility closet, was taken.

The police broke Sergeant Corrigan's eyeglasses and left them on the floor. The cops also knocked over the feeding mechanism for the tropical fish in the sergeant's 6-foot-long aquarium. When he was finally released from jail two weeks later, all of his expensive pet fish were dead.

The police turned on the electric stove and did not turn it off. They left without securing the broken door. When Sommons came back to her house later that day, she looked into Sergeant Corrigan's apartment and described it as "ransacked."

"It made me lose respect for the police officers involved," Sommons told me. "Here was Matt, who spent a year fighting for our country in Iraq—where these police would never set foot in—and they treat him like trash off the street."

Sergeant Corrigan spent two nights in the VA hospital. When he was released on February 5, police officers were waiting. They handcuffed him and finally read the soldier his Miranda rights, according to court papers, charging him with three counts of unregistered guns and seven counts of possession of ammunition—all based on evidence obtained without a warrant.

The police took the reservist to the 5th District station, where they put him in an open booking cell before questioning him. Sergeant Corrigan's then-girlfriend, now-wife, Chetna Lal drove to the station but was told she couldn't see him. She said the police told her to wait at D.C. Superior Court for an arraignment.[7]

After a while, Sergeant Corrigan agreed to sign a waiver to be interrogated. Officers asked the drill sergeant for details about each gun, such as where he had bought it and what it was for. He was called out of his cell once more to be taken to a city mental health clinic to be evaluated. The doctor determined that he was not a suicide risk and sent him back to the police station.

Because of "Snowmageddon," Sergeant Corrigan said, most of the other people in police custody were released with an order to come back for arraignment at a later date. He said he asked an officer to check on his case and was told, "You know what you're in here for. There's no way you're being released."

Finally, in the evening, the police put those remaining in custody in a van to be transferred to the courthouse. On the way, officers told them that the court had closed early because of the weather. When he arrived, Sergeant Corrigan was booked and put in the central jail to wait for a hearing. Lal, who had been waiting all day at the court to see Corrigan, was never allowed to see him.

"They said that maybe they would be able to arraign us on Saturday morning," recalled Sergeant Corrigan. "Then Saturday came, and they said court was closed, and it would have to wait until Tuesday because Monday it was closed because of the snow."

In all, Sergeant Corrigan spent four nights in the D.C. Central Detention Facility without being allowed even a phone call. While the soldier had spent a month living on a rooftop in Iraq, he called D.C. central jail, "the worst place" with "roaches everywhere you looked" and "rats running between the cells." The only food provided was a bologna sandwich on white bread with mayonnaise and a cup of Kool-Aid. He said the worst part was trying to sleep through the "nighttime screamers."

By Monday, he was still in jail, unable to even make a call to explain not being at work. On Tuesday morning, Sergeant Corrigan finally had his first hearing. Since he hadn't been allowed to make a call to hire a lawyer, he was assigned a public defender who asked him a few basic questions. But when the case was called, the court-appointed lawyer did not appear. Another public defender, who knew nothing about the case, merely entered a not guilty plea. The judge set the next court date and remanded Sergeant Corrigan to a halfway house.

The reservist was then told that because of the snowstorm, there was no room for him in a halfway house, and he had to go to the D.C. jail. He was forced to turn in his clothes, change into an orange jumpsuit, go through a medical evaluation, and be classified.

All this time, Sergeant Corrigan's family and friends were desperate to find him. They were unable to do so because city bureaucrats had not entered his correct name or birth date into the jail system. The Superior Court arrest affidavit gave the defendant's name as "Matthew Carrigan." The arrest warrant also has the wrong birth day and month. The police arrest report from Officer Dino McFadden also had the same incorrect information.[8]

The police knew Sergeant Corrigan's actual name. Lieutenant Glover's report to Chief Lanier (which he wrote on February 9, while the soldier was still in jail) gave the soldier's correct name and birth date. The emergency response team's incident report also has the correct information.

Sergeant Corrigan protested when the jail administrator wrote another variation of his last name—"Carrington"—on his prison wrist badge. He said no one would be able to find him with the wrong name on his records. But he was assured that he could be found with his prison identification number. Not so, as his jail I.D. was associated with the wrong name and birth date.

Lal said she was turned away from the prison four times as she frantically attempted to find her then-boyfriend. "I think this kind of thing would happen in India," she said of the country of her birth. "But not in a billion years would I think this would happen in the United States of America."

Possessing firearms in the District makes you a target for criminals. When Sergeant Corrigan was arraigned, the line of other defendants in court waiting their turn heard the gun charges against him. Word quickly spread through the jail population that the soldier was a source for illegal guns. The inmates nicknamed him "21 Guns" and constantly badgered him for help in securing firearms for them on the outside.

The gun association would normally make an inmate safer on the inside, but as part of the processing, the administrators repeatedly asked Sergeant Corrigan for personal information in front of the other inmates, including his home address. The soldier now called "21 Guns" quickly realized that the criminals in jail asking him to get them weapons on the outside could easily show up at his home later, demanding a firearm.

After about five days of badgering from other inmates, Sergeant Corrigan asked to be put in protective custody. The conditions there turned out to be worse than among the general population, he said. He was locked in his cell for twenty-three hours a day. When he was taken to any kind of administrative appointment within the jail, he was shackled.

Sergeant Corrigan had his own cell for a few days, and then he got a cellmate he described as looking like John Walker Lindh, the American Taliban. One night the sergeant woke up in his bottom bunk to find his cellmate trying to strangle him with a towel. The experienced military man was able to keep off the deranged attacker until the guards made their regular rounds.

Finally, a friend who is a Navy JAG officer succeeded in tracking down Sergeant Corrigan in the jail. Then Lal was able to hire an attorney, who secured the soldier's release on his own recognizance at 12:30 a.m. on February 20.

He returned home seventeen days after his arrest to an apartment that had been destroyed by the police. There he discovered a notice saying that if he didn't pick up his dog, Matrix, within three days, the canine could be "euthanized." Thankfully, Lal had rescued the soldier's beloved dog just in time.

Sergeant Corrigan returned immediately to his job and his military duties, but the charges were a black cloud hanging over his head. From February 2010 to May 2012, Sergeant Corrigan was forced to abide by the conditions of his court release. That meant checking into the courthouse weekly, attending mandatory mental health appointments, and undergoing weekly urine testing for drugs.

The D.C. court also banned him from touching a firearm. "They basically took away my military career for two years," he said. That is a recurring theme in Washington. Our armed forces trusted Sergeant Corrigan to carry deadly weapons—the reservist continues to serve one weekend a month and two weeks in the summer—but the District bureaucrats did not.

Gardiner, who Corrigan had by then hired, had filed a motion in August 2010 to suppress the evidence because the police had violated his client's constitutional right to be free of unreasonable search and seizure.

"When I was secured, a warrant could have been obtained," the soldier told me. "When I offered not to give my consent to enter my place, a warrant could have been obtained. When the first weapon in plain view was alleged seen, a warrant could have been obtained. When they did not 'have an initial on explosives,' a warrant could have been obtained. During each of these incidents what was the exigency that prevented a warrant from being obtained?"

The assistant attorney general for the case, Avril Luongo, opposed the motion to throw the unregistered guns out of evidence. She said exigent circumstances justified the search. By this, she was referring to a November 2010 filing that said Sergeant Corrigan was an expert in planting explosives and that there was a smell of gas in the building. The document also claimed that police had "gained intelligence about the defendant, including information that the defendant was an Iraqi war veteran with specialized training (believed to be training in connection with deploying 'booby traps')."

The government's court filing concluded, "Under the totality of the circumstances—the smell of natural gas, the information that the defendant had a military background and experience with booby traps, the defendant's call to the suicide hotline—the officers reasonably believed a crisis situation existed. Thus the urgency of that crisis, including the need to secure the premises, was the basis of their decision to perform a warrantless search."

Both of the supposedly exigent circumstances—the smell of natural gas and experience with booby traps—were fabricated.

The EOD team on the scene said there was no evidence of explosives at the apartment. The same experts declined to use a dog trained to sniff out explosives, and instead brought in a special gun-searching dog.

In the discovery phase of the proceedings, Gardiner asked for copies of the police notes and documents from that evening, and found they contained no reference to "booby traps." He asked Luongo for the rest of the evidence supporting her theory, but that was all she had. The prosecutor told the defense attorney that she would talk directly to the police officers to get the answers. "She never told me what was said, but the next thing she filed was the notice to withdraw the claims of booby traps because the police couldn't substantiate it," said Gardiner.

The prosecution began to fold. Before a hearing on the motion to suppress on April 18, 2012, D.C. Attorney General Irvin Nathan wrote the court, "Upon further investigation, the government is no longer relying on the proffer that the Metropolitan Police Department was aware that the defendant had training in the deployment of 'booby traps.'" At the hearing, the attorney general's office only had the supposed "smell of gas" to prove their search was based on an exigent circumstance.[9]

Lieutenant Glover's report to Chief Lanier noted a "strong odor of natural gas emanating from the immediate area in and around the target address." But this excuse fell apart quickly. Sommons took the stand and testified she told the police that night that there is no gas in the basement of the row house. In court, Gardiner questioned Officer Carlos Heraud, who was one of the first on the scene and had interviewed Sommons about the gas. Asked on the stand if he smelled gas that night, Officer Heraud said he did not. There was no mention of gas or explosions in the officer's handwritten notes from that night. Furthermore, an hour or two before the police woke up Sergeant Corrigan and arrested him, they had Washington Gas turn off the line to the building.

The judge found this evidence overwhelming. On April 19, D.C. Superior Court Judge Ryan granted the defense's motion to suppress the evidence because the search had violated the Fourth Amendment. The prosecutor asked for thirty days to determine whether the city would appeal the ruling. The judge granted the request, then set the next status hearing for May 21.

The city was finally forced to stop persecuting Sergeant Corrigan. Luongo called Gardiner a week before the hearing to inform him that the city had decided against appealing the decision. She also said that all the charges against Sergeant Corrigan would be dropped because of the lack of evidence.

Gardiner then petitioned the court to return his clients' property—guns and ammunition. (The lawyer had just gotten back the guns of his other active-duty veteran client, Lieutenant Kim, after two years.) Judge Ryan initially protested that Sergeant Corrigan would be violating D.C.'s registration laws if the guns were returned to him. Gardiner told the judge that his client is now a resident of Virginia, where registration is not required.

A new prosecutor assigned to the case told the judge that he was unprepared to discuss this issue. Judge Ryan gave the city three days to file a response, and said he would rule within a week. When the attorney general's office filed the documents, it repeated the discredited claim that Sergeant Corrigan was planting booby traps and that the police smelled gas on the property.

Gardiner was "amazed" by this development. He asked the judge's clerk if he could file a reply. "I wrote that the opposition is unethical because he presents facts to a judge that he knows are not true because the assistant attorney general previously filed a notice to the court that withdrew these claims," he said.

The court did nothing from May until August, when it asked Gardiner to provide additional documentation that Sergeant Corrigan could legally own guns in Virginia. Again, the court delayed until December, when it asked Gardiner to file a statement indicating "whether Mr. Corrigan has complied with any applicable requirements for possessing said ammunition."[10]

Not until April 9, 2013—nearly a year after the charges were dropped against the war veteran—did the court issue an order to release the illegally seized property. Finally, a month later, the District of Columbia got around to returning Sergeant Corrigan's firearms. The veteran was notified that his belongings would be sent via FedEx to the Loudoun County Sheriff's office.

Sadly, just like Lieutenant Kim, Sergeant Corrigan found his property damaged. "The sheriff told me that the rifle and handguns were sent in the same tube, bouncing around with each other. He said there was some paper, but not enough to matter," Sergeant Corrigan reported back to me after picking up his guns. "They moved the handguns into the box with the bagged brass so they wouldn't get beat up any more than they already were."[11] Both the pistols and the rifle had numerous chips that were not there before. The Sig had a stock-size smash mark. The officers had etched their initials and case numbers on them.

"I carried an M4 for fourteen months of a combat deployment, toting it around every day, getting in and out of vehicles, searching homes, and setting up overwatch positions. My battle rifle from combat had fewer dings and scratches than the one that was in D.C.'s possession for three years and three months," said Sergeant Corrigan.

"I had an expectation that the weapons would be defaced from Lieutenant Augustine Kim's story. I was hoping it would not be that big a deal, that getting the property and its value back was more important," Sergeant Corrigan explained to me. "It became immediately apparent that it is a huge deal. Every time I go to the range to shoot or clean my weapons, I'll be reminded of this debacle, of everything that happened to me."

The veterans I profiled followed each other's stories. When other soldiers come to me for help in similar situations (in D.C. or a state that has radical gun control laws) but do not want to go public for fear of their careers, I help get legal counsel and also connect them with other victims of these draconian laws so they can support and advise each other.

Sergeant Corrigan was going to try to have the guns fixed and the etching removed. He told me, "I want these guns to represent the accomplishments in my life again and not the initials and numbers of the D.C. officers that violated my civil rights."

The damage to the veteran was beyond repair. Sergeant Corrigan filed a civil suit in February 2012 against the District asking a minimum of $500,000 for violating his Fourth Amendment right to be free from unreasonable searches and seizures.[12] Gardiner added some of the individual officers to the lawsuit in mid-2013.

I asked Sergeant Corrigan why he was pursuing this civil case after winning the criminal case. "Everything from this point on is to hold those responsible accountable. Because you know if they did it to me with this amount of finesse and police report padding, they have done it to others. I think, in general, this is why a growing portion of the public is fed up with the current enforcement mechanisms."

The Iraq vet added, "I adhere to the Constitution—both here and overseas. I expect that the authorities that I served for would do the same thing. The facts are they didn't uphold that piece of paper that I have defended through service for the last seventeen years. I expect better, and I demand better."

CHAPTER 20

GUN CONTROL BATTLES MOVE TO THE COURTS

A s quickly as gun-grabbing governors snatched away citizens' Second Amendment rights in the states, gun owners filed lawsuits to get them back.

The Supreme Court's landmark decisions in *District of Columbia v. Heller* and *McDonald v. Chicago*—allowing Americans to "keep" arms in the District of Columbia and the states, respectively—encouraged advocates for the Second Amendment to trust that whatever unconstitutional gun laws get enacted can ultimately be reversed.

The NRA is staying vigilant on Capitol Hill, but prioritizing the restoration of Second Amendment rights in the states through the courts. "Where we have lost in the political or legislative agenda, you can count on us using the legal process," said Chris Cox. "Freedom lost is much harder to regain. We're dedicated to protecting the rights of our members in New York, as much, if not more so, than expanding the rights of our members in Alabama or Idaho."

In Connecticut, plaintiffs including the NRA filed suit in federal court in June 2013 challenging the constitutionality of Governor

Malloy's dramatically titled "Act Concerning Gun Violence Prevention and Children's Safety."[1]

Scott Wilson, the president of the Connecticut Citizens Defense League, one of the plaintiffs, told me in an interview that the law puts people in more danger. "They are trying to legislate utopia. They think passing a law and putting up these magical 'gun-free zones' will work," Wilson said. "But it's just an invitation for a killer to come in because there will be no resistance." The gun rights group, which was started in 2009, saw its membership triple in the six months after the Sandy Hook Elementary School shooting.[2]

In Colorado, a powerful coalition of plaintiffs—fifty-four county sheriffs, the NRA, NSSF, Magpul Industries, and disabled individuals—filed a federal lawsuit on May 17 to challenge Governor Hickenlooper's new gun control regulations. Of the new ban on "high-capacity" magazines, the complaint says, "The Sheriffs have limited resources and limited public funds to spend on investigations. They cannot expend those resources to conduct investigations that would be necessary to monitor compliance with the new magazine restrictions."[3]

New York Governor Cuomo's SAFE law is also being challenged in court.[4] The New York State Sheriffs' Association and five individual sheriffs have joined in the lawsuit filed by the New York State Rifle and Pistol Association, the NRA, and others. The group asked the court to rule that the law violates the Second Amendment by prohibiting law-abiding citizens from keeping "commonly possessed firearms in the home for defense of self and family and for other lawful purposes."[5]

Unfortunately, it takes years for these kinds of lawsuits to be decided. In the meantime, citizens of these states are forced to either live without their full Second Amendment rights recognized or move.

The *Heller* and *McDonald* decisions determined that the right to "keep" arms—possess handguns at home—could not be infringed by state laws. Another major Second Amendment issue that the judiciary branch will have to decide is the extent to which the right to "bear" arms can be limited. Until the end of 2012, there were two places in the country where bearing arms was outright banned: Illinois and the District of Columbia.

Alan Gura won District residents the right to own handguns in D.C. from the Supreme Court, but now he is fighting to get them the right to carry them outside the home. "The courts will have to step in because the city will need to be dragged kicking and screaming all the way to accepting this is a normal feature of the Bill of Rights," the attorney told me in an interview in June 2013. "They are not going to simply comply with the spirit and the meaning of the Second Amendment. They will have to be sued—repeatedly—and courts will have to take those cases seriously."[6]

In 2008, Gura—along with co-counsels Robert Levy and Clark Neily—convinced the Supreme Court to force city officials to recognize the right to keep arms through the *Heller* case.[7]

However, the high court did not rule on two Second Amendment issues which it is likely to weigh in on in the next few years: whether federal or state laws could set limits on the type of guns, and if the right to bear arms could be restricted.

"It would have been very strange for the Supreme Court to announce *Heller* and *McDonald*, and then retreat forever from the Second Amendment," said Gura. "They opened a door to a new area of constitutional litigation, and as the *Heller* decision itself predicted, they would have future opportunities to weigh in on Second Amendment conflicts."[8]

Gura is the Second Amendment Foundation's lead attorney for different right-to-bear-arms cases that the organization has working through the courts in D.C. and four states.

The biggest win for carry rights to date is *Moore and Shepard v. Madigan* on December 11, 2012, when the Seventh U.S. Circuit Court of Appeals decision struck down the carry ban in Obama's home state of Illinois. The case was a landmark because, as Second Amendment Foundation founder Alan Gottlieb told me, "Illinois' ban on carrying a loaded firearm for self-protection is now history, and now no other state can come back and ban carry."[9] The right to bear arms had been affirmed.

The NRA hired attorney Chuck Cooper to argue on behalf of Mary Shepard, who is licensed to carry a concealed handgun in both Utah and Florida but not her home state of Illinois. The Second Amendment Foundation had Alan Gura represent Michael Moore, an Illinois resident who had been allowed to carry a firearm off duty as a corrections officer but was denied a permit to do the same as a civilian jail superintendent. Lisa Madigan is the attorney general for Illinois.

Judge Richard A. Posner wisely pointed out in his decision, "A woman who is being stalked . . . has a stronger self-defense claim to be allowed to carry a gun in public than the resident of a fancy apartment building (complete with doorman) has a claim to sleep with a loaded gun under her mattress." Posner also noted that carrying guns can deter crime because "knowing that many law-abiding citizens are walking the streets armed may make criminals timid."[10]

Illinois filed a petition for a rehearing en banc, which was denied in February 2013.[11] Under Posner's direction, the state legislature had 180 days to "craft a new gun law that will impose reasonable limitations, consistent with the public safety and the Second Amendment as interpreted in this opinion, on the carrying of guns in public."

Attention then turned to whether the Illinois legislature would write the new carry law along the lines of those in the "may issue" states such as Maryland. "If Illinois puts in an overly restrictive law, we'll go back to court again," Gottlieb warned. On June 1, 2013, its last day in session, the General Assembly passed a law that made it difficult for citizens to get permits, but did not require them to show need.[12] Both residents and non-residents, as long as they don't fall into a category of "prohibited person," who take a sixteen-hour training course and pay fees ($150 or $300) can get a license valid for five years. The license can be renewed after taking a three-hour training course.

Democratic Governor Pat Quinn tried to stand in the way of the federal courts and his own legislature. He issued an amendatory veto in early June that would have given Illinois one of the most restrictive carry laws in the country. On July 9, the Illinois House and Senate overturned the governor's veto. The Second Amendment Foundation's Alan Gottlieb cheered, "We welcome Illinois to the United States of America."[13]

Madigan asked the Supreme Court twice for more time to decide whether to appeal, which Justice Elena Kagan granted. As this book went to press, Madigan had until July 22, 2013, to file an appeal.

Woollard v. Sheridan, which challenged Maryland's "may issue" style of requiring carry permit applicants to show a "good cause," excited the pro-Second Amendment activists when the U.S. District Court ruled in March 2012 that the law was unconstitutional.

Judge Benson Everett Legg wrote, "At bottom, this case rests on a simple proposition: If the Government wishes to burden a right guaranteed by the Constitution, it may do so provided that it can show a satisfactory justification and a sufficiently adapted method. The showing, however, is always the Government's to make. A citizen may not be required to offer a good and substantial reason why he should be permitted to exercise his rights. The right's existence is all the reason he needs."[14]

In July, Legg denied a stay requested by Maryland, to continue to refuse citizens the right to carry concealed weapons while the appeal was pending. Gura argued the case before the Fourth Circuit Court of Appeals, but unfortunately it overturned the lower court's decision in March 2013. The Fourth Circuit concluded that the "good-and-substantial-reason requirement is reasonably adapted to Maryland's significant interests in protecting public safety and preventing crime."[15] Gura appealed the decision to the Supreme Court.

———

The Supreme Court's landmark decisions in *Heller* and *McDonald* gave gun rights supporters confidence that the Second Amendment can prevail in the courts. Both of those landmark decisions, however, were 5 to 4, with Justices Samuel Alito, Anthony Kennedy, Antonin Scalia, Clarence Thomas, and Chief Justice John Roberts voting in the majority. That means if any one of these five justices retires and is replaced with a liberal by President Obama, the court will flip to be anti-gun.

Obama's reelection empowered the left to start laying the groundwork for the case that the Constitution allows banning "assault weapons" and "high-capacity" magazines, as well as restrictions on carrying guns outside the home.

After the Aurora movie theater shooting in July 2012, Mayor Bloomberg brought Senator Frank Lautenberg and Representative Carolyn Maloney to New York's city hall to introduce a new bill to expand the "high-capacity" magazine ban. Their legislation would require buyers to show a photo I.D. at the time of purchase, effectively banning people from buying their ammunition online or by mail. It would also require the dealer to report any purchase exceeding 1,000 rounds to law enforcement within five business days.

In the statement describing the timing for his ammunitions bill, Senator Lautenberg said he counted conservative Supreme Court Justice

Antonin Scalia among those who had "publicly expressed acceptance or support for some form of gun regulation since the Colorado shooting."[16]

That was far from an accurate description of Scalia's comments the day before on *Fox News Sunday*.[17] "What the opinion *Heller* said is that it will have to be decided in future cases—what limitations upon the right to bear arms are permissible," Scalia had said. "Some undoubtedly are because there were some that were acknowledged at the time [the Second Amendment was ratified]. For example, there was a tort called affrighting, which [was] if you carried around a really horrible weapon just to scare people, like a head axe or something. That was, I believe, a misdemeanor. So yes, there are some limitations that can be imposed. What they are will depend on what the society understood was reasonable limitation."

"But what about these technological limitations?" asked Wallace. "We're not talking about a handgun or a musket. We're talking about a weapon that can fire a hundred shots in a minute." (Wallace should have clarified that the only thing that makes a semiautomatic firearm shoot one hundred rounds in sixty seconds is someone who can pull the trigger repeatedly extremely fast.)

"Obviously, the amendment does not apply to arms that cannot be hand-carried. It's to keep and bear. So, it doesn't apply to cannons," said the justice. "I suppose there are hand-held rocket launchers that can bring down airplanes—it will have to be decided."

"How do you decide if you're a textualist?"

"Very carefully," said Scalia. "My starting point and ending point probably will be what limitations are within the understood limitations that the society had at the time. They had some limitation on the nature of arms that could be born. So, we'll see what those limitations are as applied to modern weapons."

Justice Scalia's originalist interpretation of the scope of the Second Amendment was clear. When he said that there "are some limitations that can be imposed," he only referred to those that were understood as reasonable at the time the Constitution was written.

But the liberal media tried to make the public believe that the court was about to shift in favor of banning guns. MSNBC's Lawrence O'Donnell crowed, "Justice Antonin Scalia is now the beaming source of hope that the government might someday do something to reduce the chances of you and your family being shot to death by a madman when you go to the movies in America."[18]

After Newtown, the politicians stepped up their efforts to reinterpret the high court's rulings on guns. Senator Dianne Feinstein cited *Heller* in the February hearing on her Assault Weapons Ban of 2013. "That decision clearly stated, 'The right secured by the Second Amendment is not unlimited.'"

She did not mention that the court had listed the types of acceptable limitations: certain state restrictions on carrying concealed weapons, "longstanding prohibitions on the possession of firearms by felons and the mentally ill, or laws forbidding the carrying of firearms in sensitive places such as schools and government buildings, or laws imposing conditions and qualifications on the commercial sale of arms."[19]

Feinstein went on to say, "Justice Scalia, the author of that opinion wrote that, 'Dangerous and unusual weapons could be prohibited.'"[20] She stopped reading from the decision at that point because the rest of the passage didn't fit her argument.

The ruling went on to say that even military weapons (which are already highly regulated) would be allowed because "the conception of the militia at the time of the Second Amendment's ratification was the body of all citizens capable of military service, who would bring the sorts of lawful weapons that they possessed at home to militia duty. It may well be true today that a militia, to be as effective as militias in the eighteenth century, would require sophisticated arms that are highly unusual in society at large. Indeed, it may be true that no amount of small arms could be useful against modern-day bombers and tanks."

Feinstein claimed that her "assault weapon" ban would be held up by the courts because, "Even with *Heller*, I see no really regular use of an AR-15—'common use' in society. It may be a small group of people that use it for target practice or—God forbid—they use it for hunting—they're not much of a hunter. But the irreparable damage that's done to bodies from this weapon and other high-velocity rifles, that tears peoples' bodies apart, I do not know why as a matter of public policy we can't say they don't belong."[21]

On the contrary, the AR-15 is commonly used by millions of law-abiding Americans for target shooting, hunting, and self-defense. The weapons are used by criminals to kill an average of thirty-five people a year, according to Feinstein's own figures.

Heller made it clear that the Second Amendment protected all weapons that the citizens at that time of its adoption kept at home to be ready to fight in battle. "The traditional militia was formed from a pool of men bringing arms 'in common use at the time' for lawful purposes like self-defense." Scalia wrote in the decision that the only guns that the Second Amendment does not protect are "those weapons not typically possessed by law-abiding citizens for lawful purposes, such as short-barreled shotguns."

A couple months later at a White House event with Attorney General Eric Holder, Vice President Biden used the White House bully pulpit to help reinforce the gun-grabbers' misinterpretations of Scalia's remarks. "Justice Scalia, who is a brilliant conservative mind on the court, pointed out the government has the right to prohibit the sale of certain types of weapons. It's constitutionally permitted. Senator Feinstein has an amendment to keep those weapons of war off the streets and not aimed at you," he said.

The anti-gun politicians and their allies in the media are trying to establish the public perception that the Supreme Court will rule in favor of gun control if Obama gets to replace a conservative with a liberal on the high court. Pro-Second Amendment activists, on the other hand, hope that the Supreme Court takes up cases on the right to carry arms and on banning "assault weapons" and "high-capacity" magazines before the president has the chance to change the make-up of the court.

I met Justice Scalia at the White House Correspondents' Dinner in April 2013. I was with my good friend, Shannon Bream, who covers the Supreme Court for Fox News. At this annual confab of media, politicians, and Hollywood celebrities, everyone mills around the tables before the dinner starts to make small talk with acquaintances or meet new contacts. Bream and I were heading to our tables when she stopped to greet Scalia. After chatting a few minutes, she turned to introduce me.

Supreme Court justices are rarely seen at public events. Because of their lifetime appointments, the necessity for total confidentiality about proceedings, and security concerns, they generally only go to events with their close friends and family. So it was a big deal to meet a justice, and particularly, for me, the one who wrote the *Heller* decision.

However, the justices are skilled at talking without giving away any information on what is happening inside that exclusive white-columned building to the east of the Capitol.

"Thank you so much, sir, for giving me back the right to have a gun in D.C.," I told Justice Scalia. "I bought a handgun, and I owe that to you. Thank you for writing *Heller*." He smiled and nodded. "So when will we get the right to bear arms? Will you take up a case soon?" I asked.

Justice Scalia shook his head. "I don't know," he said. "We'll see." It appeared to me that his expression indicated that the Supreme Court would not be taking up one of the "bear" cases in the immediate term.

"You have to do it before Obama stacks the court," I pleaded. "We'll never get back our carry right if you five don't give it to us."

"What we really need to look at first is this semiautomatic case," he said.

I was not sure what he was referring to, but didn't want to press him because it would have been inappropriate in that setting. He could be talking about the so-called Heller 2 case that challenges the District's registration laws.

I lightened up on my interrogation. "I hope you are staying healthy. We need you to stay on the court for a long time," I said. He laughed good-naturedly, clearly amused at the unexpected female reporter in a strapless black-tie dress begging him for help to be gun toting around D.C.

"I'm okay. You don't need to worry about me," he said, laughing.

"What about those?" Bream asked, pointing to the cigar sticking out of Scalia's tuxedo jacket.

He laughed. "Only on special occasions," he said.

"Make sure you get regular exercise," I added as we said goodbye.

There's no doubt where the four liberal justices stand on the gun bans that have been instituted on the state level, and which Obama wants on the federal level as well. Former Justice John Paul Stevens, the author of the minority opinions in the *Heller* and *McDonald* cases, made some radical statements at an event hosted by the Brady Campaign to Prevent Gun Violence in October 2012.

"The Second Amendment provides no obstacle to regulations prohibiting the ownership or the use of the sorts of automatic weapons used in the tragic multiple killings in Virginia, Colorado, and Arizona in recent years," said Stevens, incorrectly lumping semiautomatics together with automatic weapons, which are already heavily regulated. "Maybe you have some kind of constitutional right to have a cellphone with a pre-dialed 911 in the number at your bedside. And that might provide you with a little better protection than a gun which you're not used to using."[22]

Stevens's suggestion that a mobile phone is a more than adequate substitute for the arms the Second Amendment gives us the right to keep and bear should have scared enough people to the voting booth the next month to prevent Obama from appointing any more justices. Unfortunately, it did not.

Instead, gun owners have to hope that all five pro-Second Amendment justices on the high court stay healthy until at least 2016.

CHAPTER 21

SENSELESS PANIC: SOLDIER THROWN IN JAIL FOR JUST UNREGISTERED AMMO

The cases of First Lieutenant Kim and Sergeant Corrigan were shameful, but at least those men were actually in possession of firearms and could conceivably be considered a threat. Former Army Specialist Adam Meckler, on the other hand, never had a gun but was still charged under the same law, which comes with a maximum penalty of a year in jail. Specialist Meckler's story was the final straw that got the city's anti-gun politicians to ease off a little on prosecuting good people.

I learned of Specialist Adam Meckler's case when Diamond found it mentioned on the website AR15.com. I went into the forum and asked that the person get in touch with me. Specialist Meckler emailed me after a fellow member of the forum contacted him on my behalf. I was stunned when he told me his story.[1]

Specialist Meckler was only fifteen days out of active duty and still living at Fort Belvoir when he had to go into the District to turn in his medical records on September 18, 2011. The veteran of the wars in

Afghanistan and Iraq went to the VFW, which is located inside the Veterans Affairs D.C. regional office four blocks from the White House.

His loose papers created a mess going through the scanner conveyer belt. So when he had to return with more documents the next day, the Army medic took his first aid backpack to keep the papers from flying around again at security. He had used this same bag when he served as a medic at the shooting range for his Army job, and also when he shot recreationally. Specialist Meckler owned his military-issued sidearm, the Beretta M9, and a Springfield XD(M) in 9mm.

He took the Metro into the city. At the entrance of the Eye Street building, he got in line to go through the magnetometers again. When it was his turn, the Kentucky native put the backpack on the conveyer belt. Expecting to be waved through the checkpoint, he was shocked when the security guard held him in place.

"The guard looking at the monitor screen had this crazy look on his face," Specialist Meckler recalled when I interviewed him. The head security guy walked over to look at the screen. Unbeknownst to Specialist Mecker, the guard saw some loose rounds of 9mm ammunition in the bag. He yelled out, "Cuff him!" A guard told Specialist Meckler to put his hands behind him, then slapped steel cuffs tightly on his wrists.

Instead of simply confiscating the ammo, the guards created a huge, unnecessary scene in the federal government building. "They yelled for the people in line behind me at security to back out of the building," said the combat vet. "As people were coming off the elevator, they were telling them to get back on. They shut down the lobby. It was like I had explosives or something in my bag."

During this melee, Specialist Meckler had no idea what was happening. "I was thinking, what is in my bag? I thought, there is no way it's a gun, all my guns are locked up. I'd made sure there were no knives in the bag."

The guards told him that they had found ammunition, and that did not surprise him. "I have plenty of bags with random ammo in them. It never crossed my mind to look for them before going into D.C.," he explained.

In retrospect, Specialist Meckler thinks he probably threw the ammunition in the bag haphazardly after a recreational shoot. "I think the last time I went to the range to shoot, my father-in-law gave me some rounds. And I emptied a magazine and tossed them in the bag," he said. A spokesman for the District's Office of the Attorney General told me that they discovered fourteen rounds of 9mm ammunition in the bag.[2]

Massachusetts, Illinois, New York City, and D.C. are the only places in the country where you have to have a registered firearm in order to possess ammunition legally. (Although a case like Meckler's could also happen in Illinois, Massachusetts, or New Jersey if the person didn't have the required state permit, license, or I.D. card.)[3]

Specialist Meckler apologized profusely to the guards and tried to explain the mistake. One of the guards at the VFW initially sounded reasonable. "He said, 'This happened a couple of weeks ago with another soldier. We'll get this straightened out.'" The soothing words were far from the mark.

The security officer walked Specialist Meckler down the hall, with one guard in front and one behind. As people came out of their offices, the guards yelled for them to get back in and close the doors. "It was embarrassing," the veteran recalled. "People looked at me like I was a terrorist."

As he was being marched in restraints by armed guards, Specialist Meckler was thinking about both of his fifteen-month tours in Iraq and Afghanistan. "I can't tell you how many people we PUCed—we put in flexi cuffs—and took them out of the village because we found explosives on them, but not for having some rounds on them."

He told me his unit raided villages in Afghanistan and detained people with massive weapons caches containing anti-aircraft rounds and piles of RPG rounds. In Iraq, he went on "countless missions" to grab high-value targets and restrain them in a similar manner.

Though Specialist Meckler had tangled with terrorists on foreign soil, he was being humiliated by our government for merely possessing some bullets.

Inside the security office, Specialist Meckler was handed off to uniformed federal police officers from Veterans Affairs. "I was completely submissive. I didn't want to be a problem," the nine-year Army vet recalled. The federal police officer asked Specialist Meckler if he knew that ammunition was illegal in the District. He said he did not. The officer replied that it was and began to read Meckler his Miranda rights. Specialist Meckler said he interrupted to ask, "Am I really going to be arrested for this?'" The officer confirmed he was.

Specialist Meckler kept trying to explain the simple misunderstanding, but the officers were not listening. He told me later that, "I understand that it was my fault that the rounds were in the bag. I understand the lengths the security officers went to to make sure that I was not a threat," he told me later. "What I don't understand is that, after everyone completely understood the situation that I had accidentally put myself into, I was still arrested."

While waiting to be transferred to jail, he asked the officers to loosen his handcuffs, but they refused. "I'm a big guy," he said. "I've been in those flex cuffs before in training, but I've never been in those steel kind." The handcuffs left marks on his wrists. The federal officers led him out of the federal building—which was on lockdown since the ammunition was found—and into a truck that he recalled said "Homeland Security" on the side.

He was thrown in jail at police headquarters without being allowed a phone call. Specialist Meckler recalled feeling relieved to be in the holding cell because the tight handcuffs were finally removed. He spent about two hours alone in the cell. He told me that he kept thinking, "I can't believe this is happening."

One of the officers agreed with him. "The processing officer said, 'I can't believe they did this. They usually just take the ammo and let you go. I don't know why they brought you in like this,'" he recalled.

As I explained earlier, another unique part of Washington's firearms laws is that the only people who could possess ammo in D.C. are licensed dealers (and Charles Sykes doesn't sell ammo); residents who have a firearms registration certificate for a firearm in the same caliber or gauge as the ammunition; local or federal officers or employees acting within the scope of their duty; and those who had an ammunition collector's certificate on September 24, 1976.

(The new registration law passed by the city council in April 2012 allowed registered gun owners to possess ammo in other calibers or gauges than their own gun. As if this makes any difference.)

Specialist Meckler's was one of 594 ammunition-related arrests in 2011, according to the police. Of those, sixty-four had the illegal possession of ammunition as the top charge. Almost all were District residents. Only the soldier and eight others were non-residents. (The D.C. police department has refused to respond to my Freedom of Information Act requests for numbers of arrests in 2012 and 2013.)[4]

═══════

After hours in jail, the police handed Specialist Meckler a paper with the charge of "unregistered ammunition" and a court date.[5] They gave him back his bag and released him, so he was able to then use his cell phone to call his wife.

The Attorney General for the District of Columbia, Irvin Nathan, wouldn't drop the charges for the harmless "crime."[6] Prosecution for unregistered ammunition in D.C. is "common," according to the prosecution's spokesman.[7] Unregistered ammunition, though, is a charge generally tacked on to a higher charge, such as possession of an unregistered firearm. The maximum penalty for the charge is the same as for an unregistered firearm—a $1,000 fine and one year in jail.

Specialist Meckler was represented by his wife's uncle, Jim Henderson, a constitutional lawyer. The soldier said he did not fight the charges because he didn't have the time or money. "I just wanted to get it past me," he said. But he was concerned about landing a job with a criminal conviction on his record. "I was getting out of the military and had a bunch of job applications out and the forms for government jobs all asked if I had ever been convicted of anything."

As it happened, he almost lost the offer for his present job—as a telehealth clinical technician at the Veterans Health Administration in Jacksonville, N.C.—when his security clearance kicked back over the ammunition charge. He was able to get the job only after providing a thorough explanation to his superiors.

Without money to hire an attorney who specialized in firearms cases, the veteran gave in and accepted a deal from the city. He would plead guilty to one misdemeanor of "possession of unregistered ammunition" and get thirty days unsupervised probation, perform community service, pay a $100 fine, and make a $100 "donation" to the Victims of Violent Crimes fund.

Specialist Meckler went to court on December 5, 2011, and D.C. Superior Court Judge Richard Ringell accepted the deal the prosecution had offered, except the judge struck out the community service requirement and added being put on the District's Gun Offender Registry.

D.C. Council member Phil Mendelson's committee created the registry in 2009 for the police department's internal use. It was intended to provide enhanced monitoring of those convicted of firearm laws and provide a deterrent for offenders. By law, it can only be shared with other government agencies. Every name on the list is supposed to be removed after two years. The police spokesman, Crump, said the registry is not available to the public.[8]

Specialist Meckler went straight from the court to police headquarters down the street to register himself. An officer there told him of a case of an Army staff sergeant who was caught with a non-functioning weapon from a family member and was charged and also forced to register on this offenders list.

Meckler was photographed and his fingerprints were taken. He was upset and embarrassed by the process. "I felt like I was registering as a sex offender," he said.

———

While Attorney General Nathan prosecuted a humble veteran of America's wars for unknowingly breaking an obscure firearms law, he let the powerful NBC anchor David Gregory go scot-free for doing it deliberately.

The *Meet the Press* anchor brandished an illegal thirty-round magazine to push his anti-gun agenda in an interview with the NRA's Wayne LaPierre a few weeks after Newtown. At NBC's Washington bureau, Gregory held up what the city considers a "high-capacity" magazine on live national TV.

The anchor said, "Isn't it possible that, if we got rid of these, if we replaced them and said, 'Well, you could only have a magazine that carries five bullets or ten bullets,' isn't it just possible that we can reduce the carnage in a situation like Newtown?" He then waved a smaller, legal magazine at LaPierre.[9]

Gregory knew he was breaking the law. The Friday before, an NBC producer—whose name was redacted in documents I received through a FOIA request—had emailed the police, "Meet the Press is interviewing a person on the show this Sunday in studio—Producers for the show would liek [sic] to have a clip (standard and high power), without ammunition in studio to use on the show. There will be no gun, no bullets, just clips. Is this legal?"

That night, someone in the police department—again, the name was blacked out—replied: "No, possession of high capacity magazines is a misdemeanor under Title #7 of the D.C. Code. We would suggest utilizing photographs for their presentation."[10]

A photograph would not have been as powerful a weapon to use against LaPierre, so Gregory went ahead with his publicity stunt, in spite of the police warning.

A criminal investigation was launched once the show ended, but Gregory was given special treatment. While others have been thrown in jail for the exact same crime in D.C. and other jurisdictions in the U.S., the NBC anchor left for vacation. Several law enforcement sources told me in the days after the show aired that, if this were anyone else, a warrant would already have been drafted for an arrest for a crime that carries a maximum penalty of $1,000 fine and one year in jail.[11]

Yes, this is a stupid law and no one was in any danger, but by deliberately breaking it for his own agenda, Gregory forced police to waste manpower. As the head of the police union, Kris Baumann, said to me during the investigation period, "The argument defending Gregory—that don't the police have something better to do? The answer is, yes we do. And thank you for making it more difficult to get to those things."[12]

After a few weeks of silence, D.C. police spokesperson Gwendolyn Crump told me that the police had "completed the investigation into this matter" and turned the case over to the Office of the Attorney General "for a determination of the prosecutorial merit of the case." That meant that, unlike Specialist Meckler, Gregory was never arrested or thrown in jail. Just two days later, Nathan, the attorney general for D.C., announced he would not press charges against NBC News or David Gregory. The prosecutor wrote to Gregory's attorney that his office had "made this determination, despite the clarity of the violation of this important law, because under all of the circumstances here a prosecution would not promote public safety."[13]

By that reasoning, city officials believe prosecuting a war veteran for accidentally bringing bullets to the VFW somehow promoted public safety. The decision sent out the clear message that there are two systems of justice in the city.

"This is a perfect example of what is wrong with local D.C. politics," Officer Baumann said in an interview. "There are two sets of rules. One set for us common people, and a second set for the politically connected. It is indefensible that the criminal justice process could be manipulated to protect one individual. It undermines public confidence in the District, law enforcement, and the criminal justice system."[14]

While Gregory broke the firearms law and went on vacation, the police arrested 105 other people in 2012 on charges that included possession of "high-capacity feeding device or extended clip,"[15] and the attorney general charged fifteen of them.[16]

One of those cases was James Brinkley, an Army veteran and federal employee I profiled in the *Washington Times.*

Brinkley was arrested on September 8 in D.C. as he was dropping his wife and young children off at the White House for a tour. He was handcuffed, taken to jail, and charged with possessing two "high-capacity" magazines and an unregistered firearm. All this was over an unloaded Glock 22 that was in a padlocked box in the trunk of his car with the two standard-issue fifteen-round magazines outside the gun.

In contrast to the Gregory case, Attorney General Nathan's office refused to drop the charges, despite overwhelming evidence that Brinkley was legally transporting through Washington. Brinkley refused to accept a plea bargain and went to the expense of taking the matter to court, where he was acquitted of all charges.[17]

I asked Specialist Meckler for his take on the NBC case. "Admittedly, I made a mistake. By carrying those overlooked, loose rounds in my backpack, I unknowingly broke the law. Mr. Gregory knowingly broke the law. While both are seemingly harmless, both acts were deemed illegal under the District's obscure firearms laws," Meckler told me. "At the very least, he should be put on probation, pay a fine, and be added to the District's Firearms Offender Registry, as I was ordered to do."[18]

———

In the course of my investigation, I discovered that you can be arrested under the District's law for something even less dangerous than empty magazines or ammunition. The police are on the lookout for anyone in Washington, D.C., with shell casings or empty shotgun shells.

Police Chief Lanier sent out a "roll call training"—a script for what the police should do in various situations, including driving with "a fired .45 ACP cartridge case in the cup holder."

Empty brass casings in the cup holder are illegal? I asked police spokesperson O'Meara if I was misunderstanding and the training was really referring to live ammo. Nope.

"Strictly speaking, the casings fall within the definition of ammunition," she told me. The penalty is the same as for breaking any of the firearms and ammunitions laws—a $1,000 fine and a year in jail.

This is hands-down the stupidest of all the District's firearms laws. A brass candlestick can do more harm than an empty brass casing. I often have empty casings in my bags and clothes from when they fly off at the range, or as souvenirs.

The police guidance advised officers to "exercise discretion in making arrests under this scenario or other similar occurrences."

But O'Meara insisted to me in email that "there may be scenarios where someone is not eligible to register a gun and having a bunch of spent cartridge cases would have a different meaning. For example, if someone has a previous conviction for violent gun crimes and is found with cartridge cases, the implications would be more serious."

Criminals aren't going to the range to train. If they shoot, they will leave the casing. There are very few scenarios in which someone who is banned from owning a gun would happen to have empty casings in a cup holder. This law will almost only apply to the law-abiding.

I was especially concerned how the guidance could cause innocent tourists trouble with the police. Most gun owners in America can't prove that their gun is legal at home, since few states require a registration certificate.

––––––––

By the time Specialist Meckler and I spoke in May 2012, he was still feeling bad about the decision to take a plea deal. He has never denied fault for not knowing D.C.'s unique firearm-related laws, but he feels they are unjust. "Because of my personal situation, I couldn't have stood up at the time, but now is my chance to tell my story so no one else goes through the same thing," he said. Specialist Meckler accomplished exactly that.

Just days after my story about the soldier was published, an aide to D.C. Council Chairman Mendelson contacted me about another new bill, being introduced that week, to partially decriminalize possession of unregistered firearms and ammunition. The legislation would allow for the D.C. attorney general—Nathan—to offer offenders an administrative disposition (a fine, no criminal record) instead of a criminal charge.

In September, Mendelson opened the hearing on the bill by reading my accounts of Lieutenant Kim and Specialist Meckler as examples of the types of cases that should not result in criminal prosecution.

Most witnesses at the hearing were in favor of the change. Even the executive director of the Coalition to Stop Gun Violence, Josh Horwitz, did not oppose the change, though he found it necessary to note in his testimony that the bill is "not an attempt to placate the NRA."[19]

Dick Heller, the man who had successfully sued Washington and put an end to its unconstitutional thirty-year handgun ban, told Mendelson his bill was a "mere micro step in the right direction in the slow slog toward true firearms freedoms in our city."[20]

The biggest opposition came from Andrew Fois, one of D.C. Attorney General Nathan's deputies, who said his office opposed the measure because administrative disposal "is not appropriate for firearms-related offenses for anyone." His testimony was of concern to gun rights advocates because of the possibility that the prosecutors might never take advantage of the option for administrative disposal and a fine.

In December, Mendelson released a final version of the legislation. It allowed prosecutors to take into account whether the person being charged was a District resident at the time of arrest and "had knowledge of" the gun laws. The prosecutors could then choose to give a violator a fine (to be determined by the court) with no criminal record, but only if the accused wasn't charged with another crime from the same incident.

I was surprised when Mendelson brought this bill up for a vote on Monday, December 17—just three days after the Newtown shooting. With that terrible event at the forefront of everyone's minds and with calls for more gun control coming from the White House to the city level, I assumed Mendelson would be afraid to go forward with a public vote. But the city council voted unanimously in favor.[21]

This new law would never have been proposed, much less have been passed, if veterans such as Specialist Meckler, Lieutenant Kim, and Sergeant Corrigan had not been courageous enough to go public with their stories. They all did so for one reason: to help other responsible and law-abiding gun owners avoid getting caught in the crosshairs of Washington's outrageous anti-gun laws.

They and all our military are heroes for serving our country and fighting for freedom and the preservation of our constitutional rights. That's why all Americans should know about their cases before President Obama and Mayor Bloomberg succeed in extending this kind of extreme anti-gun regime across the country.

CHAPTER 22

"SHALL NOT BE INFRINGED"

I decided to get a gun after being a victim of a frightening crime. While I could not foresee it, that choice drove me to fight to stop D.C. from infringing on Washingtonians' rights to keep and bear arms. And, in turn, that led to a deep understanding that the Second Amendment is a pillar of our democracy.

I awoke to the value of this constitutional right at almost the exact moment the other 100 million gun owners in America faced the most concerted, well-financed, and determined attack on the Second Amendment in the history of our country.

Less than two months after I started exposing the District of Columbia's outrageous registration laws, the city council moved to reduce some of the seventeen steps to gun ownership. The bill passed the liberal city council unanimously and was signed into law in May 2012.[1] The most significant change was the elimination of the five-hour gun class. That alone saves residents over $200 and a day off work. The ballistics test was also scrapped, as was the vision test.

I asked Dick Heller what he thought of the new process. "It's a little easier now, but it still infringes on our Second Amendment rights," said Heller. "I would like to think the NICS test is enough if it was perfected. But D.C. still fingerprints the good citizens like criminals. Cops don't even fingerprint drivers at a traffic stop, but they still can find out if they are fugitives."[2]

Also, the new registration law attempted to protect residents should the only D.C. gun dealer, Charles Sykes, get zoned out of business or otherwise close again. It would require Mayor Vincent Gray—who, when campaigning, wouldn't even talk to me about making it easier to get a gun in the District—to become a Federal Firearms Licensee for District residents. I love Sykes, but if he chooses to retire, I will be very amused to see Gray forced into being a legal gun dealer.

While I was pleased that the city had decreased the steps it took to register a gun from seventeen to eleven and the cost from $435 to $173, the registration requirement should be eliminated.

———

Undaunted by his temporary loss in the Senate, Obama promises to continue pushing to restrict gun rights. "And as we saw earlier this year with the gun safety debate, sometimes this stuff takes time, and it's frustrating," Obama told supporters at a reception for "LGBT Pride Month" in the East Room of the White House on June 13, 2013. "You take two steps forward and sometimes there's a step back."[3]

While Obama bides his time on gun control legislation on Capitol Hill, he is aiming at restricting gun rights by supporting the United Nations Arms Trade Treaty. This treaty is intended to regulate the dangerous global arms trade, but also covers civilian firearms under "small arms and light weapons." And it does not include a provision making clear that individuals have the inherent right to keep and bear arms.

Obama knew this would be unpopular with the public, so when negotiations were moving quickly in the U.N. in the summer before the 2012 election, the U.S. asked for a delay. Then, just hours after he was reelected in November 2012, the president authorized U.N. Ambassador Susan Rice to support the treaty. The U.S. voted in favor of it in the General Assembly in March 2013.[4]

When the treaty was opened for signatures on June 3, Secretary of State John Kerry said that the U.S. would sign it once it had been translated, adding the claim that it does not infringe on Second Amendment rights.[5]

The White House will have a steep climb to get two-thirds of the Senate to ratify it. Senator Jerry Moran, Kansas Republican, sponsored a resolution saying that the president should not sign the arms treaty, but if he does, the Senate ought not ratify it.[6] The resolution has thirty-five co-sponsors, which is more than enough to block the treaty in the Senate.

The House, which has the power of the purse, passed an amendment on June 16 to prohibit federal funding for the treaty's implementation.[7] Nevertheless, Obama appears intent on signing the global document, which will go into effect after fifty countries ratify it. The president's signature alone could give the international community the false impression that Americans are ceding their right to keep and bear arms.

———

So far, the Republican House and the red-state Democrats in the Senate have kept Obama from achieving his gun control agenda. This reflects the will of the people, yet the left continues to blame it on scare tactics by gun groups.

President Bill Clinton said on MSNBC in June 2013 that lawmakers were voting out of fear of attack ads by NRA and Gun Owners of America.

"These organized interest groups don't want anything done because it's a big source of their money and support to terrify people living out there in the country and try to make them think there's this big conspiratorial federal government trying to take all their guns away," said Clinton, who signed the last federal gun ban. "I think if you could get a clear-headed vote on the issue standing alone, the overwhelming majority of Americans in every state would be for it."[8]

Clinton, like our current president, is out of touch with the American people on this issue. The liberal politicians just can't seem to accept that the majority of Americans do not believe restricting gun rights will reduce crime. And for good reason. As we have seen, crime has been going down even as gun ownership has been going up every year.

The voters don't think well of the politicians, either. Only one out of three Americans rated Obama's handling of gun control as good or excellent according to a July 2013 survey by Rasmussen. Forty-two percent said the president's performance on this issue was poor.[9]

What is most unfortunate about Obama playing politics with gun control is that he is holding hostage measures that have bipartisan support and would actually make our nation safer.

We have a serious problem with mental health in this country—both with respect to treatment and inpatient facilities, but also in simply getting mental health records into the NICS system to prevent the mentally ill from buying guns.

Also, people with criminal records, fugitives from justice, and domestic abusers all need to be put into the FBI database to make the laws we already have effective. Prosecuting those who try to get a gun illegally would not only stop those particular criminals, but also have a ripple effect through the criminal underworld.

The other way to make people safer—schoolchildren in particular—is to eliminate gun-free zones. While it's impossible to know what goes through the deranged minds of mass murderers, all the recent mass shootings—with the single exception of the attack on Gabrielle Giffords in Tucson—occurred in places where the law-abiding were disarmed.

For the same reason, some of the devastating injuries and deaths might have been averted in Aurora. "In that movie theater, everyone was sitting there totally helpless. And this guy is just popping them off one after another," Donald Trump told me.

The billionaire real estate developer has a concealed-carry permit in New York City and owns an H&K in .45 caliber and a .38 Smith & Wesson. "Frankly, at some of these terrible shootings, if others had guns, they would have been able to shoot the criminals."[10]

The tragic murders at the Sandy Hook Elementary School broke the heart of every American, and that includes gun owners. Those of us who live in the almost half of homes in the nation with a gun are mothers, fathers, sisters, brothers, grandparents, aunts, and uncles who thought of the precious children in our families when we mourned the terrible scenes from Newtown.

I don't think we should be using these people's pain to push for any legislation or policy. We should let them grieve in peace. However, since the anti-gun forces jumped so quickly to exploit their loss to push for more gun control laws, it is worth debating what could be done to prevent the same horror from happening again to another child.

Sandy Hook Elementary School was also a gun-free zone, meaning Adam Lanza knew that no one could shoot back when he entered the school or the classroom.

When a person determined to do harm cannot get a gun legally, he will obtain it illegally. Even if the 300 million guns in America were rounded up and thrown into the ocean, there will still be murders.

In 1995 Timothy McVeigh and Terry Nichols used simple fertilizer in Oklahoma City to kill 168 people, including nineteen children under the age of six. In gun-free Japan in 2008, a former school janitor stabbed eight children to death in their elementary school.

The worst mass killing in a school in American history did not involve a single firearm. In 1927, a school's treasurer in Bath Township, Michigan, used bombs made with dynamite and pyrotol to kill thirty-eight elementary school children. We can't outlaw fertilizer or explosives or knives. And even if we could, the bad guys would just find another way to kill, such as the pressure cookers used in the terrorist attack in Boston.

The only thing that might have stopped Adam Lanza was an armed guard. Do you really think he would have gone into that school if there was a police car parked outside? Would he have broken past the front door if he thought a staff member might have a gun to shoot back? There does not need to be an armed guard at every school, but those schools that choose to have that extra level of security should be allowed.

Wayne LaPierre suggested the same thing after Newtown. Bloomberg, congressional Democrats, and MSNBC hosts called the idea everything from "irresponsible" to "shameful." However, once the hysteria died down, even the White House seemed to realize it was a worthwhile idea.

In a *Parents* magazine interview at the White House, Vice President Biden said that when he wrote the "Biden crime bill" in 1994 as a senator from Delaware, it included a provision for putting police officers in schools. "We found that those school resource officers were of value in many schools," he told the audience. "We haven't been funding them of late. We think they should be funded."[11]

The COPS in Schools program gives grants to help law enforcement agencies hire school resource officers for community policing in and around primary and secondary schools. The program, begun during the Clinton administration, awarded $753 million to hire more than 6,500 school resource officers around the country between 1999 and 2005. Congress never shut down the program, so restarting it would only require the Appropriations Committee shifting funding, without adding to the national debt, to resume it.[12]

Freshman Representative Mark Meadows, a North Carolina Republican, introduced legislation in February 2013 that would allocate an initial $30 million of unspent funds to restart the COPS in Schools program.[13] "We're trying to find something that had bipartisan support, that is outside politics, that can make our schools safer," the North Carolina Republican told me in an interview. "When funded in the past, school resource officers had a positive effect in reducing gun violence. It's a common sense, practical measure to protect our kids and teachers in school."[14]

There are already armed guards in nearly one-third of the nation's 23,000 public schools, according to the Department of Education.[15] Sixty percent of schools with over one thousand students have security with a gun. And the concept is popular with the public. By a 2 to 1 margin, Americans favor armed security guards and police in more schools, according to the Pew Research Center.[16]

In addition to eliminating the criminals' playground of gun-free zones, another thing that would make America safer would be to have more law-abiding gun owners carrying handguns. It's just common sense that a criminal is less likely to attack a person he thinks might have a gun. It's a deterrent. The Senate should pass the national concealed-carry reciprocity bill that the House passed, so that law-abiding people who have handgun permits issued in their own states can travel the country legally with their handguns.

———

When our Founding Fathers declared independence on July 4, 1776, they said, "We hold these truths to be self-evident, that all men are created equal, that they are endowed by their Creator with certain unalienable Rights." That means the Framers believed God gave us certain rights as human beings, and the government exists to ensure those rights are upheld. They withdrew from the control of the British King George III because of his "absolute Tyranny over these States."

The Founding Fathers explained in the preamble to the Bill of Rights that they were adding "further declaratory and restrictive clauses" to the Constitution in order to prevent the government from "misconstruction or abuse of its powers." They believed so strongly that the right to keep and bear arms was imperative to prevent government tyranny that they listed it second, after the First Amendment's guarantees of freedom of speech, religion, assembly, and the press.

But liberal politicians refuse to accept the fact that the framers' primary purpose for the Second Amendment was to prevent government tyranny. "As Americans we have the right to arm ourselves against criminals, but we do not need the ability to arm ourselves against the army," said Senate Majority Leader Harry Reid during the gun control debate. "The United States military is not out to get us. Federal law enforcement and local police departments are not out to get us. These conspiracy theories are dangerous and they should be put to rest."[17]

This is why Reid couldn't twist enough arms to pass gun control. He and Obama and the rest of their liberal wing of the Democratic Party are totally out of touch with mainstream America. Two out of three voters say the Second Amendment was, in fact, intended to protect them from tyranny, according to a Rasmussen poll. Only 17 percent disagreed.[18]

Since I wrote so publicly about registering a gun in D.C., several otherwise law-abiding people have confided in me that they have unregistered firearms in the city. Some ask me for information on the worst-case scenario if they get caught.

I tell them that the maximum penalty for breaking any of the firearms-related laws—whether you have an AR-15 rifle or only an empty brass casing—is a $1,000 fine and a year in jail. They usually look terrified. I clarify that they will likely get a deal for a lesser plea, but warn they will spend at least a few hours in D.C. jail, be out legal fees, and have a criminal record.

I asked one friend why he doesn't just register his guns. "I don't want the government knowing I have a gun," he replied.

"Which government? Federal? City?" I asked.

"Any of 'em," the respected, professional, church-going man answered.

"What are you afraid will happen?"

"If they change the law, they'll come take my guns," he replied. Most others gave me the same reason for not registering their firearms. Some just don't have time or patience to go through the—now eleven—steps to register.

The liberal media and politicians mock gun owners who are concerned that gun control will ultimately lead to registration, and registration will lead to confiscation.

"They say the NRA is trying to scare people to raise money. No, the NRA is trying to prevent bad things from happening because this is what we're tasked to do," said Chris Cox. "Throughout the history of the world, you've seen gun control proposals lead to confiscation. It's happened here. When California passed their first assault weapons ban, if you were in possession, and you didn't turn them over, they came and took them. You saw it when they confiscated guns from law-abiding people after Hurricane Katrina in New Orleans." Cox noted, "Confiscation is not our word—that's their word. 'Mandatory gun buy-backs'— those are their words."

And as a matter of fact that was the interpretation of Obama's Justice Department on how their "universal background check" bill would be effective.[19] "The challenge to implementing this more broadly is that most states do not have a registry of firearm ownership. Currently NICS background checks are destroyed within twenty-four hours. Some states maintain registration of all firearms. Gun registration aims to 1) increase owner responsibility by directly connecting an owner with a gun, 2) improve law enforcement's ability to retrieve guns from owners prohibited from possessing firearms."

The left tries to make gun owners seem paranoid and delusional for thinking that a registry will lead to the government taking our firearms—but this secret memo showed that among themselves they discuss "law enforcement's ability to retrieve guns from owners."

The shocking scandals in the first year of Obama's second term only confirmed gun owners' reasonable fears. The IRS used its extraordinary powers to prevent conservative groups from getting tax-exempt status to operate during the 2010 election cycle, and we still don't know how high up in Washington this abuse of power was initiated.

Then we found out that the Justice Department has been secretly monitoring the phone calls, emails, and computer traffic of reporters from the Associated Press, Fox News, and CBS News. Next it came out that the National Security Agency has been collecting records of the phone, email, and internet activity of all Americans for a new spy program called PRISM.

"People don't trust the Obama world that they are starting to see, and I don't think gun control is any different," said Reince Priebus, chairman of the Republican Party. "Obviously, the IRS scandal and NSA issue only make the idea of more government lists that have no information to even be useful for the goals they espouse isn't going to fly either. I think that it's par for the course for these guys." Priebus added that the president is "driven by ego and hatred for dissent."[20]

These scandals show that the federal government under Barack Obama violated the rights Americans have under the First and Fourth Amendments. If it had access to a list of the 300 million firearms in the country, who could trust that this government would think twice before infringing on our Second Amendment rights?

Since I started writing about the hoops I had to go through to get a legal gun in D.C.,[21] the one question I get most often from readers has been, Why don't you just move?

Well, I might one day, but I want to stay in D.C. to have standing to fight for the Second Amendment for everyone in the nation's capital. The most gratifying part of doing this series has been hearing from Washington residents who have gotten guns to protect themselves after reading my series. I hope that they never have to use their firearms, but if the worst happens, I am glad to know that they have a better chance at defending themselves in such a dangerous city.

While I feel safer at home now that I have a loaded gun at the ready, I feel just as vulnerable as before when I leave my home. A scary incident that happened just as I was finishing up this book reminded me how important it is for Second Amendment advocates never to give up until the District allows residents to "bear" as well as "keep" their arms.

It also reminded me that we should never allow the gun-grabbing politicians to make American citizens in the rest of the country as vulnerable to criminals as the ridiculous gun control laws in Washington, D.C., make us.

A strange man at my apartment building, who turned out to be a non-uniformed mover who was working for a neighbor, took violent offense when I closed the propped-open front security door of the apartment building. I stood in the lobby of my building, where I am not allowed to carry my gun, and was terrified as he violently banged on the glass door, screaming, "What the f--- you doing? You f---ing bitch open the door. I'm going to get you, you f---ing bitch."

No one else was around, and I was scared that if I left the lobby, someone would let him in and he'd carry out his threats. I called 911. I waited exactly fifteen minutes, but he had not stopped screaming and trying to get in the building. I called 911 again. The police finally showed up twenty minutes after the incident started. They took a police report and told the man to stay away from me and the building.

A few hours later, I had to leave to go to the photo shoot at the NRA range for the cover of this book. I was transporting my gun legally, which meant it was unloaded. I walked out of my building to find the man still there, staring at me. I held the lockbox in front of me, in the hopes he would even consider that I had some protection, which I did not. It seemed the police warning was enough to keep him away from me.

The incident reinforced my belief that there is no reason that any of us should be more vulnerable to potential thugs outside our homes than inside. We should not live in fear. So I'm staying in D.C. to stand up for the rights of everyone to keep arms without going through an arduous registration process as well as the right to bear arms.

And I will fight for anyone across the nation who is facing gun-grabbing politicians who restrict the rights of the law abiding in a futile effort to stop the criminals.

God gave us the right to defend ourselves—whether from dangerous citizens or a tyrannical government. Our Founding Fathers said those rights cannot be infringed.

I generally don't call myself "pro-gun." I chose to describe myself as "pro-Second Amendment."

A gun is just a tool. The fight is for freedom.

APPENDIX A

Secret Justice Department Memo on Obama's Gun Control Agenda from January 4, 2013

This secret document from the Justice Department was unearthed by the National Rifle Association's Institute for Legislative Action. In this memo, the deputy director of the National Institute for Justice analyzed Obama's gun control agenda before its public rollout and advised that none of it could be effective in reducing crime without implementing much more radical gun control provisions, including a national gun registry and confiscation by law enforcement.

Summary of Select Firearm Violence Prevention Strategies

Greg Ridgeway, Ph.D.
Deputy Director
National Institute of Justice

January 4, 2013

On average there are about 11,000 firearm homicides every year. While there are deaths resulting from accidental discharges and suicides, this document will focus on intentional firearm homicides. Fatalities from mass shootings (those with 4 or more victims in a particular place and time) account on average for 35 fatalities per year. Policies that address the larger firearm homicide issue will have a far greater impact even if they do not address the particular issues of mass shootings.

This document provides a cursory summary of select initiatives to reduce firearm violence and an assessment of the evidence for the initiative.

Gun buybacks
Twitter summary: Buybacks are ineffective unless massive and coupled with a ban

Goal: Reduce access to firearms by incentivizing owners to dispose of their unwanted guns rather than transfer them to a more risky possessor

Evidence: Gun buybacks are ineffective as generally implemented. 1. The buybacks are too small to have an impact. 2. The guns turned in are at low risk of ever being used in a crime. 3. Replacement guns are easily acquired. Unless these three points are overcome, a gun buyback cannot be effective.

The 1997 Australia gun buyback and its associated regulations is an exception to this. 1. It was large, buying back 20% of the firearm stock. 2. It targeted semi-automatic weapons. 3. It coupled the buyback with a ban on certain weapons and a nationwide registration and licensing program. There is strong evidence that it reduced mass killings (before the initiative massacres occurred on average once per year and none have occurred in the 15 years since).

The Australia buyback appears to have had no effect on crime otherwise. One study (Leigh & Neill 2010) has proven confusing in that its abstract suggests that Australia's gun buyback reduced firearm homicide rates by 80%, but the body of the report finds no effect. Others (Reuter & Mouzas 2003) have used the same data and also found no effect on crime although they also noted that mass shootings appear to have disappeared in Australia. A third study (Chapman et al 2006) using Australian data from 1979 to 2003 shows that the firearm homicide rate was already declining prior to the firearm reforms and that there is no evidence that the new legislation accelerated the declines. This remains true when data through 2007 are added to the analysis (conducted by G. Ridgeway on 1/3/2013 at NIJ).

Large capacity magazines restrictions

Twitter summary: Great potential to reduce lethality; requires a massive reduction in supply

Goal: Reduce the lethality of guns by reducing the number of rounds that can be quickly fired.

Program: Restrictions on the manufacture, sale, transfer, and possession of large capacity magazines (usually defined as holding more than 10 rounds).

Evidence: Mass shootings predominantly involve the use of large capacity magazines. The most lethal ones all involve large capacity magazines. In addition large capacity magazines were used in nearly 25% of all crimes in 1993 just prior to the ban. There is reason to believe that reducing the availability of large capacity magazines could have an effect on the total number of homicides.

In five cities studied closely found no change in the criminal use of large capacity magazines during the ten year ban. However, a Washington Post analysis for Virginia continued the analysis where the research team left off. The data indicate that the percentage of crime guns using large capacity magazines declined from 18% in 1999 (when magazine imports were highest) to its lowest level in 2004 (10% of crime guns had large capacity magazines). The percentage doubled between 2004, when the ban expired, and 2010.

The 1994 ban on large capacity magazines had limited effectiveness because 1) Large capacity clips are a durable good 2) There were an estimated 25 million guns with large capacity magazines in 1995 3) The 1994 law exempted magazines manufactured before 1994 so that the importation of large capacity magazines manufactured overseas before 1994 continued through the ban 4) while the price of the clips increased dramatically (80% during the ban) they were not unaffordable. A 2004 study of the 1994 law found: "because the ban has not yet reduced the use of [large capacity magazines] in crime, we cannot clearly credit the ban with any of the nation's recent drop in gun violence." The 1994 ban essentially did little to affect the supply of large capacity magazines.

In order to have an impact, large capacity magazine regulation needs to sharply curtail their availability to include restrictions on importation, manufacture, sale, and possession. An exemption for previously owned magazines would nearly eliminate any impact. The program would need to be coupled with an extensive buyback of existing large capacity magazines. With an exemption the impact of the restrictions would only be felt when the magazines degrade or when they no longer are compatible with guns in circulation. This would take decades to realize.

Ammunition logs

Twitter summary: Increases opportunities to detect illegal firearm possessors

Goal: 1) Reduce flow of ammunition to the illicit market and 2) develop leads for illegal weapons.

Program: Laws that prohibit certain individuals from owning firearms also pertain to ammunition (18 USC 922g&n). Whereas direct retail sales of firearms to criminals are regularly disrupted by instant background checks, sales of ammunition are essentially unchecked. Ammunition purchase logs are a means of checking for illegal purchases and for developing intelligence on illegal firearms.

Alternatively, several states do not record purchases, but rather require the purchaser to show a permit to purchase ammunition and only of the same caliber or gauge as their firearm. While purchasing a firearm is a one-time action, repeated purchases of ammunition create more complications for prohibited firearm possessors.

Evidence: A study used criminal background checks conducted on individuals purchasing ammunition in Los Angeles in April and May 2004. 2.6% of transactions involved prohibited purchasers. They purchased 5,000 rounds of ammunition per month during this period. Rather than institute instant checks on ammunition purchases, local police began regularly checking the logs for illegal purchases, using it as an intelligence tool to find not only ammunition but also the illegally possessed weapons. Sacramento instituted a similar program and identified 13 illegal purchasers per month in the first year, recovering an average of 7 illegal firearms per month.

There is evidence that the program can be used to identify prohibited purchasers and can aid in the recovery of illegal firearms. The volume of recoveries is not of a scale likely to impact the illegal firearm trade, but could disrupt some criminal activity.

In 2009 California passed AB 962 that would make the ammunition logs statewide. It has since been held up in court due primarily to the use of the phrase "handgun ammunition," which is not a well-defined phrase.

Universal background checks

Twitter summary: Effectiveness depends on the ability to reduce straw purchasing, requiring gun registration and an easy gun transfer process

To understand the value of background checks it is essential to understand the source of crime guns. Several sporadic attempts have been made to learn how criminals acquire guns. For example, a 2000 study by the ATF found the following distribution of sources

Source	Percentage
Straw purchase	47%
Stolen	26%
Store	14%
Residence	10%
Common carrier	2%
Unregulated private seller	20%
Gun shows/flea markets	13%
Retail diversion	8%

Note: Percentages do not add up to 100% since some sources fall into multiple categories (e.g. unregulated seller at a flea market)

These figures indicate informal transfers dominate the crime gun market. A *perfect* universal background check system can address the gun shows and might deter many unregulated private sellers. However, this does not address the largest sources (straw purchasers and theft), which would most likely become larger if background checks at gun shows and private sellers were addressed. The secondary market *is* the primary source of crime guns. Ludwig and Cook (2000) compared states that introduced Brady checks to those states that already had background checks and found no effect of the new background checks. They hypothesized that the background checks simply shifted to the secondary market those offenders who normally purchased in the primary market.

Supply sources can vary in different parts of the country. An NIJ funded study of the Los Angeles illicit gun market noted: "Results showed that many crime guns were first purchased at local—that is, in county—licensed dealers, rather than from out of state. That is, contrary to the conventional wisdom that crime guns were being trafficked across state borders from places with less stringent regulations, such as Arizona and Nevada, we found that a majority of the guns used in crimes were purchased in Los Angeles County." Thus, gun markets can be highly local.

Understanding gun sources requires a sustained and localized surveillance program. For example, the program could interview new arrestees at intake about how they acquired their gun, cost, and general gun availability. This could be conducted in conjunction with BJA's plans to target local violence prevention programs in 20 cities. This is similar to the ADAM program for monitoring drug markets and could, in fact, complement any restart of ADAM. In the coming years such data could become available through BJS efforts; BJS will include a series of questions in its 2013/2014 national inmate survey.

Target straw purchasers

Straw purchasers are the primary source of crime guns. Importantly, straw purchasers have no record of a prohibiting offense. As a result, they are quite different from those who actually commit crimes. Consistent with criminological theory, because the person conducting the straw purchase does not have a criminal history forbidding him or her from making legal purchases, this population could potentially be deterred from initiating this illegal activity.

Because straw purchasers are the largest source for the illicit market and these purchasers likely can be deterred, effort should be focused here. There is little evidence on what works. The ATF and NSSF sponsored the "Don't Lie for the Other Guy" public awareness campaign starting in 2000 but there are no evaluation reports of its effectiveness.

A Los Angeles program to target straw purchasers sent new gun buyers a letter, signed by prominent law enforcement officials, indicating that law enforcement had a record of their gun purchase and that the gun buyer should properly record future transfers of the gun. The letters arrived during buyers' 10-day waiting periods, before they could legally return to the store to collect their new gun. An NIJ-funded study found that the letter could modify gun owner behaviors. The study found that the rate at which guns are reported stolen for those who received the letter is more than twice the rate for those who did not receive the letter. While this does not show an effect on crime, it does show that a simple letter to those at risk of diverting guns to the illicit market can modify their behavior.

Require all gun transfers to occur at an FFL

Some states, such as California, require all transfers of guns to be properly documented (since 1923). This usually requires the involvement of a federally licensed dealer in the transaction. Despite this, straw purchasing continues largely unabated. Wachtel (1998) describes some straw purchasing of crime guns for Los Angeles between 1988 and 1995. There are disincentives to following the law in California ($35 and a waiting period). Such a process can discourage a normally law-abiding citizen to spend the time and money to properly transfer his or her firearm to another. To be effective, requiring all transfers to occur at an FFL needs to be coupled with all the necessary incentives (or at least no disincentives) for unlicensed sellers to follow the law. Sanctions and threats of penalties are insufficient.

Gun shows

Gun shows do provide firearms to the illicit market, but the problem is not uniquely about gun shows but rather secondary transfers of unregulated private sellers. Gun shows simply convene numerous private sellers along with FFLs. Gun shows in states requiring all transfers to be documented have fewer illegal gun sales according to Wintemute et al 2007.

Gun registration and continuous checks for possession eligibility

Universal checks are insufficient for ensuring that firearm owners remain eligible. Convictions, mental health issues, and restraining orders can develop after the background checks.

Recovering guns from those that become ineligible is likely effective. There is evidence from three studies that policies that check domestic violence perpetrators for firearm possession are effective at reducing intimate partner violence. Vigdor and Mercy (2006) found a 7% reduction in intimate partner homicide in states that allowed guns to be confiscated on site of domestic violence incidents. Zeoli and

Webster (2010) found that state statutes restricting those under restraining orders from accessing firearms are associated with reductions of 20%-25% in total and firearm intimate partner homicide. Bridges et al (2008) found that most domestic violence laws do not effect intimate partner homicide *except* those relating to firearms. All three studies use methods that make alternative explanations unlikely.

The challenge to implementing this more broadly is that most states do not have a registry of firearm ownership. Currently NICS background checks are destroyed within 24 hours. Some states maintain registration of all firearms. Gun registration aims to 1) increase owner responsibility by directly connecting an owner with a gun, 2) improve law enforcement's ability to retrieve guns from owners prohibited from possessing firearms.

Gun registration also allows for the monitoring of multiple gun purchases in a short period of time.

Assault weapon ban

Twitter summary: Assault weapons are not a major contributor to gun crime. The existing stock of assault weapons is large, undercutting the effectiveness of bans with exemptions

Goal: Limit access to assault weapons.

Program: Ban the manufacture, sale, transfer, or possession of assault weapons.

Evidence: Guns are durable goods. The 1994 law exempted weapons manufactured before 1994. The exemption of pre-1994 models ensures that a large stock, estimated at 1.5 million, of existing weapons would persist. Prior to the 1994 ban, assault weapons were used in 2-8% of crimes. Therefore a complete elimination of assault weapons would not have a large impact on gun homicides.

A National Academy study of firearms and violence concluded that the weaknesses of the ban and the scientific literature suggest that the assault weapon ban did not have an effect on firearm homicides.

There is some evidence that the assault weapons bans can affect the availability of assault weapons. A 2004 study found that "Following implementation of the ban, the share of gun crimes involving [assault weapons] declined by 17% to 72% across the localities examined for this study (Baltimore, Miami, Milwaukee, Boston, St. Louis, and Anchorage)... This is consistent with patterns found in national data on guns recovered by police and reported to ATF." Weil and Knox (1997) found a sharp reduction in the number of assault weapons recovered by Baltimore police in the six months following Maryland's ban on assault weapons. The federal ban came into effect a few months after Maryland's ban, but Maryland's ban had no provision grandfathering in already owned assault weapons.

Since assault weapons are not a major contributor to US gun homicide and the existing stock of guns is large, an assault weapon ban is unlikely to have an impact on gun violence. If coupled with a gun buyback and no exemptions then it could be effective. The 1997 Australian gun buyback was massive in scale and, while it appears to have had no effect on gun homicide, Australia has had no mass shootings since the ban was put in place.

Smart guns

Twitter summary: Most appropriate for making guns child safe or preventing police officers from being assaulted with their own firearm. Unlikely to affect gun crime

Goal: Prevent gun use by unauthorized users, particular to prevent diversion of legally acquired firearms to the illicit market.

Program: Between 1994 and 2004, the National Institute of Justice conducted a research effort to develop a technology that would preclude anyone but the owner of a gun from using it. If a gun were stolen with this technology installed, it would become inoperable. The focus of this effort was to preclude a law enforcement officer's gun from being used if it were wrested from them during an assault. This technology was commonly referred to as 'smart' gun technology because it enabled the gun to 'recognize' its owner.

In its 2005 assessment of this effort "Technological Options for User-Authorized Handguns: A Technology-Readiness Assessment" the National Academy of Engineering estimated that it would cost an additional $30 million and take 5 to 10 additional years to bring a 'smart' gun to market. The most likely approach to achieving this capability would be through use of radio frequency identification (RFID) technology.

Evidence: The development of the technology has focused on making the guns child-proof or providing law enforcement officers with a firearm that could not be used against them. The realization of this technology would not prevent such shootings perpetrated by the owners of the guns involved. In addition this would not eliminate the illicit market, but rather alter it. There would remain an illicit market for guns that did not have this technology installed or for smart guns in which the technology had been neutralized.

APPENDIX B

D.C. Police Training on Arrests for Empty Cases and Shells

Empty shell casings are considered ammunition in Washington, D.C., so they are illegal to possess unless you are a resident and have a gun registration certificate. The empty brass or plastic has to be transported like live ammunition, in the trunk. This directive was sent out to the D.C. police force in July 2012 to train them to look for empty casings when pulling over drivers. Kelly O'Meara, one of police chief Cathy Lanier's chief advisors, sent me this document to demonstrate that the cops are instructed not to arrest legal gun owners—who live in D.C.—caught with casings in the car. What is shocking and frightening about this guidance is what is missing from it. The police are still under orders to arrest tourists or other legal gun owners from out of state who wouldn't think to remove empty brass from their cars or pockets.

July 1, 6, 11, 16, 21, 26, 31, 2012

Firearms Transportation Laws

You have stopped an SUV with District plates for a traffic violation. While you are obtaining the driver's information, you notice a fired .45 ACP cartridge case in the cup holder. You immediately ask the person if they have any weapons in the car and the driver tells you that they have a pistol in the rear space of the SUV and the driver gives you permission to retrieve it. In the rear cargo area of the SUV, you locate a gym bag. The bag contains a box of 9 mm ammunition and a hard plastic box, which is secured with a lock. The box contains a 9 mm pistol and two empty magazines for the pistol. The driver provides you an exact copy of the District of Columbia registration certificate for the pistol.

How should you address the issues related to the firearms?

Under District and federal law, if someone is transporting a firearm in a vehicle that does not have a compartment separate from the driver's compartment, the unloaded firearm or ammunition shall be contained in a locked container other than the glove compartment or console. If the vehicle does have a separate compartment, like a trunk, then, the firearm shall be unloaded, and neither the firearm nor any ammunition being transported shall be readily accessible or directly accessible from the passenger compartment of the transporting vehicle. When transporting a firearm, District residents are required to carry either the actual District of Columbia registration certificate (PD Form 219) or an exact photocopy at all times.

In this particular circumstance, the driver has an exact photocopy of the District of Columbia registration certificate, and he also has the pistol and the box of ammunition stored properly inside his vehicle. The only issue is the single .45 ACP cartridge case in the cup holder. While the driver is lawfully in possession of the cartridge case, he is not transporting in accordance with the law. In order to comply with the law, the cartridge case should be stored so it is not accessible from the passenger compartment and the driver is, in fact, violating the law and could be placed under arrest for this action.

Members of the department should generally exercise discretion in making arrests under this scenario or other similar occurrences. In this particular set of circumstances, you should not make an arrest. Rather, you should explain to the driver that the cartridge casing is considered ammunition under DC law and should be transported so it is not accessible from the passenger compartment, and have the driver move it to the rear cargo area. Be sure you also address the traffic violation which was the basis of your stop in accordance with departmental policy.

DRCT July 2012
Firearms Transportation Laws

References:
DC Code §7-2501.01.
DC Code § 7-2506.01.
DC Code § 22-4504.02.
Bill 19-748; Firearms Emergency Amendment Act of 2012, May 11, 2012.
GO-SPT-303.01; Traffic Enforcement, April 30, 1992.
GO-SPT-303.02; Notice of Infraction Procedures, December 29, 1979.
TT 05-071-12; Legislation Signed by Mayor Vincent Gray on May 11, 2012, May 11, 2012.

APPENDIX C

My Gun Registration Certificate

It took me four months, $435 in fees, four work days, and endless frustration to get this document, which only allows me to have a gun in my home. I have to renew it every four years.

APPENDIX D

Senator Dianne Feinstein's Real "Assault Weapons" Ban Plan

Senator Dianne Feinstein released a summary of her new "assault weapons" ban legislation immediately following the Newtown tragedy in December 2012. It would have required anyone who owned one of the guns which she outlawed to register it with the federal government. That sparked strong recoil, so she released a new bill in January 2013 that grandfathered in existing firearms and did not require a national gun registry. Feinstein tried to hide the original version by taking it off her website, but the National Rifle Association's Institute for Legislative Action kept a copy and is allowing me to share it.

Summary of 2013 Feinstein Assault Weapons Legislation

Bans the sale, transfer, importation, or manufacturing of:

- 120 specifically-named firearms

- Certain other semiautomatic rifles, handguns, shotguns that can accept a **detachable magazine** and have **one military characteristic**

- Semiautomatic rifles and handguns with a **fixed magazine** that can accept **more than 10 rounds**

Strengthens the 1994 *Assault Weapons Ban* and various state bans by:

- Moving from a 2-characteristic test to a **1-characteristic** test

- Eliminating the easy-to-remove bayonet mounts and flash suppressors from the characteristics test

- Banning firearms with "**thumbhole stocks**" and "**bullet buttons**" to address attempts to "work around" prior bans

Bans large-capacity ammunition feeding devices capable of accepting more than 10 rounds.

Protects legitimate hunters and the rights of existing gun owners by:

- **Grandfathering** weapons legally possessed on the date of enactment

- **Exempting** over 900 specifically-named weapons used for hunting or sporting purposes and

- **Exempting** antique, manually-operated, and permanently disabled weapons

Requires that grandfathered weapons be **registered** under the **National Firearms Act**, to include:

- o **Background check** of owner and any transferee;

- o **Type and serial number** of the firearm;

- o **Positive identification**, including photograph and fingerprint;

- o Certification from **local law enforcement** of identity and that possession would not violate State or local law; and

- o Dedicated funding for ATF to **implement registration**

APPENDIX E

Increase in Crime in the District of Columbia, 2011–2012

The Washington Metropolitan Police Department has a "crime mapping" database in which the public is able to see crime numbers in real time. This report shows a dramatic rise in crime in D.C. in 2012 compared to the previous year. Pay close attention to increase in firearms-related crimes in the jurisdiction that has the strictest gun control laws in the country.

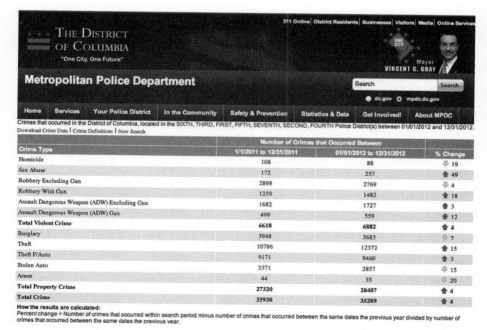

Crimes that occurred in the District of Columbia, located in the SIXTH, THIRD, FIRST, FIFTH, SEVENTH, SECOND, FOURTH Police District(s) between 01/01/2012 and 12/31/2012.
Download Crime Data | Crime Definitions | New Search

Crime Type	Number of Crimes that Occurred Between		% Change
	1/1/2011 to 12/31/2011	01/01/2012 to 12/31/2012	
Homicide	108	88	⬇ 19
Sex Abuse	172	257	⬆ 49
Robbery Excluding Gun	2898	2769	⬇ 4
Robbery With Gun	1259	1482	⬆ 18
Assault Dangerous Weapon (ADW) Excluding Gun	1682	1727	⬆ 3
Assault Dangerous Weapon (ADW) Gun	499	559	⬆ 12
Total Violent Crime	**6618**	**6882**	⬆ 4
Burglary	3948	3683	⬇ 7
Theft	10786	12372	⬆ 15
Theft F/Auto	9171	9460	⬆ 3
Stolen Auto	3371	2857	⬇ 15
Arson	44	35	⬇ 20
Total Property Crime	**27320**	**28407**	⬆ 4
Total Crime	**33938**	**35289**	⬆ 4

How the results are calculated:
Percent change = Number of crimes that occurred within search period minus number of crimes that occurred between the same dates the previous year divided by number of crimes that occurred between the same dates the previous year.

APPENDIX F

States Ranked by the Number of Mental Health Records per Capita They Report to NICS

The National Instant Criminal Background Check System (NICS) is not catching the mentally ill because states are refusing to put records into the federal database. Instead of letting Obama expand this broken system, the states need to be forced to put in the mental health and felony records. And the Obama administration has to prosecute those caught lying to get an illegal gun. The National Shooting Sports Foundation put together an infographic map and ranking of states listed by the number of mental health records they submitted to NICS.

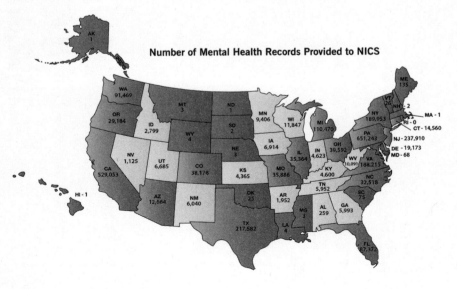

Number of Mental Health Records Provided to NICS

Mental Health Records Submitted by State

	Number of Mental Health Records	Number Rank	Per capita rank
Pennsylvania	651,243	1	1
California	529,053	2	5
New Jersey	237,910	3	2
Texas	217,582	4	9
New York	189,953	5	8
Virginia	188,215	6	3
Michigan	110,470	7	7
Washington	91,469	8	6
Florida	87,372	9	14
Ohio	39,592	10	16
Colorado	38,178	11	10
Missouri	35,886	12	12
Illinois	35,364	13	19
North Carolina	32,518	14	17
Oregon	29,184	15	11
Delaware	19,173	16	4
Connecticut	14,560	17	15
Arizona	12,664	18	23
Wisconsin	11,847	19	22
West Virginia	10,091	20	13
Minnesota	9,406	21	25
Iowa	6,914	22	21
Utah	6,685	23	20
New Mexico	6,040	24	18
Georgia	5,993	25	31
Tennessee	5,952	26	28
Indiana	4,623	27	29
Kentucky	4,600	28	27
Kansas	4,365	29	26
Idaho	2,799	30	24
Arkansas	1,952	31	30
Nevada	1,125	32	32
Alabama	259	33	34
Maine	135	34	33
Mississippi	3	43	46
Nebraska	3	41	42
Montana	3	42	40
New Hampshire	2	45	43
South Dakota	2	44	41
Massachusetts	1	47	49
Hawaii	1	48	48
Alaska	1	49	45
North Dakota	1	46	44
Rhode Island	0	50	50

ACKNOWLEDGMENTS

Several authors warned me against writing an acknowledgments page because I might inadvertently leave out people who are important to me. However, my first book was such a collaborative effort in the text, the production, and my personal support system that I had take this risk to express my gratitude to so many.

So I apologize to the person who was so helpful but whom I've forgotten to name here due to sleep deprivation. I wrote this book in seven weeks while working full time. That is my excuse.

Thank you to all the wonderful folks at Regnery Publishing for your hard work, creativity, and encouragement in the whole process. Marji Ross gave a shot to a first-time author and never seemed to doubt that I would finish. Harry Crocker guided me from day one and took my panicked calls in stride, calmly and authoritatively getting me back on track. The rest of the awesome team: Mark Bloomfield, Amber Colleran, Monica Crump, Anna Dillon, Patricia Jackson, Elizabeth Kantor, Amanda Larsen, Katharine Mancuso, Ryan Pando, Lindsey Reinstrom, Brittany

Roh, Alberto Rojas, Maria Ruhl, Hannah Sternberg, Karen Woodard, and the big boss (and a great friend), Jeff Carneal.

My bosses at the *Washington Times* were so understanding while I was balancing the newspaper and writing this book. Thank you Larry Beasley, John Solomon, Wes Pruden, and Tom McDevitt for being so generous and enthusiastic about this project. My colleagues have kindly put in a great deal of time and effort to make sure people know about this book: John Martin, Tom Culligan, Howard Bomstein, Brian Baumann, Joe Szadkowski, and Ian Bishop.

This book only exists because Brett Decker hired me at the *Washington Times* and then recommended that Regnery give me a shot. Richard Diamond wisely edited every word and theme of the original series and also taught me to shoot. Few journalists can say that about an editor.

I am indebted to David Limbaugh—specifically, I owe him 15 percent for negotiating my contract and countless hours at a rate of $300 as, variously, my psychiatrist, manager, and advisor. David is my role model for giving to others with no thought of getting anything in return. Brad Thor, a patriot, has that same spirit of selfless giving.

Thank you to those of you who got daily or hourly calls and emails from me asking for help. Just look at the endnotes to see how often I have called Larry Keane with questions. He always took time to give me a contextual answer on the industry and issues. John Frazer is an encyclopedia of gun laws, legislation, and policy. He generously and patiently shared his knowledge with me. Dave Workman offered to read and edit much of this material and offered valuable suggestions. Andrew Arulanandam, who never seems to sleep, cheerfully helped me with everything from research to time at the NRA range.

To those I interviewed on the record, thank you for your time and sharing your insights and expertise: James Baker, Kris Baumann, James Brinkley, Pete Brownell, Chris Cox, Miles Hall, Dick Heller, Richard

Gardiner, Alan Gottlieb, Representative Morgan Griffith, Alan Gura, David Keene, George Kollitides, Mark Malkowski, Representative Mark Meadows, Ted Nugent, Governor Rick Perry, Reince Priebus, Jeff Reh, Senator Tim Scott, Patrick Shomo, Richard Sprague, Michael Stock, Donald Trump, and Scott Wilson.

First Lieutenant Augustine Kim, Sergeant Matt Corrigan, and former Specialist Adam Meckler, thank you for your service to our country and fighting overseas for our freedoms. Bless you for courageously telling your stories publicly to help others avoid the travesties that happened to you.

Thank you to each one of these people for teaching me something, giving me information, or getting their bosses to talk to me for this book: Joe Allbaugh, Chris Amon, Mike Bazinet, Matt Beyon, Kevin Bishop, the Reverend Kenn Blanchard, Lisa Boothe, Drew Brandewie, Mike Campbell, Allison Castle, Mike Collins, Chuck Cunningham, Jim Curcuruto, Wesley Denton, Geoffrey Dickens, Steve Fischer, Jeff Freeman, Ted Gest, Rhona Graff, Jeff Grappone, Antonio Goicochea, Josh Havens, Jessica Jacobs, Elizabeth Karasmeighan, Kirsten Kukowski, Ed Leary, Beth Levine, George Lyon, Tom Marr, Megan Mitchell, Teddy Novin, Sam Nunberg, Kelly O'Meara, Andie Pivarunas, General Colin Powell, Matteo Recanatini, Genevieve Rozansky, Ken Shepherd, Roger Smith, Sean Smith, Sean Spicer, Mike Stock, Erica Suares, Charles Sykes, Gayle Trotter, Michael Turbyfill, Dianne Vrablic, and Larry Weeks.

To all those who made this cool cover photo shoot at the NRA range come to life: Katherine Lambert, Kevin Wright, Michael Johns, Victoria Stiles, Jonathan Larsen, and Nicholas Perrine.

The only reason I finished this book is because I am blessed with the most kindhearted girlfriends. They gave me daily encouragement, care packages, feedback on drafts, prayers, letters, and gracious understanding when I had to miss so many get-togethers. I love you, Lily Arteaga,

Jo Maney, Shannon Bream, S.O.S., Heather Florance, Laura Smith, Rebecca Houston, Laura Wille, Martha Ann Alito, Susanna Quinn (not Champ), and Molly Henneberg.

The Reverend Stuart Kenworthy and my parish family at Christ Church Georgetown provide me with a safe home in Washington.

My family is my rock. Lois, thank you for understanding that I'm never too old to need mothering. Dad, Karen, Barry, and Christopher— I love you so much.

NOTES

CHAPTER 1

1. Author interview of Kelly O'Meara, executive director of Strategic Change, Metropolitan Police Department, May 10, 2013.
2. Author interview of Dick Heller, July 10, 2013.
3. "Table 4: Crime in the United States by Region, Geographic Division, and State, 2010–2011," Federal Bureau of Investigation Uniform Crime Report, http://www.fbi.gov/about-us/cjis/ucr/crime-in-the-u.s/2011/crime-in-the-u.s.-2011/tables/table-4.
4. Metropolitan Police Department Crime Mapping Data for 2012, http://crimemap.dc.gov/Report.aspx.
5. Emily Miller, "Gun Owners Win a Round: Second Amendment Rights Advance in District and Maryland," *Washington Times*, March 6, 2012, http://www.washingtontimes.com/news/2012/mar/6/gun-owners-win-a-round/.
6. CompStat, Chicago Police Department, 2012 Year End, https://portal.chicagopolice.org/portal/page/portal/ClearPath/News/Crime%20Statistics/Crime%20Statistics%20Year%20End/1_pdfsam_compstat_public_2012_yearend_31dec2012.pdf.

CHAPTER 2

1. "Remarks by the President and Governor Romney in Second Presidential Debate," Hofstra University, Hempstead, New York, October 16, 2012, transcript, WhiteHouse.gov, http://www.whitehouse.gov/the-press-office/2012/10/17remarks-president-and-governor-romney-second-presidential-debate.

2. 1996 Independent Voters of Illinois-Independent Precinct Organization questionnaire to candidates, available on Politico's website: http://www.politico.com/static/PPM41_obamaquestionaire2.html.

3. Independent Voters of Illinois-Independent Precinct Organization 2004 US Senate Candidate Instructions, available here: Lynn Sweet, "Obama's IVI-IPO Questionnaire May Be Getting Closer Scrutiny. Read Document Here," *Chicago Sun-Times*, December 11, 2007, http://blogs.suntimes.com/sweet/2007/12/sweet_column_obamas_2003_iviip.html.

4. Ibid.

5. Ibid.

6. U.S. Senate Roll Call Votes 109th Congress—1st Session, vote summary on the Kennedy Amdt. No. 1615 to S. 397, July 29, 2005, United States Senate website, http://www.senate.gov/legislative/LIS/roll_call_lists/roll_call_vote_cfm.cfm?congress=109&session=1&vote=00217.

7. "Barack Obama's Small Town Guns and Religion Comments," YouTube video, from a speech given by Barack Obama on April 6, 2008, posted by "potus08blog," April 11, 2008, http://www.youtube.com/watch?v=DTxXUufI3jA.

8. "'Bittergate' Sparks New Look at Candidates and Guns," CNN, April 15, 2008, http://edition.cnn.com/2008/POLITICS/04/15/candidates.guns/.

9. Ibid.

10. "Wayne LaPierre at CPAC 2011 in Florida," NRA website, originally aired September 23, 2011, http://home.nra.org/home/video/wayne-lapierre-at-cpac-2011-in-florida/list/wayne-lapierre.

11. "Reality No Salve for Gun Rights Paranoia," *The Rachel Maddow Show*, MSNBC, September 30, 2011, http://video.msnbc.msn.com/rachel-maddow-show/44738478#44738478.

12. "Wayne's World," *The Daily Show with Jon Stewart* website, September 29, 2011, http://www.thedailyshow.com/watch/thu-september-29-2011/wayne-s-world.

13. *Hardball with Chris Matthews*, MSNBC, September 27, 2011, http://www.nbcnews.com/id/44700395/ns/msnbc-hardball_with_chris_matthews/#.UeWI-hYmQ5Q.

14. Fox News poll conducted by Anderson Robbins Research (D) / Shaw & Company Research (R), March 2013, http://www.foxnews.com/politics/ interactive/2013/03/22/fox-news-poll-support-for-gun-control-measures/.

15. Gallup, Jeffrey M. Jones, "Men, Married, Southerners Most Likely to Be Gun Owners," February 1, 2013, http://www.gallup.com/poll/160223/ men-married-southerners-likely-gun-owners.aspx?.

16. "Gun Control: States' Laws and Requirements for Concealed Carry Permits Vary across the Nation," U.S. Government Accountability Office, July 17, 2012, http://www.gao.gov/products/GAO-12-717.

17. Gallup, "Men, Married, Southerners Most Likely to Be Gun Owners."

18. Author interview of Reince Priebus, Republican National Committee chairman, June 12, 2013.

19. "Rick Perry: What to Do on a Day Off," YouTube, posted by "RPerry2012," September 28, 2011, http://youtu.be/riIYx6RJHI8.

20. Author interview of Rick Perry, governor of Texas, February 2012.

21. "Remarks by the President to the People of Mexico," Anthropology Museum, Mexico City, Mexico, WhiteHouse.gov, May 3, 2013, http:// www.whitehouse.gov/the-press-office/2013/05/03/remarks-president-people-mexico.

22. Author interview of Rick Perry, governor of Texas, May 2012.

23. Jason Horowitz, "Over a Barrel? Meet White House Gun Policy Adviser Steve Croley," *Washington Post*, April 11, 2011, http://www.washingtonpost. com/lifestyle/style/over-a-barrel-meet-white-house-gun-policy-adviser-steve-croley/2011/04/04/AFt9EKND_story_2.html.

24. "Remarks by the President and Governor Romney in Second Presidential Debate," WhiteHouse.gov.

25. "National Firearms Act (NFA)," Bureau of Alcohol, Tobacco, Firearms and Explosives, http://www.atf.gov/firearms/nfa/index.html.

26. Author interview of confidential sources.

27. Michael R. Bloomberg, "Statements of Mayors Against Illegal Guns Co-Chairs on Newtown, Connecticut Shooting," press release, Mayors Against Illegal Guns, December 14, 2012, http://www.mayorsagainstillegalguns. org/html/media-center/pr013-12.shtml.

28.   "The Ed Show for Friday, December 14th, 2012," MSNBC News, December 17, 2012, transcript, http://www.nbcnews.com/id/50228638/ns/msnbc-the_ed_show/t/ed-show-friday-december-th/#.UdxQ6D5UNz0.

29.   "Press Briefing by Press Secretary Jay Carney, 12/14/2012," James S. Brady Press Briefing Room, WhiteHouse.gov, December 14, 2012, http://www.whitehouse.gov/the-press-office/2012/12/14/press-briefing-press-secretary-jay-carney-12142012.

30.   *Face the Nation*, CBS News, December 16, 2012, transcript, http://www.cbsnews.com/8301-3460_162-57559465/face-the-nation-transcripts-december-16-2012-newtown-tragedy/.

31.   "December 16: Dannel Mallow, Michael Bloomberg, Dianne Feinstein, Bill Bennett, David Brooks, Randi Weingarten, Tom Ridge, Michael Eric Dyson, Pete Williams," *Meet the Press*, NBC News, December 16, 2012, transcript, http://www.nbcnews.com/id/50214941/ns/meet_the_press-transcripts/t/december-dannel-malloy-michael-bloomberg-dianne-feinstein-bill-bennett-david-brooks-randi-weingarten-tom-ridge-michael-eric-dyson-pete-williams/#.UdxRYz5UNz0.

32.   "Remarks by the President at Sandy Hook Interfaith Prayer Vigil," Newtown High School, Newtown, Connecticut, WhiteHouse.gov, December 16, 2012, http://www.whitehouse.gov/the-press-office/2012/12/16/remarks-president-sandy-hook-interfaith-prayer-vigil.

33.   Jerome P. Bjelopera et al., "Public Mass Shootings in the United States: Selected Implications for Federal Public Health and Safety Policy," Congressional Research Service, March 18, 2013, http://www.fas.org/sgp/crs/misc/R43004.pdf.

34.   "Table 20: Murder by State, Types of Weapons, 2011" in "Crime in the United States 2011," Federal Bureau of Investigation Uniform Crime Report, http://www.fbi.gov/about-us/cjis/ucr/crime-in-the-u.s/2011/crime-in-the-u.s.-2011/tables/table-20. Please note the report does not include Florida. Illinois numbers are only for Chicago, not the rest of the state.

35.   Donna L. Hoyert and Jiaquan Xu, "Deaths: Preliminary Data for 2011," in "National Vital Statistics Reports," table 2, Centers For Disease Control and Prevention, October 10, 2012, http://www.cdc.gov/nchs/data/nvsr/nvsr61/nvsr61_06.pdf.

36. Bjelopera et al., "Public Mass Shootings in the United States."

37. "Remarks by the President in a Press Conference," James S. Brady Press Briefing Room, WhiteHouse.gov, December 19, 2012, http://www.white-house.gov/the-press-office/2012/12/19/remarks-president-press-conference.

38. Author interview of David Keene, NRA President, January 8, 2012.

39. "Now Is the Time: The President's Plan to Protect Our Children and Our Communities by Reducing Gun Violence," WhiteHouse.gov, January 16, 2013, http://www.whitehouse.gov/sites/default/files/docs/wh_now_is_the_time_full.pdf.

40. "Remarks by the President and the Vice President on Gun Violence," South Court Auditorium, WhiteHouse.gov, January 16, 2013, http://www.whitehouse.gov/the-press-office/2013/01/16/remarks-president-and-vice-president-gun-violence.

41. "Now Is the Time: Gun Violence Reduction Executive Actions," White-House.gov, January 16, 2013, http://www.whitehouse.gov/sites/default/files/docs/wh_now_is_the_time_actions.pdf.

42. "Remarks by the President and the Vice President on Gun Violence," WhiteHouse.gov.

CHAPTER 4

1. "Remarks by the President on Reducing Gun Violence—Denver, Colorado," Denver Police Academy, Denver, Colorado, WhiteHouse.gov, April 3, 2013, http://www.whitehouse.gov the-press-office/2013/04/03/remarks-president-reducing-gun-violence-denver-colorado.

2. "Assault Weapons and Accessories in America," Violence Policy Center, 1988, http://www.vpc.org/studies/awacont.htm; "2012 Gun Violence Prevention Grantees," The Joyce Foundation, http://www.joycefdn.org/programs/gun-violence-prevention/gun-violence-prevention-grantees/.

3. "Q: How Can an Individual Legally Acquire NFA Firearms?" Bureau of Alcohol, Tobacco, Firearms and Explosives, http://www.atf.gov/firearms/faq/national-firearms-act-firearms.html#legally-acquire-nfa.

4. "Firearms Commerce in the United States: Annual Statistical Update," Bureau of Alcohol, Tobacco, Firearms and Explosives, 2013, https://www.

atf.gov/sites/default/files/assets/pdf-files/052013-firearms-commerce-in-the-us-annual-update.pdf.

5. Author interviews of firearms industry, ATF, and retailers.

6. "Michelle Obama: Doesn't Want to Disappoint U.S. Kids," ABC News, February 26, 2013, http://abcnews.go.com/GMA/video/michelle-obama-interview-2013-gma-lady-disappoint-us-18596599; transcript of full interview here, ABC News, February 26, 2013, http://abcnews.go.com/Politics/lady-michelle-obama-sees-movement-improving-child-obesity/story?id=18593148 &page=2#.UdxbVD5UNz0.

7. "Remarks by the President at a DCCC Event—San Francisco, CA," Private Residence, San Francisco, California, WhiteHouse.gov, April 4, 2013, http://www.whitehouse.gov/the-press-office/2013/04/04/remarks-president-dccc-event-san-francisco-ca.

8. Author interview of Lawrence Keane, senior vice president and general counsel, National Shooting Sports Foundation, Inc., June 26, 2013.

9. "School Shooter Adam Lanza Used Military-Style Bushmaster Rifle," *Huffington Post*, December 16, 2012, http://www.huffingtonpost.com/2012/12/16/school-shooter-adam-lanza_n_2312818.html; Jacques Billeaud, "Mark Kelly's Purchase of Rifle Draws Criticism," Associated Press, March 12, 2013, http://bigstory.ap.org/article/mark-kellys-purchase-rifle-draws-criticism.

10. States with "assault weapons" bans: CA, CT, DC, HI (Assault Pistols only), MD, MA, NJ, and NY—from interview with Director of State and Local Affairs, National Rifle Association Chuck Cunningham, May 22, 2013.

11. Firearm Safety Act of 2013, Senate Bill 281, available on the Maryland General Assembly website, http://mgaleg.maryland.gov/2013RS/bills/sb/sb0281E.pdf.

12. Rasmussen Reports poll, December 21, 2012, http://www.rasmussenreports.com/public_content/politics/general_politics/december_2012/55_favor_assault_weapons_ban_but_62_oppose_complete_gun_ban.

13. Gallup poll, October 26, 2011, http://www.gallup.com/poll/150341/Record-Low-Favor-Handgun-Ban.aspx.

14. "Americans on Domestic Policy," *New York Times*, May 1, 2013, http://www.nytimes.com/interactive/2013/05/01/us/domestic-poll-graphic.html.

15. *Washington Post*-ABC Poll, January 2013, available here, "Q: Would You
     Support or Oppose a Law Requiring a Nationwide Ban on the Sale of
     Assault Weapons?" *Washington Post*, April 12, 2013, http://www.
     washingtonpost.com/politics/polling/would-nationwide-requiring-
     support/2013/04/12/d6e2fec4-5e95-11e2-8acb-ab5cb77e95c8_page.html.

16. "Fox News Poll: During a Manhunt, 69 Percent of Voters Want a Gun,"
     Fox News, April 23, 2013, http://www.foxnews.com/politics/interactive/
     2013/04/23/fox-news-poll-during-manhunt-6-percent-voters-want-gun/.

17. See Appendix D, "Summary of 2013 Feinstein Assault Weapons Legisla-
     tion."

18. "Senators Feinstein and Blumenthal React to NRA," C-SPAN Video
     Library, December 21, 2012, http://www.c-spanvideo.org/program/
     310086-1.

19. SA 711, amendment to S. 649, Assault Weapons Ban of 2013, sponsored
     by Senator Dianne Feinstein (D-CA), available on the Library of Congress
     website, http://thomas.loc.gov/cgi-bin/bdquery/z?d113:sp711:.

20. Federal News Service transcript, "Press Conference with Senator Dick
     Durbin (D-IL); Senator Dianne Feinstein (D-CA); Senator Chuck Schumer
     (D-NY); et al.," Subject: Introduction of Assault Weapons Ban 2013 Leg-
     islation; Location: G-50 Dirksen Senate Office Building, Washington, D.C.,
     January 24, 2013.

21. Ibid.

22. "Remarks by the President on Preventing Gun Violence in Minneapolis,
     MN," Special Operations Center, Minneapolis Police Department, Min-
     neapolis, Minnesota, WhiteHouse.gov, February 4, 2013, http://www.
     whitehouse.gov/the-press-office/2013/02/04/remarks-president-preventing-
     gun-violence-minneapolis-mn.

23. "Law Enforcement Officers Killed and Assaulted 2011," U.S. Department
     of Justice—Federal Bureau of Investigation, November 19, 2012, http://
     www.fbi.gov/about-us/cjis/ucr/leoka/2011.

24. "Gun Policy & Law Enforcement: Survey Results," PoliceOne.com, survey
     conducted between March 4 and March 13, 2013, http://ddq74coujkv1i.
     cloudfront.net/p1_gunsurveysummary_2013.pdf.

25. "Jared Lee Loughner Pleads Guilty to Federal Charges in Tucson Shooting: Loughner Faces Life in Prison without Possibility of Release," Office of the United States Attorney, John S. Leonardo, District of Arizona, August 7, 2012, http://www.justice.gov/usao/az/press_releases/2012/AUG/PR_08072012_Loughner.html.

26. Documents pertaining to Aurora Police Department Case 12-28-181 are available on 9news.com, http://www.9news.com/assetpool/documents/130404065204_12CR1522%20Search%20Warrant%202000%20Hyundai%20Tiburon%202%20door.pdf.

27. Greg McCune, "Gun Type Used in Sikh Shootings Used in Other Attacks," Reuters, August 7, 2012, http://www.reuters.com/article/2012/08/07/us-usa-wisconsin-shooting-weapon-idUSBRE8760T820120807.

28. "Minneapolis Office Gunman Was Fired Day of Attack," Jefferson City *Star Tribune*, September 29, 2012, http://www.newstribune.com/news/2012/sep/29/minneapolis-office-gunman-was-fired-day-attack/.

29. "Update: State Police Identify Weapons Used in Sandy Hook Investigation; Investigation Continues," State of Connecticut Department of Emergency Services and Public Protection, January 13, 2013, http://www.ct.gov/despp/cwp/view.asp?Q=517284.

30. "Expanded Homicide Data Table 8: Murder Victims by Weapon, 2007–2011," in "Crime in the United States 2011," Federal Bureau of Investigation Uniform Crime Report, http://www.fbi.gov/about-us/cjis/ucr/crime-in-the-u.s/2011/crime-in-the-u.s.-2011/tables/expanded-homicide-data-table-8.

31. Ibid.

32. Federal News Service transcript, "Hearing of the Senate Judiciary Committee," Subject: The Assault Weapons Ban of 2013, Chaired by: Senator Dianne Feinstein (D-CA), 216 Hart Senate Office Building, Washington, D.C., February 27, 2013.

33. Author interview of Brian Weiss, communications director, Senator Dianne Feinstein, February 27, 2013.

34. "First Reports Evaluating the Effectiveness of Strategies for Preventing Violence: Firearm Laws," Centers for Disease Control and Prevention, Mortality and Morbidity Report, October 3, 2013, http://www.cdc.gov/mmwr/preview/mmwrhtml/rr5214a2.htm.

35.   Federal News Service transcript, "Press Conference with Senator Dick
      Durbin (D-IL); Senator Dianne Feinstein (D-CA); Senator Chuck Schumer
      (D-NY); et al.," Subject: Introduction of Assault Weapons Ban 2013 Leg-
      islation; Location: G-50 Dirksen Senate Office Building, Washington, D.C.,
      January 24, 2013.

36.   "Modern Sporting Rifle (MSR), Comprehensive Consumer Reporter 2010:
      Ownership, Usage and Attitudes towards Modern Sporting Rifles,"
      National Shooting Sports Foundation, 2010, http://www.nssf.org/MSR/
      PDF/NSSF_MSR_Report2010.pdf.

37.   Anthony Licata, "The F&S Gun Rights Interviews: Joe Biden, Vice Presi-
      dent of the United States," Field & Stream, February 25, 2013, http://www.
      fieldandstream.com/articles/guns/2013/02/gun-control-joe-biden-interview.

38.   "Testimony of Gayle S. Trotter, Senior Fellow, Independent Women's
      Forum, Partner and Co-Founder, Shafer & Trotter PLC, before the United
      States Senate Committee on the Judiciary 'What Should America Do about
      Gun Violence?'" Washington, D.C., January 30, 2013, prepared testimony
      available on the United States Senate Committee on the Judiciary website,
      http://www.judiciary.senate.gov/pdf/1-30-13TrotterTestimony.pdf.

39.   Federal News Service transcript, "Hearing of the Senate Judiciary Commit-
      tee; Subject: 'What Should America Do about Gun Violence?'; Chaired by:
      Senator Patrick Leahy (D-VT), Witnesses: Captain Mark Kelly, USN (Ret.),
      Americans for Responsible Solutions; Professor David Kopel, Adjunct
      Professor of Advanced Constitutional Law Denver University, Strum Col-
      lege of Law; James Johnson, Chief of Police, Baltimore County Police
      Department, and Chair, National Law Enforcement Partnership to Prevent
      Gun Violence; Gayle Trotter, Attorney and Senior Fellow, Independent
      Women's Forum; Wayne LaPierre, Executive Vice President and Chief
      Executive Officer, National Rifle Association;" Location: 216 Hart Senate
      Office Building, Washington, D.C.; January 30, 2013.

40.   "Crime in Connecticut 2011," Annual Report of the Uniform Crime
      Reporting Program, State of Connecticut Department of Emergency Ser-
      vices and Public Protection, Crimes Analysis Unit (one by rifle), http://www.
      dpsdata.ct.gov/dps/ucr/data/2011/Crime%20In%20Connecticut%20
      COMPLETE%202011.pdf; "Crime in Maryland, 2011 Uniform Crime

Report," Maryland State Police, June 20, 2012, (two by rifle), http://www.goccp.maryland.gov/msac/documents/2011_Crime_In_Maryland.pdf; New York 2011—5 rifle, author interview of Janine Kava, Director of Public Information, New York State Division of Criminal Justice Services, January 9, 2013.

41. U.S. Senate Roll Call Votes 113th Congress—1st Session—Vote number 101 on Feinstein Amendment Number 711, Vote 40–60, United States Senate website, http://www.senate.gov/legislative/LIS/roll_call_lists/roll_call_vote_cfm.cfm?congress=113&session=1&vote=00101.

42. Greg Ridgeway, Deputy Director of the National Institute of Justice, "Summary of Select Firearm Violence Prevention Strategies," U.S. Department of Justice, January 4, 2013. Memo acquired by National Rifle Association Institute for Legislative Action, http://www.nraila.org/media/10883516/nij-gun-policy-memo.pdf. See Appendix A.

CHAPTER 5

1. Author interview of Kelly O'Meara, Executive Director of Strategic Change, Metropolitan Police Department, total firearms registered 2009–2012 in Washington, D.C., May 24, 2013.

2. "Statement of Eligibility," Metropolitan Police Department Gun Control and Firearms Registration, http://mpdc.dc.gov/sites/default/files/dc/sites/mpdc/publication/attachments/Firearms_Statement_of_Eligibility.pdf.

3. "Fact Sheet" about the National Instant Criminal Background Check System, Federal Bureau of Investigation, http://www.fbi.gov/about-us/cjis/nics/general-information/fact-sheet.

CHAPTER 6

1. States with "high-capacity" magazine bans fifteen—CO and NJ; ban, but doesn't apply to certain license holders in these states: CA, CT, DC, HI, MD, and MA; NY (can possess ten-round magazines, but, in general, they may only be loaded with seven rounds). Author interview of Chuck Cunningham, Director of State and Local Affairs, National Rifle Association, May 22, 2013.

2. "Remarks by the President before Meeting with Law Enforcement Officials," Roosevelt Room, WhiteHouse.gov, January 28, 2013, http://www.

whitehouse.gov/the-press-office/2013/01/28/remarks-president-meeting-law-enforcement-officials.

3. Fredric U. Dicker, "Gov Faking Care of Business, Execs Fume," *New York Post*, March 25, 2013, http://www.nypost.com/p/news/local/gov_faking_care_of_business_execs_9uIcEq5lJPk96ayylaRAGL.

4. Christopher S. Koper, with Daniel J. Woods and Jeffrey A. Roth, "An Updated Assessment of the Federal Assault Weapons Ban: Impacts on Gun Markets and Gun Violence, 1994–2003," Jerry Lee Center of Criminology, University of Pennsylvania, June 2004, http://www.feinstein.senate.gov/public/index.cfm/files/serve/?File_id=b531daeb-a954-41f8-a21c-268ccec-cb4c4.

5. Federal News Service transcript, "Remarks by Vice President Joseph Biden and Attorney General Eric Holder;" Subject: Reducing Gun Violence Introduction by: Sheriff Melvin High, Prince George's County, Maryland; Location: South Court Auditorium, Dwight D. Eisenhower Executive Office Building, Washington, D.C.; April 9, 2013.

6. "First Reports Evaluating the Effectiveness of Strategies for Preventing Violence: Firearms Laws; Findings from the Task Force on Community Preventive Services," Centers for Disease Control and Prevention Morbidity and Mortality Weekly Report, October 3, 2003, http://www.cdc.gov/mmwr/preview/mmwrhtml/rr5214a2.htm.

7. Michael Planty and Jennifer L. Truman, "Firearm Violence, 1993–2011," National Crime Victimization Survey, U.S. Department of Justice, Bureau of Justice Statistics, May 7, 2013, http://www.bjs.gov/index.cfm?ty=pbdetail &iid=4616.

8. Federal News Service transcript, "Prepared Remarks of Senate Majority Leader Harry Reid (D-NV) on the Floor of the U.S. Senate; Subject: 'Support of Assault Weapons Ban, Limits on High-Capacity Magazines;'" Location: Senate Chamber, The Capitol, Washington, D.C.; April 17, 2013.

9. "Criminal Victimization in the United States, 2008; Statistical Tables," National Crime Victimization Survey, U. S. Department of Justice, Bureau of Justice Statistics, May 2011, http://www.bjs.gov/content/pub/pdf/cvus0802.pdf.

10. Greg Ridgeway, Deputy Director of the National Institute of Justice, "Summary of Select Firearm Violence Prevention Strategies," U.S. Department

of Justice, January 4, 2013. Memo acquired by National Rifle Association Institute for Legislative Action, http://www.nraila.org/media/10883516/nij-gun-policy-memo.pdf. See Appendix A.

11.   "Remarks by the President and the Vice President on Gun Violence," South Court Auditorium, WhiteHouse.gov, January 16, 2013, http://www.whitehouse.gov/the-press-office/2013/01/16/remarks-president-and-vice-president-gun-violence.

12.   Federal News Service transcript, "Remarks by Vice President Joseph Biden at a Meeting with Law Enforcement and Cabinet Officials;" Subject: The Administration's Response to Newtown; Location: Eisenhower Executive Office Building, Washington, D.C.; December 20, 2012.

13.   Pew Research, "After Newtown, Modest Change in Opinion about Gun Control," December 20, 2012, http://www.people-press.org/2012/12/20/after-newtown-modest-change-in-opinion-about-gun-control/.

14.   Gallup, "Americans Back Obama's Proposals to Address Gun Violence," January 23, 2013, http://www.gallup.com/poll/160085/americans-back-obama-proposals-address-gun-violence.aspx.

15.   Author interviews of Stephen G. Fischer Jr., chief, Multimedia Productions, FBI—CJIS Division, January 29, 2013, and Michael Campbell, deputy chief, ATF Public Affairs Division, January 28, 2013 and June 5, 2013.

16.   "Rumor Control: Ammo Shortages Revisited," National Rifle Association Institute for Legislative Action, May 31, 2013, http://www.nraila.org/news-issues/articles/2013/5/rumor-control-ammo-shortages-revisited!.aspx.

17.   Firearm Owners Protection Act 1986, 18 U.S.C. § 921(d)(3), 922(o), U.S. House of Representatives Office of the Law Revision Counsel website, http://law2.house.gov/download/pls/18C44.txt.

18.   *Piers Morgan Tonight*, CNN, July 23, 2012, http://transcripts.cnn.com/TRANSCRIPTS/1207/23/pmt.01.html.

19.   "Assessing and Reducing the Threat to Law Enforcement Officers from the Criminal Use of Firearms and Ammunition: Report Responding to Section 809 of the Antiterrorism and Effective Death Penalty Act of 1996," U.S. Department of Treasury, Bureau of Alcohol, Tobacco and Firearms, April 1997, page 17.

20. "Gun Policy & Law Enforcement: Survey Results," PoliceOne.com, survey conducted between March 4 and March 13, 2013, http://ddq74coujkv1i. cloudfront.net/p1_gunsurveysummary_2013.pdf.

21. "Growing List of Sheriffs, Associations and Police Chiefs Saying 'No' to Obama Gun Control," Constitutional Sheriffs and Peace Officers Association, May 23, 2013, http://cspoa.org/sheriffs-gun-rights/.

CHAPTER 8

1. "Remarks by the President on Preventing Gun Violence in Minneapolis, MN," Special Operations Center, Minneapolis Police Department, Minneapolis, Minnesota, WhiteHouse.gov, February 4, 2013, http://www. whitehouse.gov/the-press-office/2013/02/04/remarks-president-preventing-gun-violence-minneapolis-mn.

2. Gallup poll, "Americans Back Obama's Proposals to Address Gun Violence," January 23, 2013, http://www.gallup.com/poll/160085/americans-back-obama-proposals-address-gun-violence.aspx?.

3. Author interview of Chris Cox, executive director, National Rifle Association, Institute for Legislative Action, May 30, 2013.

4. Frank Luntz, "Gun Owners Poll," Mayors Against Illegal Guns, July 2012, http://www.mayorsagainstillegalguns.org/downloads/pdf/poll-07-24-2012. pdf.

5. On Message, Inc., "NRA National Member Survey Final," NRA-ILA, January 2013, http://www.nraila.org/media/10850041/113topline.pdf.

6. "Independence USA PAC Expenditures," OpenSecrets.org, http://www. opensecrets.org/pacs/expenditures.php?cycle=2012&cmte=C00532705.

7. Schoen, LLC Polls for Mayors Against Illegal Guns, http://www. demandaction.org/polls.

8. *Fox News Sunday*, Fox News, Chris Wallace, March 31, 2013, http:// www.foxnews.com/on-air/fox-news-sunday-chris-wallace/2013/03/31/ mark-kelly-whether-call-action-gun-control-fading-cardinal-donald-wuerl-new-pope#p//v/2268240676001.

9. "New Poll Finds 94 Percent in Florida Favor Mandatory Background Checks for All Gun Buyers," Mayors Against Illegal Guns, March 5, 2013,

http://libcloud.s3.amazonaws.com/9/f4/9/1392/FL_MAIG_ Release_030513.pdf.

10. "New Poll Finds 100 Percent in New Jersey's 4th Congressional District Favor Mandatory Background Checks for All Gun Buyers," Mayors Against Illegal Guns, March 5, 2013, http://libcloud.s3.amazonaws. com/9/34/e/1434/NJ_4_MAIG_Poll_Release_030513.pdf.

11. Gun Control Act of 1968, text: 18 USC Sec. 922, January 3, 2012, http:// uscode.house.gov/uscode-cgi/fastweb.exe?getdoc+uscview+t17t20+540+ 0++%28gun%20control%20act%201968%29; see also 18 USC § 922– Unlawful Acts, http://www.law.cornell.edu/uscode/text/18/922.

12. "Prohibiting Categories Defined by Statute," National Instant Criminal Background Check System, Federal Bureau of Investigation, http://www. fbi.gov/about-us/cjis/nics/general-information/nics-index.

13. Brady Handgun Violence Prevention Act of 1993, text available on the Library of Congress website, http://thomas.loc.gov/cgi-bin/ bdquery/z?d103:H.R.1025:.

14. "Fact Sheet," National Instant Criminal Background Check System, Federal Bureau of Investigation, http://www.fbi.gov/about-us/cjis/nics/general-information/fact-sheet.

15. "Remarks by the President and the Vice President on Gun Violence," South Court Auditorium, WhiteHouse.gov, January 16, 2013, http://www. whitehouse.gov/the-press-office/2013/01/16/remarks-president-and-vice-president-gun-violence.

16. "Guns in America: National Survey on Private Ownership and Use of Firearms," Office of Justice Programs, National Institute of Justice, May 1997, http://www.nij.gov/pubs-sum/165476.htm.

17. Michael Planty and Jennifer L. Truman, "Firearm Violence, 1993–2011," U.S. Department of Justice, May 2013, http://www.bjs.gov/content/pub/ pdf/fv9311.pdf.

18. Greg Ridgeway, Deputy Director of the National Institute of Justice, "Summary of Select Firearm Violence Prevention Strategies," U.S. Department of Justice, January 4, 2013. Memo acquired by National Rifle Association Institute for Legislative Action, http://www.nraila.org/media/10883516/ nij-gun-policy-memo.pdf. See Appendix A.

19. Author interview of George Kollitides, CEO of Freedom Group, June 6, 2013.

20. Author interview of Chris Cox, Executive Director, National Rifle Association, Institute for Legislative Action, May 30, 2013.

21. Author interview of Bob Templeton, President, National Association of Arms Shows, Inc., June 9, 2013.

22. "Pelosi: 'We Have to Pass the Bill so that You Can Find Out What Is in It,'" YouTube, March 9, 2010, http://www.youtube.com/watch?v=hV-05TLiiLU.

23. S. 374, Protecting Responsible Gun Sellers Act of 2013 (Schumer), http://www.judiciary.senate.gov/legislation/upload/ALB13180.pdf.

24. Federal News Service transcript, "Hearing of the Senate Judiciary Committee. Subject: 'What Should America Do about Gun Violence?'; Chaired by: Senator Patrick Leahy (D-VT); Witnesses: Captain Mark Kelly, USN (Ret.), Americans for Responsible Solutions; Professor David Kopel, Adjunct Professor of Advanced Constitutional Law Denver University, Strum College of Law; James Johnson, Chief of Police, Baltimore County Police Department, and Chair, National Law Enforcement Partnership to Prevent Gun Violence; Gayle Trotter, Attorney and Senior Fellow, Independent Women's Forum; Wayne LaPierre, Executive Vice President and Chief Executive Officer, National Rifle Association;" Location: 216 Hart Senate Office Building, Washington, D.C.; Wednesday, January 30, 2013.

25. Ibid.

26. "How to Become a Federal Firearms Licensee (FFL)," Bureau of Alcohol, Tobacco, Firearms and Explosives, http://www.atf.gov/firearms/how-to/become-an-ffl.html; "Important Notice to Applicants for Federal Firearms License (FFL)," Bureau of Alcohol, Tobacco, Firearms and Explosives, http://www.atf.gov/forms/download/atf-f-5310-12-notice.html.

27. Exhibit 10, "Federal Firearms Licensees Total (1975–2012)" in "Firearms Commerce in the United States; Annual Statistical Update, 2013," United States Department of Justice, Firearms Commerce in the U.S., Bureau of Alcohol, Tobacco, Firearms and Explosives, 2013, https://www.atf.gov/sites/default/files/assets/pdf-files/052013-firearms-commerce-in-the-us-annual-update.pdf.

28.   Greg Ridgeway, Deputy Director of the National Institute of Justice, "Summary of Select Firearm Violence Prevention Strategies," U.S. Department of Justice, January 4, 2013. Memo acquired by National Rifle Association Institute for Legislative Action, http://www.nraila.org/media/10883516/nij-gun-policy-memo.pdf. See Appendix A.

29.   "Gun Policy & Law Enforcement: Survey Results," PoliceOne.com, survey conducted between March 4 and March 13, 2013, http://ddq74coujkv1i.cloudfront.net/p1_gunsurveysummary_2013.pdf.

30.   New York State Sheriffs' Association, Inc., letter to New York Governor Andrew M. Cuomo, January 24, 2013, http://www.nssf.org/share/PDF/NYSSA%20Response%20to%20NY%20SAFE%20Act_021113.pdf.

31.   "Remarks by the President at Organizing for Action Event," Adour Restaurant, Washington, D.C., WhiteHouse.gov, March 13, 2013, http://www.whitehouse.gov/the-press-office/2013/03/13/remarks-president-organizing-action-event; "Remarks by the President on Gun Safety," East Room, WhiteHouse.gov, March 28, 2013, http://www.whitehouse.gov/the-press-office/2013/03/28/remarks-president-gun-safety; "Statement by the President," Rose Garden, WhiteHouse.gov, April 17, 2013, http://www.whitehouse.gov/the-press-office/2013/04/17/statement-president.

32.   "Fatal Gaps: How Missing Records in the Federal Background Check System Put Guns in the Hands of Killers," Mayors Against Illegal Guns, November 2011, http://www.mayorsagainstillegalguns.org/downloads/pdf/maig_mimeo_revb.pdf.

33.   Ibid.

34.   Author interview of Lawrence Keane, senior vice president, assistant secretary and general counsel, National Shooting Sports Foundation, Inc., January 27, 2013.

35.   Ronald J. Frandsen, "Enforcement of the Brady Act, 2010: Federal and State Investigations and Prosecutions of Firearm Applicants Denied by a NICS Check in 2010," Regional Justice Information Service, August 2012, https://www.ncjrs.gov/pdffiles1/bjs/grants/239272.pdf.

36.   Author interview of Jeffrey Reh, general counsel and vice-general manager of Beretta USA, May 3, 2013.

37. Profile No. 38, "Project Exile, U.S. Attorney's Office—Eastern District of Virginia," Office of Juvenile Justice and Delinquency Prevention, http://www.ojjdp.gov/pubs/gun_violence/profile38.html.

38. "Targeting Criminals, Not Gun Owners," National Rifle Association, Institute for Legislative Action, August 17, 2006, http://www.nraila.org/news-issues/articles/2006/targeting-criminals,-not-gun-owners.aspx?s=%22Crime+%26+Criminal+Justice%22&st=&ps=.

39. Project Exile, U.S. Attorney's Office—Eastern District of Virginia, Profile No. 38, http://www.ojjdp.gov/pubs/gun_violence/profile38.html.

40. Author interview of James J. Baker, director, National Rifle Association Federal Affairs Division, June 5, 2013.

41. "Weapons Prosecutions Decline to Lowest Level in a Decade," Transactional Records Access Clearinghouse, April 13, 2011, http://trac.syr.edu/tracreports/crim/249/.

42. Federal News Service transcript, "Hearing of the Senate Judiciary Committee; Subject: 'What Should America Do About Gun Violence?' Chaired by: Senator Patrick Leahy (D-VT) Witnesses: Captain Mark Kelly, USN (Ret.), Americans for Responsible Solutions; Professor David Kopel, Adjunct Professor of Advanced Constitutional Law Denver University, Strum College of Law; James Johnson, Chief of Police, Baltimore County Police Department, and Chair, National Law Enforcement Partnership to Prevent Gun Violence; Gayle Trotter, Attorney and Senior Fellow, Independent Women's Forum; Wayne LaPierre, Executive Vice President and Chief Executive Officer, National Rifle Association;" Location: 216 Hart Senate Office Building, Washington, D.C., Wednesday, January 30, 2013.

CHAPTER 10

1. The Public Safety and Second Amendment Rights Protection Act, Sponsored by Senator Joe Manchin, Senator Pat Toomey, Senator Charles Schumer, and Senator Mark Kirk. The text of the bill is available on Senator Joe Manchin's website, http://www.manchin.senate.gov/public/index.cfm/files/serve?File_id=8134649f-6d23-4ef2-882f-6a4555ff4889&SK=BDEA0DD2B0F4D93F905B5BC8DF6F76B6; the status of the bill is available here, "Bill Summary & Status, 113th Congress (2013–2014),

S.AMDT.715," Library of Congress website, http://thomas.loc.gov/cgi-bin/bdquery/z?d113:SP00715:.

2. Greg Ridgeway, Deputy Director of the National Institute of Justice, "Summary of Select Firearm Violence Prevention Strategies," U.S. Department of Justice, January 4, 2013. Memo acquired by National Rifle Association Institute for Legislative Action, http://www.nraila.org/media/10883516/nij-gun-policy-memo.pdf. See Appendix A.

3. Author interview of Chris Cox, executive director, National Rifle Association, Institute for Legislative Action, May 30, 2013.

4. Press Release, "Mayors Against Illegal Guns to Air Ads in Key States During Congressional Recess Demanding Washington Take Action to Reduce Gun Violence," March 23, 2013, http://e2.ma/message/pjn5b/5zq7xb.

5. "Remarks by the President on Gun Safety," East Room, WhiteHouse.gov, March 28, 2013, http://www.whitehouse.gov/the-press-office/2013/03/28/remarks-president-gun-safety.

6. "Mayors Against Illegal Guns Thanks Senator Toomey," Demand Action to End Gun Violence, http://www.demandaction.org/Toomey.

7. "Senator Flake's Opposition to Background Checks Drives down His Job Approval Ratings among Arizona Voters," Mayors Against Illegal Guns press release, April 15, 2013. To see the MAIG ads targeting Flake, go to "Demand Action from Senator Flake," Demand Action to End Gun Violence, http://www.demandaction.org/Flake.

8. "Fox News Poll: During a Manhunt, 69 Percent of Voters Want a Gun," Fox News, April 23, 2013, http://www.foxnews.com/politics/interactive/2013/04/23/fox-news-poll-during-manhunt-6-percent-voters-want-gun/.

9. "President Obama Speaks on Common-Sense Measures to Reduce Gun Violence," YouTube, April 17, 2013, http://youtu.be/yr9x1CzW2Yw; remarks here, "Statement by the President," Rose Garden, WhiteHouse.gov, April 17, 2013, http://www.whitehouse.gov/the-press-office/2013/04/17/statement-president.

10. Protecting Communities and Preserving the Second Amendment Act of 2013, introduced by Senator Chuck Grassley (aka "Grassley Cruz"); the text of the bill is available here, http://thomas.loc.gov/cgi-bin/query/

R?r113: FLD001:S02753; the status of the bill is available here, http://thomas.loc.gov/cgi-bin/query/B?r113:@FIELD(FLD003+d)+@FIELD(DDATE+20130417).

11. S.AMDT.719 Constitutional Concealed Carry Reciprocity Act of 2013, introduced by Senator John Cornyn; the text of the bill is available here, http://thomas.loc.gov/cgi-bin/bdquery/z?d113:SP00719:; the status of the bill is available here, http://thomas.loc.gov/cgi-bin/query/B?r113:@FIELD(FLD003+d)+@FIELD(DDATE+20130417).

12. SA 717 Protecting the Privacy and Safety of Law-Abiding Gun Owners, introduced by Senator John Barrasso; the text of the bill is available here, http://thomas.loc.gov/cgi-bin/query/C?r113:./temp/~r11355exxZ; the status of the bill is available here, http://thomas.loc.gov/cgi-bin/query/B?r113:@FIELD(FLD003+d)+@FIELD(DDATE+20130418).

13. "Map: Where Are the Gun Permits in Your Neighborhood?" lohudd.com (powered by the *Journal News*), December 22, 2012, http://www.lohud.com/interactive/article/20121223/NEWS01/121221011/Map-Where-gun-permits-your-neighborhood-?gcheck=1&nclick_check=1.

14. SA 730 Mental Health Awareness and Improvement Act of 2013, introduced by Senator Tom Harkin; the text of the bill is available here, http://thomas.loc.gov/cgi-bin/bdquery/z?d113:SP00730:; the status of the bill is available here, "Bill Summary & Status, 113th Congress (2013–2014), S.AMDT.730, Library of Congress website, http://thomas.loc.gov/cgi-bin/bdquery/z?d113:SP00730:.

15. "Statement by the President," Rose Garden, WhiteHouse.gov, April 17, 2013, http://www.whitehouse.gov/the-press-office/2013/04/17/statement-president.

16. Author interview of Reince Priebus, Republican National Committee Chairman, on June 12, 2013.

17. "Congressional Record, Proceedings and Debates of the 113th Congress, First Session, Senate," U.S. Government Printing Office, April 18, 2013, http://www.gpo.gov/fdsys/pkg/CREC-2013-04-18/pdf/CREC-2013-04-18-senate.pdf.

18. Author interview of Chris Cox, executive director, National Rifle Association, Institute for Legislative Action, May 30, 2013.

19.   Author interview of Donald Trump, chairman and president of The Trump
       Organization, June 10, 2013.

CHAPTER 11

1.   "Poll: Which Gun Should Emily Buy?" *Washington Times*, December 12,
      2011, http://www.washingtontimes.com/polls/2011/dec/12/which-gun-
      should-emily-buy/.
2.   "Results of the poll: Which Gun Should Emily Buy?" *Washington Times*,
      December 19, 2011, http://www.washingtontimes.com/polls/2011/dec/12/
      which-gun-should-emily-buy/results/.
3.   Federal Bureau of Investigation, National Instant Criminal Background
      Checks System, participation map of Point-Of-Contact capacity, http://
      www.fbi.gov/about-us/cjis/nics/general-information/participation-map.
4.   Author interview of John Frazer, Director, Research and Information Divi-
      sion, National Rifle Association Institute for Legislative Action, July 9,
      2013.

CHAPTER 12

1.   Grace Rauh, "Bloomberg Predicts Gun Background Checks Veto Could
      Influence 2014 Elections," NY 1, April 18, 2013, http://manhattan.ny1.
      com/text/?ArID=180671&SecID=3.
2.   Author interview of Chris Cox, executive director, National Rifle Asso-
      ciation, Institute for Legislative Action, May 30, 2013.
3.   "Demand Action in New Hampshire," Demand Action to End Gun Vio-
      lence, http://www.demandaction.org/Ayotte.
4.   "New Polls: Americans Overwhelmingly Support Background Checks,"
      Demand Action to End Gun Violence, http://www.demandaction.org/polls.
5.   Email from Pia Carusone, executive director, Americans for Responsible
      Solutions, April 30, 2013.
6.   "Americans for Responsible Solutions Launches Accountability
      Campaign," Americans for Responsible Solutions, April 24, 2013, http://
      americansforresponsiblesolutions.org/news/americans-for-responsible-
      solutions-launches-accountability-campaign/.

7. "Demand Action in New Hampshire," Demand Action to End Gun Violence.

8. Kelly Ayotte, "I Voted to Improve Background Check System," Senator Kelly Ayotte's website, May 6, 2013, http://www.ayotte.senate.gov/?p=news&id=937.

9. Author interview of Matthew E. Beynon, president, Madison Strategic Ventures, LLC, June 19, 2013.

10. "Stand with Ayotte," YouTube, May 8, 2013, http://www.youtube.com/watch?v=5iABFuDyN4U&feature=youtu.be.

11. "Quite," YouTube, May 13, 2013, http://youtu.be/7nXGiWrSnaI.

12. Chaska Police Department, http://www.chaskamn.com/cityhall/ns_police-home.cfm.

13. Author interview of Reince Priebus, Republican National Committee Chairman, on June 12, 2013.

14. Samantha Allen, "Nashua Mayor Pulls Name from Controversial Gun Control Group that Identified Criminals as Victims of Gun Violence," *The Nashua Telegraph*, June 25, 2013, http://www.nashuatelegraph.com/news/1008955-469/nashua-mayor-pulls-name-from-controversial-gun.html.

15. "Demand Action from Senator Flake," Demand Action to End Gun Violence, http://www.demandaction.org/flake.

16. See Senator Flake's Facebook page, https://www.facebook.com/JeffFlake1.

17. "Senators Facing Backlash over Background Check Votes," Public Policy Polling, April 29, 2013, http://www.publicpolicypolling.com/pdf/2011/PPP_Release_BackgroundChecks_429.pdf.

18. See Senator Flake's Facebook page, https://www.facebook.com/JeffFlake1.

19. "Demand Action from Senator Flake," Demand Action to End Gun Violence.

20. See Senator Flake's Facebook page, https://www.facebook.com/JeffFlake1.

21. "Checking on Background Checks," FactCheck.org, May 24, 2013, http://factcheck.org/2013/05/checking-on-background-checks/.

22. Senator Pryor, "It's Time to Take Another Look at Comprehensive Background Checks," Mayors Against Illegal Guns website, www.TakeAnother LookMark.org.

23. "Real Solutions," YouTube, May 30, 2013, http://youtu.be/m5JDuT-kHt20.

24. "National Drive to Reduce Gun Violence website," Mayors Against Illegal Guns website, http://nomorenames.org/.

25. "Analysis of the Slate List of Killings since Newtown June 24," from John Frazer, Director, National Rifle Association Institute for Legislative Action, Research and Information Division.

26. Alex Altman, "Chuck Schumer and the Art of the Deal," *Time*, June 13, 2013, http://swampland.time.com/2013/06/13/chuck-schumer-and-the-art-of-the-deal/#ixzz2WOAYdA1P.

27. Greg Sargent, "The Morning Plum: Holding Dems Who Vote Wrong Way on Guns Accountable," *Washington Post*, June 12, 2013, http://www.washingtonpost.com/blogs/plum-line/wp/2013/06/12/the-morning-plum-holding-dems-who-vote-wrong-way-on-guns-accountable/?hpid=z2.

28. Author interview of Reince Priebus, Republican National Committee chairman, on June 12, 2013.

29. "Mayor Bloomberg, Launched NYC Summer Youthwrap to Connect Teens in the Probation System with Jobs at Hurrican Sandy Restoration Projects," New York, Office of the Mayor website, http://www.nyc.gov/portal/site/nycgov/menuitem.beb0d8fdaa9e1607a62fa24601c789a0/.

30. "John Feinblatt," New York, Office of the Mayor website, http://www.nyc.gov/portal/site/nycgov/menuitem.047d873163b300bc6c4451f401c789a0/index.jsp?pageID=nyc_photo_slide&catID=1194&doc_name=http%3A%2F%2Fwww.nyc.gov%2Fhtml%2Fom%2Fhtml%2Fbios%2Fbio_om_criminalj.html.

31. "Is Michael Bloomberg Using City Resources for His 'Mayors Against Illegal Guns' Group?" Ace of Spades HQ, June 21, 2013, http://ace.mu.nu/archives/341105.php#341105.

32. "Tell Governor Sandoval to Support Background Checks," Mayors Against Illegal Guns, Demand Action to End Gun Violence website, http://www.demandaction.org/Nevada.

33. "Christopher Kocher, Special Counsel at Office of the Mayor of New York City," LinkedIn profile, http://www.linkedin.com/pub/christopher-kocher/a/9b7/67b.

34. "Preliminary Community Board #1 Committee Meeting Agendas, New York City website, November 2011, http://www.nyc.gov/html/mancb1/downloads/pdf/Commitee_Agendas/11-11.pdf.

35. Nevada Lobbyist Information, Nevada Legislature website, http://leg.state.nv.us/AppCF/lobbyist/.

36. Author interview of Carrie Herbertson, June 16, 2013.

37. Author interview of Daniel S. Reid, state liaison, National Rifle Association Institute for Legislative Action. June 16, 2013.

38. "RE: Senate Bill 221 of the 77th Legislative Session," Letter from Governor Brian Sandoval to Secretary of State Ross Miller, June 13, 2013, http://www.rgj.com/assets/pdf/J7206868613.PDF.

39. Jesse Hathaway, "Columbus Mayor's Office Conspired with Liberal Groups to Politicize School Shooting," Media Trackers, August 2, 2012, http://mediatrackers.org/ohio/2012/08/02/columbus-mayors-office-conspired-with-liberal-groups-to-politicize-school-shooting; Email from info@mayorsagainst illegalguns.org, Subject: "RE: Coalition Conference Call Re: Response to Tucson Shooting Today at 4pm (EST)," January 13, 2011, http://mediatrackers.org/assets/uploads/2012/08/Coleman_Bloomberg_MAIG_Giffords_shooting.pdf.

40. "UCP Welcomes New Political Strategist and Advocate," United Cerebral Palsy, June 6, 2012, http://www.ucp.org/media/press/2012/06/06/ucp-welcomes-new-political-strategist-and-advocate; William Swenson email, Subject: "RE: CNN Breaking News," February 27, 2012, Media Trackers, http://mediatrackers.org/assets/uploads/2012/08/Coleman_Bloomberg_ProgressOhio_Chardon.pdf.

41. Email from Lance Orchid, Subject: "Re: School Shooting Re: Ohio Bi-Weekly Call Reschedule," February 27, 2012, Media Trackers, http://mediatrackers.org/assets/uploads/2012/08/Coleman_Bloomberg_ProgressOhio_Chardon.pdf.

42. New York City Council Task Force to Combat Gun Violence report to New York City Council Speaker Christine C. Quinn, December 21, 2012, http://www.council.nyc.gov/html/pr/gvtfreport.pdf

43. "Come Hear Chris Kocher Plus Learn of Opportunities to Help," Newtown Action Alliance, March 15, 2013, http://newtownaction.org/come-hear-chris-kocher-plus-learn-of-opportunities-to-help/.

44. Christopher Kocher email, Subject: "RE: Ohio School Shooting May Draw Attention to State's Lax Gun Laws Chardon High School Shooting Backgrounder.docx," February 28, 2012, Media Trackers, http://mediatrackersorg/assets/uploads/2012/08/Coleman_Bloomberg_ Progress Ohio_Chardon.pdf.

45. Author interview of Brian Rothenberg, August 9, 2012.

46. Hunter Walker, "After Aurora: How Mayor Bloomberg Planned to Make the Next Massacre Count," New York Observer, Politicker, March 12, 2012, http://politicker.com/2013/03/after-aurora-how-mayor-bloomberg-planned-to-make-the-next-massacre-count/.

47. The John Gambling Show with Mayor Mike, WOR Radio, July 20, 2012, video available on YouTube, http://www.youtube.com/watch?v=R_Zhvk6A3kE&feature=youtu.be; text available on the New York City website, http://www.nyc.gov/portal/site/nycgov/menuitem.c0935b9a57b-b4ef3daf2f1c701c789a0/index.jsp?pageID=mayor_press_release&catID=1194&doc_name=http%3A%2F%2Fwww.nyc.gov%2Fhtml%2Fom%2Fhtml%2F2012b%2Fpr270-12.html&cc=unused1978&rc=1194&ndi=1.

48. Michael Planty and Jennifer L. Truman, "Firearm Violence, 1993–2011," U.S. Department of Justice Office of Justice Programs, May 2013, http://www.bjs.gov/content/pub/pdf/fv9311.pdf.

49. Sunlight Foundation Reporting Group, "Independence USA PAC, 2014 Cycle," http://reporting.sunlightfoundation.com/outside-spenders/2014/committee/independence-usa-pac/C00532705/.

50. Altman, "Chuck Schumer and the Art of the Deal."

51. Author interview of Chris Cox, executive director, National Rifle Association, Institute for Legislative Action, May 30, 2013.

52. Author interview of Rick Perry, governor of Texas, May 3, 2013.

53. Author interview of Chris Cox, executive director, National Rifle Association, Institute for Legislative Action, May 30, 2013.

54. Author interview of Reince Priebus, Republican National Committee Chairman, on June 12, 2013.

CHAPTER 13

1. "Records Required—Licensees," Bureau of Alcohol, Tobacco, Firearms and Explosives, http://www.atf.gov/firearms/faq/licensees-records-required. html.

2. Author interview of John Frazer, Director, Research and Information Division, National Rifle Association Institute for Legislative Action, July 5, 2012.

CHAPTER 14

1. Gallup poll, "Self-Reported Gun Ownership in U.S. Is Highest since 1993,"October 26, 2011, http://www.gallup.com/poll/150353/Self-Reported-Gun-Ownership-Highest-1993.aspx.

2. "Gun Control: States' Laws and Requirements for Concealed Carry Permits Vary across the Nation," General Accounting Office, July 17, 2012, http://www.gao.gov/products/GAO-12-717.

3. "Right-To-Carry 2012," National Rifle Association Institute for Legislative Action, February 28, 2012, http://www.nraila.org/news-issues/factsheets/2012/right-to-carry-2012.aspx.

4. Author interview of Lawrence Keane, Senior Vice President, Assistant Secretary and General Counsel, National Shooting Sports Foundation, Inc., June 10, 2013.

5. "National Shooting Sports Foundation Firearms and Ammunition Industry Economic Impact Report 2012," NSSF, 2012, http://www.nssf.org/PDF/2012EconomicImpactReport.pdf.

6. National Shooting Sports Foundation Firearms and Ammunition Industry Economic Impact Reports for 2008, 2009, 2010, and 2011.

7. National Shooting Sports Foundation® Report, U.S. Imports for Consumption: In Units.

8. "ATF Annual Firearms Manufacturing and Export Report," Bureau of Alcohol, Tobacco, Firearms and Explosives, http://www.atf.gov/files/

statistics/download/afmer/2011-final-firearms-manufacturing-export-report.pdf.

9.   "Total NICS Background Checks," Federal Bureau of Investigation, 2013, http://www.fbi.gov/about-us/cjis/nics/reports/total-nics-background-checks-1998_2013_monthly_yearly_totals-033113.pdf.

10. "FFL Newsletter: Federal Firearms Licensee Information Service," Bureau of Alcohol, Tobacco, Firearms and Explosives, March 2013, https://www.atf.gov/sites/default/files/assets/pdf-files/ffl_newsletter_march_2013_volume_1.pdf.

11. "NICS Firearms Checks: Top 10 Highest Days/Weeks," National Instant Criminal Background Check System, Federal Bureau of Investigation, http://www.fbi.gov/about-us/cjis/nics/reports/nics-firearm-background-checks-top-10-highest-days-and-weeks-033113.pdf.

12. "Adjusted NICS for May," National Shooting Sports Foundation, June 10, 2013, http://www.nssf.org/bulletpoints/view.cfm?Iyr= 2013& Bissue=061013.htm.

13. National Shooting Sports Foundation Firearms and Ammunition Industry Economic Impact Report—Excise Taxes/Projected Sales Firearms and Ammunition's 2012.

14. Sturm, Ruger & Co., Inc., "Sturm, Ruger & Company, Inc. Reports First Quarter 2012 Fully Diluted Earnings of 79 Cents per Share," press release, May 1, 2012, http://www.ruger.com/corporate/PDF/ER-2012-04-30.pdf.

15. Sturm, Ruger & Co., Inc., "Sturm, Ruger & Company, Inc. Reports First Quarter Fully Diluted Earnings of $3.60 per Share and Declares Dividend of 40.4 Cents per Share," press release, February 27, 2013, http://www.ruger.com/corporate/PDF/ER-2013-02-27.pdf.

16. Sturm, Ruger & Co., Inc., "Sturm, Ruger & Company, Inc. Reports First Quarter Fully Diluted Earnings of $1.20 per Share and Dividend of 49 Cents per share," press release, April 29, 2013, http://www.ruger.com/corporate/PDF/ER-2013-04-29.pdf.

17. Smith & Wesson Holding Corp., "Smith & Wesson Holding Corporation Reports Third Quarter Fiscal 2013 Financial Results," press release, March 5, 2013, http://ir.smith-wesson.com/phoenix.zhtml?c=90977&p=irol-newsArticle&ID=1792505&highlight=.

18. "Annual Report for the Fiscal Year—Ended: December 31, 2012," Remington Outdoor Company, Inc. (also known as Freedom Group, Inc.), December 31, 2012, http://www.freedom-group.com/FreedomGroup2012_10-K.pdf.

19. Author interview of George Kollitides, CEO, Freedom Group, June 6, 2013.

20. Author interview of Roger M. Smith, Washington Operations, Colt Defense, LLC, June 6, 2013.

21. Author interview of Jeffrey Reh, general counsel and vice-general manager of Beretta USA, June 12, 2013.

22. This estimate comes from a National Shooting Sports Foundation survey of ammunition manufacturers.

23. "National Shooting Sports Foundation Firearms Retailer Survey Report," 2012.

24. Author interview of Pete Brownell, CEO, Brownells, Inc., June 13, 2013.

25. Author interview of Miles E. Hall, founder and president, H&H Shooting Sports Complex, June 11, 2013.

26. Author interview of Richard D. Sprague, owner, Sprague's Sports Inc., June 11, 2013.

27. Mark Kelly, "NRA Leadership Should Refocus Its Priorities," *Houston Chronicle*, May 1, 2013, http://www.chron.com/opinion/outlook/article/NRA-leadership-should-refocus-its-priorities-4480769.php.

28. *Fox News Sunday*, Fox News, February 3, 2013, http://www.foxnews.com/on-air/fox-news-sunday-chris-wallace/2013/02/03/capt-mark-kelly-wayne-lapierre-chances-compromise-gun-control-debate#p//v/2139988959001.

29. Peter H. Stone and Ben Hallman, "NRA Gun Control Crusade Reflects Firearms Industry Financial Ties," *Huffington Post*, January 11, 2013, http://www.huffingtonpost.com/2013/01/11/nra-gun-control-firearms-industry- ties_n_2434142.html.

30. "Gun Safety," website of Congresswoman Carolyn McCarthy, http://carolynmccarthy.house.gov/gun-safety3/.

31. Kristin Donnelly, "Dem. Congressman: NRA Stokes Fear to Help Sell More Guns," January 30, 2013, MSNBC, http://tv.msnbc.com/2013/01/30/dem-congressman-nra-stokes-fear-to-help-sell-more-guns/.

CHAPTER 15

1. 2012 District of Columbia Code Section 7-2508.01, available on Justia.com, http://law.justia.com/codes/district-of-columbia/2012/division-i/title-7/subtitle-j/chapter-25/unit-a/subchapter-viii/section-7-2508-01.html.
2. D.C. Code § 7-2501.01 District of Columbia Official Code Division I. Government of District Title 7. Human Health Care and Safety. Subtitle J. Public Safety. Chapter 25. Firearms Control. Unit A. Firearms Control Regulations. Subchapter I. Definitions.

CHAPTER 16

1. Michael Planty and Jennifer L. Truman, "Firearm Violence, 1993–2011," U.S. Department of Justice, Office of Justice Programs, Bureau of Justice Statistics, May 2013, http://www.bjs.gov/content/pub/pdf/fv9311.pdf.
2. "Uniform Crime Reports," Federal Bureau of Investigation, http://www.fbi.gov/about-us/cjis/ucr/.
3. Geoffrey Dickens, "New Poll Proves Power of Media's Bias against Guns," Media Research Center, May 8, 2013, http://www.mrc.org/biasalerts/new-poll-proves-power-medias-bias-against-guns.
4. Pew Research, D'Vera Cohn, Paul Taylor, Mark Hugo Lopez, Catherine A. Gallagher, Kim Parker, and Kevin T. Maass, "Gun Homicide Rate down 49% since 1993 Peak; Public Unaware," May 7, 2013, http://www.pewsocialtrends.org/2013/05/07/gun-homicide-rate-down-49-since-1993-peak-public-unaware/.
5. Rasmussen Reports poll, May 10, 2013, http://www.rasmussenreports.com/public_content/politics/current_events/gun_control/64_who_favor_more_gun_control_believe_gun_crime_has_gone_up.
6. Author interview of NRA President David Keene, May 9, 2013.
7. Pete Souza, "President Barack Obama Shoots Clay Targets on the Range at Camp David, Md.," Official White House Photo, August 4, 2012, http://www.flickr.com/photos/whitehouse/8436110735/; Media reports that

called Obama's shotgun a "rifle": Peter Baker and Mark Landler, "President Claims Shooting as a Hobby, and the White House Offers Evidence," *New York Times*, February 2, 2013, http://www.nytimes.com/2013/02/03/us/politics/obamas-skeet-shooting-comments-draw-fire.html?_r=2&.; Andy Borowitz, "Gun Sales Soar on Photo of Armed Obama," *New Yorker*, February 2, 2013, http://www.newyorker.com/online/blogs/borowitzreport/2013/02/gun-sales-soar-on-photo-of-armed-obama.html.; Darlene Superville, "White House Photo Shows Obama Skeet Shooting," Associated Press, February 2, 2013, http://bigstory.ap.org/article/white-house-releases-photo-obama-firing-gun.

8.   Franklin Foer and Chris Hughes, "Barack Obama Is Not Pleased," *New Republic*, January 27, 2013, http://www.newrepublic.com/article/112190/obama-interview-2013-sit-down-president#.

9.   Editorial, "6,000 Bullets," *New York Times*, July 23, 2012, http://www.nytimes.com/2012/07/24/opinion/6000-bullets-in-colorado.html.

10.   Editorial, "Obama and Romney's Discreditable Silence on Gun Control," *Washington Post*, July 23, 2012, http://www.washingtonpost.com/opinions/obama-and-romneys-discreditable-silence-on-gun-control/2012/07/23/gJQA7ScH5W_story.html.

11.   Editorial, "Myths about Gun Regulation," *New York Times*, January 31, 2013, http://www.nytimes.com/2013/02/01/opinion/myths-about-gun-regulation.html.

12.   Editorial, "The Scourge of Concealed Weapons," *New York Times*, December 22, 2012, http://www.nytimes.com/2012/12/23/opinion/sunday/the-scourge-of-concealed-weapons.html?_r=0.

13.   Editorial, "Myths about Gun Regulation."

14.   Editorial, "The Public Wants Background Checks," *New York Times*, April 9, 2013, http://www.nytimes.com/2013/04/10/opinion/the-public-wants-background-checks-for-gun-sales.html?.

15.   Editorial, "The Moment for Action on Guns," *New York Times*, January 14, 2013, http://www.nytimes.com/2013/01/15/opinion/the-moment-for-action-on-gun-laws.html?.

16. Editorial, "The Senate Fails Americans," *New York Times*, April 17, 2013, http://www.nytimes.com/2013/04/18/opinion/the-senate-fails-americans-on-gun-bills.html.

17. "There Are Too Many Victims of Gun Violence," Brady Campaign to Prevent Gun Violence, http://www.bradycampaign.org/sites/default/files/GunDeathandInjuryStatSheet3YearAverageFINAL.pdf.

18. Editorial, "The Scourge of Concealed Weapons," *New York Times*.

19. Editorial Board, "The Damage Wrought by the Gun Lobby," *New York Times*, April 4, 2013, http://www.nytimes.com/2013/04/05/opinion/the-damage-wrought-by-the-gun-lobby.html?.

20. Joe Nocera, "The Gun Report: July 12, 2013," *Gun Report*, blog, *New York Times*, July 12, 2013, http://nocera.blogs.nytimes.com/category/gun-report/.

21. Editorial Board, "The Senate Misfires on Gun Control," *Washington Post*, April 18, 2013, http://www.washingtonpost.com/opinions/the-senates-cowardly-act-on-gun-control/2013/04/17/d8b4b108-a7aa-11e2-b029-8fb7e977ef71_story.html.

22. Editorial, "A Good Day for the Second Amendment," *Washington Times*, April 18, 2013, http://www.washingtontimes.com/news/2013/apr/18/a-good-day-for-the-second-amendment/.

23. "Gun Control Meltdown," *Wall Street Journal*, April 17, 2013, http://online.wsj.com/article/SB10001424127887323309604578429141422680354.html.

24. Geoffrey Dickens, "ABC, CBS, NBC Slant 8 to 1 for Obama's Gun Control Crusade," Media Research Center, February 5, 2013, http://www.mrc.org/media-reality-check/abc-cbs-nbc-slant-8-1-obamas-gun-control-crusade.

25. *The Last Word with Lawrence O'Donnell*, MSNBC, January 1, 2013, http://www.nbcnews.com/id/50495482/ns/msnbc/t/last-word-lawrence-odonnell-wednesday-january-th/#.UbILEvZVTop.

26. Author interview of George Kollitides, CEO of Freedom Group, June 6, 2013.

27. Editorial, "The Deadly Fantasy of Assault Weapons," *New York Times*, December 28, 2012, http://www.nytimes.com/2012/12/29/opinion/the-deadly-fantasy-of-assault-weapons.html.

28. Scott Cohn, "Owners of Some Remington Shotguns, Rifles Claim Pattern of Inadvertent Discharges," NBC, April 11, 2012, http://rockcenter.nbc-news.com/_news/2012/04/11/11148671-owners-of-some-remington-shotguns-rifles-claim-pattern-of-inadvertent-discharges?lite.

29. "NBC's Bob Costas on Gun Control following Jovan Belcher Tragedy Sunday Night Half-Time Show Tribute," YouTube, December 2, 2012, http://www.youtube.com/watch?v=uOi7If0zW9s.

30. *The Dan Patrick Show*, December 4, 2012, http://www.danpatrick.com/2012/12/04/bob-costas-explains-why-he-made-gun-commentary-at-halftime-of-sunday-night-game/.

31. *The O'Reilly Factor*, Fox News, December 5, 2012, http://www.foxnews.com/on-air/oreilly/2012/12/06/bob-costas-explains-gun-culture-comments.

32. Center for Disease Control. Detailed Tables for the National Vital Statistics Report (NVSR), "Deaths: Final, Data for 2010," Table 10. Number of deaths from 113 selected causes, Enterocolitis due to Clostridium difficile, drug-induced causes, alcohol-induced causes, and injury by firearms, by age: United States, 2010.; "Crime in the United States 2011," Federal Bureau of Investigation, http://www.fbi.gov/about-us/cjis/ucr/crime-in-the-u.s/2011/crime-in-the-u.s.-2011/tables/expanded-homicide-data-table-8.; Gary Kleck, "Armed Resistance to Crime: The Prevalence and Nature of Self-Defense with a Gun," *Journal of Criminal Law and Criminology* 86, issue 1 (1995), http://www.guncite.com/gcdgklec.html.

33. Author interview of Lawrence Keane, Senior Vice President, Assistant Secretary and General Counsel, National Shooting Sports Foundation, Inc., October 17, 2012.

34. "Piers Morgan Tonight," CNN, December 18, 2012, http://transcripts.cnn.com/TRANSCRIPTS/1212/18/pmt.01.html.

35. "Deport British Citizen Piers Morgan for Attacking 2nd Amendment," White House, petition, December 21, 2012, https://petitions.whitehouse.gov/petition/deport-british-citizen-piers-morgan-attacking-2nd-amendment/prfh5zHD.

36. *Hardball with Chris Matthews*, MSNBC, June 13, 2013, http://www.nbcnews.com/id/52204810/ns/msnbc-hardball_with_chris_matthews/#.Ub0NmPZUNz0.

37.   "Anderson Cooper 360 Degrees," CNN, March 28, 2013, http://transcripts. cnn.com/TRANSCRIPTS/1303/28/acd.01.html.

38.   "Piers Morgan Tonight," CNN, February 4, 2013, http://transcripts.cnn. com/TRANSCRIPTS/1302/04/pmt.01.html.

CHAPTER 17

1.   Metropolitan Police Department Crime Mapping Data for 2012, http:// crimemap.dc.gov/Report.aspx; see Appendix E, "Increase in Crime in the District of Columbia, 2011–2012."

2.   Emily Miller, "D.C.: District of Crime; Metropolitan Police Are Keeping Two Sets of Books," *Washington Times*, September 21, 2012, http:// www.washingtontimes.com/news/2012/sep/21/dc-district-of-crime/.

3.   "2011 Annual Report on Crime & Crime Control," Metropolitan Washington Council of Governments, September 12, 2012, http://www.mwcog. org/uploads/pub-documents/oF5dXFY20120912145153.pdf.

4.   Author interview of Gwendolyn Crump, director, Office of Communications, Metropolitan Police Department, September 14, 2012.

5.   Scott McCabe, "FBI: Crime Drops across D.C. Region," *Washington Examiner*, March 16, 2012, http://washingtonexaminer.com/article/89469.

6.   "Metropolitan Police Department Annual Report: 2011," http://mpdc. dc.gov/sites/default/files/dc/sites/mpdc/publication/attachments/ar_2011_0. pdf.

7.   Author interview of Kristopher Baumann, chairman of the Fraternal Order of Police, Metropolitan Police Department Labor Committee, July 9, 2013.

8.   Ibid.

9.   Compstat, Chicago Police Department, 2012 Year End, https://portal. chicagopolice.org/portal/page/portal/ClearPath/News/Crime%20Statistics/ Crime%20Statistics%20Year%20End/1_pdfsam_compstat_public_2012_ yearend_31dec2012.pdf.

10.   Freedom of Information Act request #130325-003 for Attorney George Lyon, May 29, 2013.

11.   Metropolitan Police Department Crime Mapping Data for 2012, http:// crimemap.dc.gov/Report.aspx.

12. Author interviews of Army First Lieutenant Augustine Kim from March 16, 2012, to May 31, 2012.

13. Firearms Owners' Protection Act of 1986, available on the U.S. House of Representatives Office of Law Revision Counsel, http://uscode.house.gov/download/pls/18c44.txt.

14. Author interview of Kelly O'Meara, Executive Director, Office of Strategic Change. Metropolitan Police Department, July 13, 2012.

15. Author interview of attorney Richard Gardiner, May 24, 2012.

16. Author interview of Gwendolyn Crump, director, Office of Communications, Metropolitan Police Department, May 14, 2012.

17. John Kelly, "'Guns into Plowshares' Sculpture Can Be Seen again—if You Can Find It, That Is," *Washington Post*, January 17, 2011, http://www.washingtonpost.com/wp-dyn/content/article/2011/01/16/AR2011011604146.html.

18. Author interview of Gwendolyn Crump, director, Office of Communications, Metropolitan Police Department, May 24, 2012.

19. Bill Text 113th Congress (2013–2014) H. R. 1290.IH, March 20, 2013, available on the Library of Congress website, http://thomas.loc.gov/cgi-bin/query/z?c113:H.R.1290:.

20. Author interview of Representative Morgan Griffith, May 24, 2012.

CHAPTER 18

1. Talk 1300 AM, http://www.talk1300.com/.; Becket Adams, "Here's the Audio of the NY Gov. Talking Gun Control: 'Confiscation Could Be an Option'," The Blaze, December 21, 2012, http://www.theblaze.com/stories/2012/12/21/heres-the-audio-of-ny-gov-talking-gun-control-confiscation-could-be-an-option/.

2. "2013 State of the State," New York Governor Andrew Cuomo, governor.ny.gov, http://www.governor.ny.gov/NY/2013-State-of-the-State.

3. "Transcript of Governor Andrew M. Cuomo's 2013 State of the State Address," governor.ny.gov, https://www.governor.ny.gov/press/01092013sostranscript.

4. "Bill No. S02230," New York State Assembly, http://assembly.state.ny.us/ leg/?default_fld=&bn=S02230&term=2013&Summary=Y&Actions=Y& Votes=Y&Memo=Y&Text=Y.

5. "2013-2014 Regular Sessions, Senate–Assembly, January 14, 2013," New York State Assembly, http://assembly.state.ny.us/leg/?sh=printbill&bn=S0 2230&term=2013.

6. "Rifles – Banned Features," NY SAFE, governor.ny.gov, http://www. governor.ny.gov/assets/documents/RiflesBannedFeatures.pdf.

7. "Gun Owners," NY SAFE, governor.ny.gov, http://www.governor.ny.gov/ nysafeact/gun-owners.

8. Author interview of Janine Kava, Director of Public Information, New York State Division of Criminal Justice Services, January 9, 2013.

9. "Gun Owners," NY SAFE, governor.ny.gov, http://www.governor.ny.gov/ nysafeact/gun-owners.

10. "Key Information For:," NY SAFE, governor.ny.gov, http://www.governor. ny.gov/nysafeact/gun-reform.

11. Bloomberg School of Public Health at Johns Hopkins University in Baltimore, Maryland, "Summit on Reducing Gun Violence," January 14, 2013. "Johns Hopkins University Holds Summit on Reducing Gun Violence," Mike Bloomberg, January 14, 2013, http://mikebloomberg.com/index. cfm?objectid=39DA7A10-C29C-7CA2-F621828953C96E97.

12. Ibid.; JohnsHopkinsSPH, "Gun Policy Summit – Day 1 – Part 1," YouTube, January 14, 2013, http://www.youtube.com/watch?v=Mit-YvWyM fk&feature=share&list=PLtgdsdWLoHgQOG17zzsqG33Qr0ooQvgAx.

13. "Crime in Maryland: 2011 Uniform Crime Report," goccp.maryland.gov, 2011, http://www.goccp.maryland.gov/msac/documents/2011_Crime_In_ Maryland.pdf.

14. Governor Martin O'Malley, "Junior Waterfowl Hunting Day and Protecting Traditions," email message, February 7, 2013.

15. Author interview of Patrick Shomo, President Maryland Shall Issue, February 11, 2013.

16. "Maryland Statewide Poll Highlights," Susquehanna Polling and Research, February 6, 2013, http://www.marylandshallissue.org/share/Poll_Memo-MarylandStatewide-Feb2013.pdf.

17. "Firearm Safety Act of 2013," Maryland General Assembly, 2013, http://mgaleg.maryland.gov/webmga/frmMain.aspx?pid=flrvotepage&tab=subject3&id=SB0281,h-0895&stab=02&ys=2013rs.

18. "Senate Bill 281," Maryland General Assembly, http://mgaleg.maryland.gov/2013RS/bills/sb/sb0281e.pdf.

19. Author interview of Jeffrey Reh, General Counsel and Vice-General Manager of Beretta USA, May 3, 2013.

20. "Senate Bill 281," Maryland General Assembly, http://mgaleg.maryland.gov/2013RS/bills/sb/sb0281e.pdf.

21. Author interview of Jeffrey Reh, General Counsel and Vice-General Manager of Beretta USA, May 16, 2013.

22. Federal News Service transcript, Remarks by Vice President Joseph Biden, "Reducing Gun Violence," Western Connecticut State University, Danbury, Connecticut, February 21, 2013.

23. "Senate Bill No. 1160, Public Act No. 13-3," cga.ct.gov, http://www.cga.ct.gov/2013/ACT/PA/2013PA-00003-R00SB-01160-PA.htm.

24. Ibid.

25. "Crime in Connecticut," Annual Report of the Uniform Crime Reporting Program State of Connecticut Department of Emergency Services and Public Protection, Crimes Analysis Unit, 2011, http://www.dpsdata.ct.gov/dps/ucr/data/2011/Crime%20In%20Connecticut%20COMPLETE%202011.pdf.

26. Author interview of Lawrence Keane, Senior Vice President, Assistant Secretary and General Counsel, National Shooting Sports Foundation, Inc., January 29, 2013.

27. *This Week*, ABC News, July 22, 2012, http://abcnews.go.com/Politics/week-transcript-tragedy-colorado/story?id=16824177&page=4#.UbUdYPZVToo.

28. "House Bill 13-1229," leg.state.co.us, http://www.leg.state.co.us/clics/clics2013a/csl.nsf/fsbillcont3/590C29B4C02AFC2F87257A8E0073C303?Open&file=1229_enr.pdf.

29. Author interview of Lawrence Keane, Senior Vice President, Assistant Secretary and General Counsel, National Shooting Sports Foundation, Inc., May 23, 2013.

30. "An Act to Strengthen and Enhance Firearms in the Commonwealth," Mass.gov, January 16, 2013, http://www.mass.gov/governor/legislation-eexecorder/legislation/an-act-to-strengthen-and-enhance-firearms-laws.html.

31. "State Rankings," FixNICS, 2013, http://www.fixnics.org/staterankings.cfm.

32. "Governor Christie: This Is about Violence Control," state.nj.us, 2013, http://www.state.nj.us/governor/news/news/552013/approved/20130117e.html.

33. "Governor Christie Acts on Violence Prevention with Comprehensive Review of the Intersection of Gun Control, Addiction, Mental Health and School Safety Issues," state.nj.us, January 17, 2013, http://www.state.nj.us/governor/news/news/552013/approved/20130117b.html.

34. "State of New Jersey, 215th Legislature," njleg.state.nj.us, June 6, 2013, http://www.njleg.state.nj.us/2012/Bills/A4500/4182_I1.PDF.; "State of New Jersey 215th Legislature," njleg.state.nj.us, May 9, 2013, http://www.njleg.state.nj.us/2012/Bills/S3000/2723_U2.PDF.

35. "Keeping New Jersey SAFE," state.nj.us, April 19, 2013, http://www.state.nj.us/governor/news/news/552013/approved/20130419a.html.

36. Association of New Jersey Rifle & Pistol Clubs, https://anjrpc.site-ym.com/.

37. "Confiscation! NJ Senators Caught Mocking Gun Owners Committee Meeting May 9, 2013," YouTube, May 9, 2013, http://www.youtube.com/watch?v=jMptQ_YfvzE.

38. "National Shooting Sports Foundation Firearms and Ammunition Industry Economic Impact Report 2012," NSSF, 2012, http://www.nssf.org/PDF/2012EconomicImpactReport.pdf.

39. Author interview of Mark Malkowski, President of Stag Arms, February 26, 2013.

40. Author interview of Jeffrey Reh, General Counsel and Vice-General Manager of Beretta USA, May 16, 2013.

41. Author interview of George Kollitides, CEO of Freedom Group, June 6, 2013.

CHAPTER 19

1.   Author interview of Sergeant Matthew Corrigan from May 21, 2012, to June 4, 2012.

2.   Washington DC VA Medical Center, Mental Health Hotline Report, Suicide Risk Assessment Note from February 2, 2010, at 11:08pm. Transcript of 911 call between "Beth" from National Veterans Suicide Hotline and District of Columbia Emergency Services, February 2, 2010.

3.   Author interview of Tammie Sommons, May 27, 2012.

4.   Email: From: Porter, Jesse (MPD); sent: Wednesday, February 03, 2010 2:51 AM; To: Glover, Robert (MPD); Q'Bryant, Kevin (MPD); Beach, Mark (MPD); Subject: CAD Printout; Importance: High; The following is the CAD data from OUE.

5.   Ibid.

6.   Metropolitan Police Department, Homeland Security Bureau Special Operations Division, Emergency Response Team, February 9, 2010; Memorandum; To: Chief of Police; Executive Office of the Chief of Police from Lieutenant Robert T. Glover; Subject: Barricade Report from 2408 North Capitol Street, NW (50) on Wednesday, February 3, 2010 (ERT#10-11).

7.   Author interview of Chetna Lal, wife of Sergeant Matt Corrigan, June 4, 2012.

8.   Superior Court of the District of Columbia; Criminal Division Affidavit in Support of an Arrest Warrant; Complainant's Name: Det D. McFadden; Defendant's Name: Carrigan, Maithew; 240-305-4839 I; Date of Offense: 2-3-10.

9.   Superior Court of the District of Columbia; Criminal Division—D.C. & Traffic Branch; District of Columbia : : Docket No. 2010 CDC 2483; V. : Trial: January 13, 2011 : Judge Morin; Matthew Corrigan : Supplement to Opposition to Defendant's Motion to Suppress.

10.   Author interview of attorney Richard Gardiner, May 18, 2013.

11.   Author interview of Sergeant Matthew Corrigan, May 16, 2013.

12.   Case 1:12-cv-00173-BAH, Document 1, Filed February 1, 2012, in the United States District Court for the District of Columbia, *Matthew Corrrigan v. The District of Columbia*, http://www.scribd.com/doc/80941044/Matthew-Corrigan-v-District-of-Columbia.

CHAPTER 20

1. Case 3:13-cv-00739-AVC, Document 10, Filed June 11, 2013, in the United States District Court for the District of Connecticut, http://www.ccdl.us/images/CCDL/amended_complaint_filed.pdf.

2. Author interview of Scott Wilson Sr., president, Connecticut Citizens Defense League, Inc., www.ccdl.us, May 24, 2013.

3. Complaint Fifty-four Sheriffs vs. John W. Hickenlooper, available on the Independence Institute website, http://www.i2i.org/files/file/54-sheriffs-complaint.pdf.

4. Case 1:13-cv-00291-WMS, Document 47-1, Filed May 14, 2013, in the United States District Court Western District of New York, Buffalo Division, https://www.nysrpa.org/files/SAFE/NY-Sheriffs-SAFE-Amicus.pdf.

5. Case 1:13-cv-00291, Document 1, Filed March 21, 2013, in the United States District Court for the Western District of New York, Buffalo Division, http://www.nysrpa.org/files/SAFE/NYSRPA-SAFE-Lawsuit.pdf.

6. Author interview of Alan Gura of Gura & Possessky on June 19, 2013.

7. *District of Columbia et al. v. Heller*, Supreme Court of the United States, argued March 18, 2008—Decided June 26, 2008, available on the Supreme Court website, http://www.supremecourt.gov/opinions/07pdf/07-290.pdf.

8. Author interview of Alan Gura of Gura & Possessky, October 1, 2012.

9. Author interview of Alan Gottlieb, founder of the Second Amendment Foundation, December 11, 2012.

10. *Michael Moore, et al., and Mary E. Shepard, et al., v. Lisa Madigan, Attorney General of Illinois, et al.*, United States Court of Appeals for the Seventh Court, Nos. 12-1269, 12-1788, Argued June 8, 2012—Decided December 11, 2012," http://media.ca7.uscourts.gov/cgi-bin/rssExec.pl?Submit=Display &Path=Y2012/D12-11/C:12-1269:J: Posner:aut:T:fn Op:N:1046906:S:0.

11. Case: 12-1269, Document: 70, Filed February 22, 2013, United States Court of Appeals for the Seventh Circuit, Chicago, Illinois, http://saf.org/legal.action/il.carry/OPINION_DENYING_REHEARING.pdf.

12. Bill HB0183 Illinois General Assembly, http://www.ilga.gov/legislation/billstatus.asp?DocNum=183&GAID=12&GA=98&DocTypeID=HB&LegID=69231&SessionID=85.

13. "SAF Applauds Illinois Lawmakers for Override Vote, Court Compliance," Second Amendment Foundation, July 9, 2013, http://www.saf.org/viewpr-new.asp?id=450.

14. *Raymond Woollard, et al. v. Terrence Sheridan, et al.*, Civil Case No. L-10-2068, Filed March 2, 2012, in the United States District Court for the District of Maryland, http://ia600501.us.archive.org/1/items/gov.uscourts.mdd.180772/gov.uscourts.mdd.180772.52.0.pdf; Case 1:10-cv-02068-BEL, Document 71, Filed July 23, 2012, in the United States District Court for the District of Maryland, http://ia700501.us.archive.org/1/items/gov.uscourts.mdd.180772/gov.uscourts.mdd.180772.71.0.pdf.

15. *Raymond Woolard; Second Amendment Foundation, Inc., v. Denis Gallagher; Seymour Goldstein; Charles M. Thomas, Jr; et al.*, United States Court of Appeals for the Fourth Circuit, Appeal from the United States District Court for the District of Maryland, at Baltimore, Benson Everett Legg, District Judge, Argued October 24, 2012, Decided March 21, 2013, http://www.ca4.uscourts.gov/opinions/Published/121437.p.pdf.

16. "Lautenberg, McCarthy, Advocates Announces New Legislation to Effectively Ban Online Ammo Sales," Frank R. Lautenberg website, July 30, 2012, http://www.lautenberg.senate.gov/newsroom/record.cfm?id=337363.

17. *Fox News Sunday*, Fox News, July 29, 2012, http://www.foxnews.com/on-air/fox-news-sunday/2012/07/29/justice-antonin-scalia-issues-facing-scotus-and-country#p/.

18. "Could Scalia Help Rewrite Gun Laws?" *The Last Word with Lawrence O'Donnell*, blog, MSNBC, July 31, 2012, http://thelastword.msnbc.com/_news/2012/07/31/13042541-could-scalia-help-rewrite-gun-laws?lite.

19. "October Term, 2007, Supreme Court of the United States, Syllabus, District of Columbia et al. v. Heller, Certiorari to the United States Court of Appeals for the District of Columbia Circuit, No. 07–290, Argued March 18, 2008—Decided June 26, 2008," http://www.supremecourt.gov/opinions/07pdf/07-290.pdf.

20. Federal News Service transcript, "Hearing of the Senate Judiciary Committee; Subject: 'The Assault Weapons Ban of 2013;'" Chaired by: Senator

Dianne Feinstein (D-CA); Location: 216 Hart Senate Office Building, Washington, D.C., February 27, 2013.

21.   Ibid.

22.   "Second Amendment and Gun Laws," C-SPAN Video Library, October 15, 2012, http://www.c-spanvideo.org/program/308809-1.

CHAPTER 21

1.   Author interviews of Adam Meckler, former Army Specialist, from March 13, 2013, to November 8, 2013.

2.   Author interview of Ted Gest, public information officer, Office of the Attorney General, District of Columbia, June 29, 2012.

3.   Author interview of John Frazer, Director of the National Rifle Association Institute for Legislative Action, Research and Information Division, June 27, 2012.

4.   Freedom of Information Act Request No. 130610-001, May 31, 2013. Request for extension for release of information on June 25, 2013. from Teresa Quon Hyden, Acting FOIA Officer, Freedom of Information Act Office, Office of the General Counsel, Metropolitan Police Department. Emails to Hyden after deadline sent July 10 and July 12, 2013 and no response.

5.   Author interview of Kelly O'Meara, executive director, Office of Strategic Change, Metropolitan Police Department, July 5, 2012.

6.   Letter from District of Columbia Attorney General Irvin Nathan to Lee Levine of Levine Sullivan Koch & Schultz, attorney for David Gregory and NBC, January 11, 2013.

7.   Author interview of Ted Gest, public information officer, Office of the Attorney General, District of Columbia, July 29, 2012.

8.   Author interview of Gwendolyn Crump, Director, Office of Communications, Metropolitan Police Department, June 22, 2013.

9.   *Meet the Press*, NBC News, December 23, 2012, http://www.nbcnews.com/id/50283245/ns/meet_the_press-transcripts/t/december-wayne-

lapierre-chuck-schumer-lindsey-graham-jason-chaffetz-harold-ford-jr-
andrea-mitchell-chuck-todd/#.UbNzffZUNz0.

10. Freedom of Information Act Request# 130327-002, Freedom of Informa-
     tion Act (FOIA) Office, Office of the General Counsel, Metropolitan Police
     Department.

11. District of Columbia Official Code § 7-2507.06 Penalties. Division I.
     Government of District Title 7. Human Health Care and Safety; Subtitle
     J. Public Safety Chapter 25. Firearms Control Unit A. Firearms Control
     Regulations Subchapter VII. Miscellaneous Provisions.

12. Author interview of Kristopher Baumann, chairman of the D.C. Police
     Union, Fraternal Order of Police, Metropolitan Police Department Labor
     Committee (FOP), December 27, 2012.

13. D.C. Attorney General Irvin Nathan letter to Lee Levine of Levine Sullivan
     Koch & Schultz, attorney for NBC and David Gregory. January 11, 2013.

14. Author interview of Kristopher Baumann, Chairman of the D.C. Police
     Union, Fraternal Order of Police, Metropolitan Police Department Labor
     Committee (FOP), December 27, 2012.

15. Author interview of Gwendolyn Crump, director, Office of Communica-
     tions, Metropolitan Police Department, January 4, 2012.

16. Author interview of Ted Gest, public information officer, Office of Attor-
     ney General for District of Columbia, January 11, 2013.

17. Emily Miller, "If You're Not David Gregory," *Washington Times*, January
     4, 2013, http://www.washingtontimes.com/news/2013/jan/4/if-youre-not-
     david-gregory/.

18. Author interview of former Army Specialist Adam Meckler, December 31,
     2012.

19. Council of the District of Columbia, Committee on the Judiciary, Chair-
     man Phil Mendelson, Public Hearing on Bill 19-888, Administrative Dis-
     position of Weapons Amendment Act of 2012, September 24, 2012.

20. Ibid.

21. Bill 19-888, Administrative Disposition for Weapons Offenses Amendment
     Act of 2012, District of Columbia, http://dcclims1.dccouncil.us/
     images/00001/20130118174512.pdf.

CHAPTER 22

1. Bill 19-614, Firearms Amendment Act of 2012, District of Columbia, http://dcclims1.dccouncil.us/images/00001/20120510092819.pdf.

2. Author interview of Dick Heller, July 11, 2013.

3. "Remarks by the President at a Reception for LGBT Pride Month," East Room, WhiteHouse.gov, June 13, 2013, http://www.whitehouse.gov/the-press-office/2013/06/13/remarks-president-reception-lgbt-pride-month.

4. "The Arms Trade Treaty," United Nations Office for Disarmament Affairs, http://www.un.org/disarmament/ATT/.

5. Secretary of State John Kerry, "United States Welcomes Opening of Arms Trade Treaty for Signature," Washington, D.C., U.S. Department of State website, June 3, 2013, http://www.state.gov/secretary/remarks/2013/06/208554.htm.

6. Bill Text, 113th Congress (2013–2014), S.CON.RES.7.IS, March 13, 2013, available on the Library of Congress website, http://thomas.loc.gov/cgi-bin/query/z?c113:S.CON.RES.7:.

7. "House Unanimously Adopts Kelly Amendment to Ban Funding for UN Arms Trade Treaty," U.S. Representative Mike Kelly's website, June 14, 2013, http://kelly.house.gov/press-release/house-unanimously-adopts-kelly-amendment-ban-funding-un-arms-trade-treaty.

8. Federal News Service transcript, *Morning Joe* MSNBC Interview with Former President Bill Clinton; June 14, 2013.

9. Rasmussen Reports poll, "Rating President Obama on the Issues: 40% Rate Obama Poorly on National Security," July 10, 2013, http://www.rasmussenreports.com/public_content/politics/obama_administration/obama_rotations/rating_president_obama_on_the_issues.

10. Author interview of Donald Trump, chairman and president of The Trump Organization, June 10, 2013.

11. Federal News Service transcript, "Facebook Town Hall with Vice President Joseph Biden;" Subject: Efforts to Reduce Gun Violence; Moderator: Michael Kress, Executive Editor, Parents Magazine and Parents.com; Location: White House, Washington, D.C., February 19, 2013.

12. "COPS in Schools (CIS)," COPS: Community Oriented Policing Services, U.S. Department of Justice, http://www.cops.usdoj.gov/default. asp?Item=54.

13. Bill Text, 113th Congress (2013–2014), H.R.751.IH, February 15, 2013, available on the Library of Congress website, http://thomas.loc.gov/cgi-bin/query/z?c113:H.R.751:.

14. Author interview of Representative Mark Meadows (R-NC), February 20, 2013.

15. "Crime and Safety Surveys," U.S. Department of Education Institute of Education Sciences National Center for Education Statistics, Table 34, http://nces.ed.gov/surveys/ssocs/tables/all_2010_tab_34.asp?referrer=css.

16. Pew Research poll, January 14, 2013, http://www.people-press. org/2013/01/14/in-gun-control-debate-several-options-draw-majority-support/.

17. Federal News transcript, "Remarks of Senate Majority Leader Harry Reid (D-NV) on the Floor of the U.S. Senate;" Location: Senate Chamber, The Capitol, Washington, D.C., Date: Wednesday, April 17, 2013.

18. Rasmussen Reports, "65% See Gun Rights as Protection against Tyranny," January 18, 2013, http://www.rasmussenreports.com/public_content/politics/current_events/gun_control/65_see_gun_rights_as_protection_against_tyranny.

19. Greg Ridgeway, Deputy Director of the National Institute of Justice, "Summary of Select Firearm Violence Prevention Strategies," U.S. Department of Justice, January 4, 2013. Memo acquired by National Rifle Association Institute for Legislative Action, http://www.nraila.org/media/10883516/nij-gun-policy-memo.pdf. See Appendix A.

20. Author interview of Reince Priebus, Republican National Committee chairman, on June 12, 2013.

21. Emily Miller, "Emily Gets Her Gun," *Washington Times*, October 5, 2011, http://www.washingtontimes.com/blog/guns/2011/oct/5/miller-emily-gets-her-gun/.

INDEX

Collins, Susan, 106
Colorado, 46, 68, 70, 80, 96, 219–20, 224, 246, 251, 255. *See also* Rocky Mountain State
Colt Defense (Colt), 160, 224
1911 .45 caliber pistol, 20
1911 pistols, 224
Carbine AR-15 rifle 6920 5.56/.223, 201
M4 Carbine, 160
revolvers, 224
Columbine High School shooting, 45
Commissioner of Emergency Services and Public Protection, 219
concealed-carry, 19, 47, 66, 77, 99, 11, 127, 156, 165, 189, 192, 250, 252, 273. *See also* "may issue"; "shall issue"
guns, 77
permit holders, 19
permits, 127, 189, 192, 273
pistols, 163
reciprocity, 189, 275
weapons, 99
Congress, 15, 17, 23–24, 27, 64, 83, 89, 103–4, 111, 132, 189, 206, 274. *See also* Capitol Hill; Senate; U.S. House of Representatives
Congressional Research Service (CRS), 25
Connecticut, 23–24, 46, 50, 159–60, 187, 217–19, 224–25, 245. *See also* Nutmeg State
Connecticut Citizens Defense League, 246
Connecticut House, 218
Connecticut State Police, 46
Conservative Political Action Conference (CPAC), 18, 20
conservatives, 30, 61, 187, 250, 253–54.

groups of, 131, 278
views of, 29
"cool down law," 153, 169
Cooper, Anderson, 194–95
Cooper, Chuck, 248
"cop-killer" bullets, 39, 66. *See also* armor-piercing ammunition
COPS in Schools, 274–75
Cornyn, John, 92, 111
Corrigan, Matt, 180, 227–43, 257, 268
cosmetic features, 36, 40–44, 46, 212, 215, 217–18. *See also* "assault weapons" ban
Costas, Bob, 193
Cox, Chris, 75, 80, 84–85, 98, 106, 113, 130, 140, 245, 277
crime, 33, 36, 40–41, 64, 82, 88, 90, 120, 127, 131, 137, 190–91, 193, 199–200, 219, 248, 250, 268
gun-related, 10, 80, 84, 91–92, 138, 185–87, 223, 266, 269
petty, 11
reducing, 11, 17, 70, 166
reports of, 186
sprees, 10
unemployment and, 11
violent crime, 5, 42, 45, 48, 66, 70, 91–92, 194, 197–98, 222, 266
Crime Bill of 1994 ("Biden crime bill"), 26, 276. *See also* Assault Weapons Ban of 1994
criminals, 3, 5, 7, 10, 21, 66, 69, 79, 113, 129, 134, 145, 215, 270, 272, 275–76, 279–80
charges of, 267
gun acquisition and, 22–23, 48, 64, 80, 84, 86, 88, 171, 237, 253
prosecution of, 91–92, 267
records of, 267–68, 272, 277

If you only follow liberal media and listen to President Obama, it would be easy to believe that gun owners are all bitter clingers, reckless hicks, or criminals. The truth is that the 100 million gun owners in America are among the most responsible, patriotic, family-oriented citizens in our nation. To dispel this mischaracterization, I'm deeply grateful to all the law-abiding gun owners who sent in photographs of themselves that are published in this book. The photos are a beautiful demonstration of Americans—men and women, young and old—exercising their Second Amendment rights.